Contents

CONTENTS

TH

OF

Glol

*You ...
I know you
good read!
Best ...
Nic X.*

For Anthony Elliott, Nicola Geraghty and Lucy James

THE TRANSFORMATION OF THE MEDIA

Globalisation, Morality and Ethics

Nick Stevenson

LONGMAN
London and New York

Pearson Education Limited
Edinburgh Gate
Harlow
Essex CM20 2JE
England
and Associated Companies throughout the world

Published in the United States of America
by Pearson Education Inc., New York

Visit us on the world wide web at:
http://www.awl-he.com

© Pearson Education Limited 1999

First published 1999

ISBN   0 582 29205 0

British Library Cataloguing-in-Publication Data

A catalogue record for this book is available from the British Library

Library of Congress Cataloging-in-Publication Data

Stevenson, Nicholas, 1961–
    The transformation of the media: globalisation, morality, and
ethics / Nicholas Stevenson.
       p.   cm.
    Includes bibliographical references and index.
    ISBN 0–582–29205–0
    1. Mass media—Moral and ethical aspects.   2. Communication,
International.   3. Mass media and culture.   I. Title.
    P94.S74   1999
    175—dc21   98-32386
                                                                      CIP

Set by 35 in 10/12pt Palatino

Printed and bound in Great Britain by
Biddles Ltd, Guildford and King's Lynn

Preface

The writing of this book has taken much longer than I originally expected. This has been for a multitude of reasons, including a changing of direction and focus by the author. What began as a moralistic polemic against certain versions of post-modernism has ended with a call for us to rethink questions of morality and ethics in an increasingly mediated age. That books are like people in that they rarely turn out as we first expected is probably a lesson with which many of us are already familiar. It is however perhaps fitting that a book concerned with 'long distance' communication should be dedicated to my friends Anthony Elliott and Nicola Geraghty who live so far away. This book is also dedicated to Lucy James. A new love who I hope will stick around long enough to become an old love.

First, I would like to mention my publisher Sarah Caro who is a gem. For support through the different stages of redrafting I would like primarily to thank Anthony Elliott, Sean Homer, Sian Makel, John Westergaard and especially in this context Mike Kenny. Their confidence in my ability and willingness to debate with me many of the issues contained within in the spirit of friendship has helped me more than they think. I would also like to thank the following scholars for their thoughts and encouragement past and present: Anthony Giddens, Jim McGuigan, John B. Thompson and Philip Schelsinger. For being such good friends and colleagues Kate Brookes, Ankie Hoogevelt, Sharon MacDonald, Diane Richardson, Maurice Roche and Peter Jackson are worthy of mention. I would also like to offer special thanks to Liza Beattie and Greg Philo of the Glasgow University Media Group for their help on the Rwanda chapter. Finally a 'big' thank you to my friends and family for all the hope and support they have offered through admittedly troubled times: Chris Baber, Lianne Batchelor, Brian Comber, Chris Docx, Gaye Flounders, Alan and Jan France, Eugene Georgaca, Jane, Steve, Charlotte and Joe Hurd, Colin Lago, Layne and Perry Lambert, Kitty L, Donna Luff, Alex MacDonald, Hazel May, Georgia Mason, David Moore, Lianne Older, Jadish Patel, Nicola Piper, Paul Ransome, David Rose, 'Bobby'

⮡ the man himself!

Simpson, William Dennis and June Stevenson, Simon Unger, Rob Unwin, Mrs Wang and Elsie Webster. Without you the world would be a smaller place.

Some of the chapters enclosed in this volume have already appeared elsewhere in a different form:

Chapter 2 appeared as 'Media, ethics and morality', in Jim McGuigan (eds) *Cultural Methodologies*, London, Sage, 1977.

Chapter 3 appeared as 'Global media and technological change: social justice, recognition and the meaningfulness of everyday life citizenship studies', *Citizenship Studies*, 1(3), 1997.

Chapter 4 appeared as 'Globalization, national cultures and cultural citizenship', *Sociological Quarterly*, 38, 1997.

All of these chapters appear here in a very different form, and Chapters 5, 6 and 7 are published for the first time.

knowing now
that the life
at which I aim
is a circumference

continually expanding
through sympathy and
understanding
rather than an exclusive centre
of pure self-feeling
the whole I seek
is centre plus circumference
and now the struggle at the centre is over
the circumference
beckons from everywhere

Kenneth White (1989)

CHAPTER 1

Introduction

The transformation of the media at the end of the twentieth century is one of the most important social changes currently facing advanced industrial and indeed global societies. These changes, as this book will make clear, have economic, political and cultural implications for our shared world. Our culture is more profoundly mediated than any other that has existed within human history. From the reporting of the sex lives of politicians to the tragic consequences of war and famine, the spatial flows of the media put us in touch with the lives of people we have never met, while stretching the outlines of our community. If we compare our 'common' world to those that lived at the end of the nineteenth century then one of the major differences we could point towards would be the genuinely mass development of public systems of communication. It is indeed hard to imagine what our lives would be like without the mass media. News from the world's four corners taking months rather than seconds to arrive, politicians escaping the visible public scrutiny of the cameras and no cinemas to visit with our friends and family. The mass media, in one shape or form, have become part of the rituals of everyday life. Yet as we come to the century's close these shared networks of communication are arguably undergoing a change as deep seated as the initial provision of mass television. The emergence of new technologies in respect of digital television, video recorders, the internet and a host of other features are reshaping our shared cultural landscape. Yet what is the 'real' significance of these changes? Do they necessarily make us a more communicative society? How do these elements bear upon the current times in which we live? It is these sorts of questions that this book seeks to map out through a range of issues and concerns.

The media: capital, nation and the public

In seeking to understand the structures and discourses that shaped the media during the twentieth century we need to investigate the interconnections between capitalism, the nation-state and notions of the public. While the specific interrelations between these concepts have impacted differently depending upon particular histories and societies it is possible to uncover a more general story. These overlapping dimensions have defined the outline of media cultures for much of the preceding century and will continue to have an important bearing upon the next. However, as we shall see throughout this book, the theoretical and practical complexity of the media has been added to by processes of globalisation and more 'uncertain' political frames of reference.

Capitalism during the twentieth century ushered in a mass culture that was based upon standardisation, commodification and conformity. Media industries were invested in in order to gain profits irrespective of questions of value. The mass culture of capitalism then was built upon the order of tried and tested packages which were deeply suspicious of cultural innovation and avant-guardist forms of experimentation. The fear that dominated this particular era was that dominant cultural producers (read the United States) would both push minority cultures to the margins while diminishing more literary and educated sensibilities. Recent transformations however have begun to ask questions of this particular narrative. The age of informational capitalism has meant that advertising, magazines and television programmes have become more explicitly targeted in terms of certain lifestyle niches. This has meant that capitalism is becoming less associated with a culture of mass conformity than with the catering of products to meet the preferences of explicit population groupings. Increasingly television programmes, advertisements, magazines and films are produced with the cultural make up of a particular audience segment in mind. Further, this inevitably creates a situation where commercial media cultures are increasingly orientated around the requirements of social groups who are in full-time employment. For example, the recent development of satellite broadcasting and pay TV can be seen in these terms. In the British context the dominance of Sky TV over certain sporting events (most importantly premiership football) has created a situation whereby access to viewing televised soccer is increasingly determined by ability to pay. We could also point towards the expansion of cable services and the internet and argue that, in addition to more explicitly targeted media cultures, 'informational' capitalism is also creating an increasing divide between the technological rich and the technological poor. This is not to argue however that the mass culture thesis has been completely displaced by a more information segmented culture. One only has to point towards Hollywood's current reworking of popular television serials from the 1960s and the 1970s (*The Avengers* and *Lost in Space* have both been released this summer) to argue

2

that it continues to rely upon previously established genres and taste communities. Here my argument is not so much that we are entering into what Poster (1995) has called a second media age, but that mass forms of culture continue to work within so-called post-modern processes of fragmentation and differentiation.

Since the advent of the printing press the idea of the nation has been a relatively permanent feature within the popular imagination. The development of the press and television have all been specifically 'national' in focus, ownership and control. Many television programmes, films and newspapers took the idea of a recognisable national identity for granted while symbolically contributing to its construction. The national 'we' is discursively present in the vast majority of the media that we consume on a daily basis. The content of the media of mass communication continues to provide a rough and ready guide as to whether the nation is defined in civic or ethnic terms. Media cultures therefore have been central in helping define the limits of the community. However, two major changes are discernible at this conjuncture. First, the media, as we shall see, are increasingly owned and controlled by large-scale trans-national concerns that only maintain the most minimal of ties to specifically national cultures. These communications conglomerates that are based upon product differentiation and the power of distribution networks are genuinely global institutions in that they sell their products the world over. This has meant that the main agent of governance in terms of communications is no longer the state but the market. The determination of our communicative futures therefore will be driven by the needs of capital rather than the state. Secondly, the transgressing of national boundaries by symbolic goods and peoples has given national cultures a more cosmopolitan orientation. Modern citizens are increasingly used to living in shared cultural environments that are composed of different ethnicities and regularly keep them up to date with developments in different corners of the globe. Arguably then, if the communications media at the beginning of the century were specifically national, at the end they have a more hybrid and global orientation. At this point however my analysis differs sharply from many of the others currently on offer in that I argue that while the nation-state has lost much of its power it is still in a position to maintain its influence. Here I argue that notions of community remain more than contingently tied to ideas of nationhood, and that states still have the ability to shape the communicative identities of their citizens. These arguments press the importance of obligations over rights and of the interconnection between state and civil society more generally.

Finally, the role of the media in the shaping of the public sphere as opposed to commercial and national cultures is an important one. Whereas commercial cultures are concerned with economic exchange, national cultures with common forms of identity and belonging, notions of the public are intimately connected to democratic will formation. That is they depend less upon a structurally determined identity and more on our shared capacity to be able to participate within public debates. This inevitably, as we shall see, opens questions of a moral and ethical nature. In other words, while notions of the public grew up with capitalism and the nation, they remain analytically separable. Ideas of the public meant that the media had an obligation to provide information that would embarrass nation-states, blow the whistle on the exploits of capital and allow a diverse community critically to debate the important issues of the day. If capitalism defined the people as consumers, the state as a nation or nation's, then notions of the public took them to be citizens with rights and responsibilities. Critical notions of the public have served to make citizens aware when their common cultures were racist or sexist, when certain broadly accepted viewpoints served powerful interest groups, or when the well-polished spin of political or scientific experts were interrupted in the interests of a broader community. Yet while the public might have been 'comfortably' identified with the nation for much of this century this is no longer the case. The public sphere is a spatially differentiated concept that works at the level of the local, national and the global. Hence public discussion of ecological issues can involve the school magazine, the national press and CNN news all at once. The media spirals of dialogue, discussion and outrage in an age of instantaneous communication also open out new temporal dimensions and less formally rationalistic perspectives. The cacophony of noise that can greet genuinely 'global events' like the impeachment of an American president or the reporting of a genocide moves us beyond spatially stable notions of the public sphere.

The more global orientation of the media also involves us in moral and ethical questions far removed from the communities we physically inhabit. Documentaries that present us with pictures of human suffering insistently ask us amongst other questions 'what should we do'? In addition, the gaze of the media has changed the balance between public and private life opening out the intimate dimensions of many people's lives about whom we know little personally. This then poses new questions in terms of what the limits of legitimate public reflection should be, why certain 'events' rather than others appear on our screen, and what a fully 'inclusive' public dialogue would look like? These questions and others form the 'heart' of the book in that they open out a number of complex moral and ethical questions posed by new media environments. However, to be clear, the debates do not so much resolve these and other questions, but open them out for wider forms of reflection, while suggesting some of the paths that we might fruitfully take.

Undoubtedly the account given above in respect of changing media cultures is Eurocentric. The narrative however continues to have a resonance inside North American and Western European societies marginalising other more differentiated histories and trajectories. Globalisation, if it has taught us anything, has asked us to think again about projecting our own backyards onto the rest of the world. In this respect, I attempt, partially at least, to deconstruct this way of thinking while recognising that it is a tradition that many of us with good reason continue to follow. For some I will have gone too far in this process, while for others I will not have gone far enough. In other words, what is contained in the following pages is an attempt to defend a pluralist public realm that may find a foothold in a variety of cultural settings. This book then is written at a particular point in the study of mass communications where old paradigms are breaking down and newer ones are just beginning to emerge into the light. Yet my overwhelming concern is not so much to map out the 'empirical' changes evident within mass forms of communication, but to ask what they mean for genuinely moral and ethical dimensions of thinking.

In this respect, the volume opens by considering whether a case can still be made for a critical public sphere through the writing of Raymond Williams and Jurgen Habermas. Here I point to the similarities and differences between these two writers when it comes to considering questions of a moral and ethical nature in terms of the media, while pointing to some of their limitations in this respect. Of key importance here is their mutual concentration upon an ethics of dialogue that needs to be rejoined with one of responsibility. In the next chapter, I argue that to be concerned with moral and ethical questions in a global media age opens up questions of justice, recognition and notions of meaningfulness in respect of contemporary media cultures. The aim here is to develop a set of moral and political criteria that takes the debate beyond earlier questions of bias in media reporting and the more contemporary stress on the fragmentation of identity fostered by post-modern accounts. These dimensions I argue are likely to become more rather than less important as the media become increasingly central to the definition of social and political life. Following on, the third chapter opens out current debates around cosmopolitanism and nationalism, policy and citizenship, and obligations and rights in respect of the working of contemporary media cultures. My argumentative strategy here is that critical questions regarding morality and ethics can no longer be contained solely within questions related to the public sphere, but must engage with a wider range of discourses and debates. These concerns enable us to formulate the concept of 'cultural citizenship' and thereby discuss processes of inclusion as well as exclusion from the cultural sphere. The fourth chapter centrally addresses the question as to how we might understand issues related to the media and globalisation in terms of a set of debates in media studies that stem from the 1960s. Here I juxtapose debates in respect of media imperialism and McLuhan's notions of the global village with more contemporary concerns in respect of post-colonialism, the risk society and the 'new' political economy of media. This neatly links into my case study about the reporting of the 1994 Rwandan genocide by both local and global media. The specific example of the political history and global position of a small African nation is used as a foil to throw light upon some of the current claims being made by both academics and media entrepreneurs alike in respect of the so-called new global media age. Finally, the last chapter considers the claims made by those who argue that the global media needs to be reformulated through the acceptance of a human rights agenda, while simultaneously considering the polarities involved in assessing the argument that a more participatory media culture is likely to be ushered in by new technologies. This section looks critically at the prospects for a more engaged and participatory public sphere emerging in the age of 'informational' capitalism. These considerations then set the scene for some 'minimal' policy recommendations in respect of contemporary media cultures.

Overall then this book is meant to contribute to both a critical theory of the media and open out new possibilities in terms of morality and ethics more generally. Whether I succeed in either of these ventures is not for me to judge.

Media and cultural studies today

Finally I would like to say something of where this text fits into the tradition of media and cultural studies as a whole. There has been much talk recently of certain absences and retreats within media and cultural studies. A point made by writers as different as Edward Said (1993) and Richard Rorty (1998) has concerned cultural studies' neglect of political economy and practical political questions in the public sphere. Here a picture is painted of university courses being excessively concerned with 'theory' at the cost of an engagement with certain more gritty realities. Whereas Said points to the academies' silence or acquiescence on issues concerning the continuation of American imperial power, most notably evident in the Gulf War, Rorty is more concerned that identity politics has come to replace a concern with class and economic divisions within America. We might add to this, in my own context, by pointing that much of the talk that goes on within cultural studies under the rubric of globalisation is bland and forecloses important political questions. Of these issues more later; for now my own argument is both sympathetic to these projections while pointing to different absences. Questions of political economy and the public sphere, as should already be obvious, are central to the issues opened out by this volume. Yet while there is much to agree with in terms of Said's and Rorty's respective claims they are at least currently finding a more receptive climate.[1]

My concern, as I have already indicated, maps on to these issues and yet has a slightly different trajectory. This is that media and cultural studies has an at best uneasy relationship with issues that are moral, ethical and 'political' in nature. I think that some of the reasons for this are evident if we consider for a moment the history of cultural and media studies in the British context. Here I want to look at the figures of Raymond Williams and E. P. Thompson who were arguably two of the most important intellectuals on the British New Left, and major theorists of the first wave of post-war

British cultural studies. Both of these writers combined a moral and political agenda that linked the study of class and culture to the need for a socialist society. While both Williams and Thompson sought to defend a romantic literary tradition that linked a range of writers from Morris to Blake, they inhabited a certain moralism when it came to the understanding of commercial forms of popular culture. To writers in the second generation of cultural studies trained in semiotics, discourse analysis and structuralism this neglected to analyse the specific ideologies, pleasures and subjectivities mobilised by popular material cultures. This neglect was taken not only to be elitist, but also lacked any appreciation of the complex and contradictory nature of much of contemporary popular culture. My argument here is not that such views are wholly mistaken, but that the critique is simultaneously accurate and somewhat overdone.[2]

For Williams and Thompson the achievement of a 'socialist' society would lead to a more complex and participatory civil society and more concerted forms of engagement with educated culture. These connections, as are my own, are the product of certain times and places. Since their time we have witnessed the collapse of state socialism, the globalisation of the media and the flows of capital, the opening up of ecological questions, more fluid gender identities, the rebirth of ethnic nationalism and the diminishing power of the state amongst other frames. This is reason enough not to start 'lifting' cultural agendas from earlier waves of theorising. Yet both Williams and Thompson were concerned to link questions of political economy, the public sphere and progressive political agendas in a way that was mostly absent from the second wave of cultural theorising. Arguably in the critique of their moralism we also discarded questions of a moral and ethical nature. Where perhaps I differ from both generations of cultural theorising is in both wanting to preserve the nature of these concerns while adding a deeper uncertainty and ambivalence in terms of the 'answers' that it leaves us with. One of the reasons why it seems so short-sighted to ignore the moral and ethical dimensions of media cultures is that in an increasingly mediated world this is precisely the domain where they are most likely to be raised publicly. Yet while wanting to open questions that are concerned with morality and ethics I am perhaps less certain as to how these dimensions might be decided, theorised and acted upon. Arguably then my concerns are not properly addressed by either of the two generations of cultural studies in that such issues open out the importance of an active civic culture that has given up the politics of certitude.

Such a view steers a critical path between the more certain moral and political universe inhabited by Williams and Thompson and the absence of moral and ethical terms in much contemporary theorising. In this respect, I am indebted to both Jurgen Habermas and Zygmunt Bauman for clearly demonstrating the continued purchase of such questions. While I am critical of their writing in many respects, I think that both writers open out a sustained concern with moral and ethical matters while pointing to the undoubted political nature of such questions. Both Habermas and Bauman, in their different ways, have sought to maintain an understanding of the 'harder' features of modernity from the colonising imperatives of capital to the dangers of bureaucratic forms of reason, while linking them to the rise of a more thoroughly mediated social world. This does not so much point to the 'impossibility' of moral and ethical dimensions, but their renewed urgency in a world that since the collapse of the Cold War is defined by more 'uncertain' political parameters. What Milan Kundera (1994) has termed the 'lightness of being' speaks as much of a shared human ontology as it does the current contours of post-traditional societies. That our shared moral and ethical futures depend as much upon the continuing structural coordinates of modernity, more uncertain post-modern frames and the ways in which we choose to act in a mediated world encompasses much of what I am trying to say.

CHAPTER 2

Media, morality and modernity

The community stagnates without the impulse of the individual, the impulse dies away
without the sympathy of the community

[William James]

In thinking about mass communication, Raymond Williams once wrote, 'it matters greatly where you start' (Williams, 1962b). Indeed in thinking about the mass media social theorists of various kinds have started from a multitude of positions. If we step back a moment it is evident that there are basically three places to start discussing the media. These include the responses of critical theory, reception analysis and those mostly concerned with the functioning of different mediums of communication. My concern here is that they very rarely give direct answers to the question as to 'what the media is for'? Arguably such a question presupposes issues that are of a moral and ethical nature. For instance, the reason that many continue to argue that the mass media should represent a plurality of viewpoints is that they take the view that democracy has a certain normative relevance. That is that most definitions of democracy are connected with the idea that power is invested in the people, rather than a social elite or a bureaucratic apparatus. Overall democratic societies would wish to uphold that the practices of collective decision making are *better* than authoritarian rule. This might be justified through a variety of arguments that would propose that democracies potentially allow for the acceptance of difference, the fostering of relations of solidarity, and the acceptance of the principles of liberty and equality. More likely such arguments would turn on the necessity of the channels of communication being kept open in order to enable processes of consensual democratic will formation. Obviously in actually existing democracies these values can come into conflict, be passed over in favour of efficiency criteria, or fall into disuse through neglect. Despite all of these obstacles substantive human values can be called upon to press the case for democracy. But, for the most part, media theory has either presupposed such values relegating them to the background of the analysis, or has ignored arguments related to the normative relevance of instituted communication networks. These reflections lead unavoidably to a consideration of the current status of media theory in respect of moral and ethical questions.

The first approach suggested by media theory offers a critical theory of mass communication, where the organisational structures, content and reception of media cultures is examined as a source of social power and ideology. Here the media are often linked to accumulation strategies on the part of capital, hegemonic attempts by powerful social groups aiming to legitimate certain 'world views' over others, or to the ways in which state power silences dissenting voices that are potentially embarrassing for the status quo. Yet, as many theorists have been aware, such arguments contain within them normative claims that pose critical questions for the dominant means of image production. For instance, there is little sense in protesting against the overwhelmingly biased nature of much media production unless we are also informed as to how such relations might be reformulated. To argue that the media currently give a distorted impression of AIDS sufferers implicitly suggests that we have some idea as to how they might be more fairly or impartially represented. In short, if we are to enter into a critique of relations of dominance, we can only do so if we make certain normative claims that we feel will find a wide acceptance in the community as a whole.

The second strand of media research is provided by a more interpretative approach. Audience research of various kinds has argued that media interactions normally take place within private as opposed to public settings, and involve complex symbolic work on the part of viewers, listeners and readers. Much of this work has uncovered the ways in which media messages are variously negotiated and resisted by audiences located within public and private networks of power and authority. Again most of this writing has been motivated by the concealed normative desire to uncover the voices and perspectives of ordinary people. These excluded perspectives, it is argued, are rarely heard in the everyday outpourings of centralised media messages. The semiotic struggle from below offers an ethics of resistance against the incorporation of 'the people' into dominant ideological strategies. Such an approach is not merely descriptive, but opens out a plurality of voices where it was previously assumed there was only one. Difference is discovered in the place of a previously prevailing sameness. The introduction of audience analysis thereby unsettled previously held assumptions that the subjectivity of the audience mirrored that of media content. Again the desire to reveal difference affirms that human individuality is worthy of our respect.

Finally, the other main strand of thinking about the media has built the development of mediums of communication into the history of modernity. Such views have argued that the mechanisms by which modern societies communicate with themselves are primary rather than secondary phenomena. The historical passage of human societies through oral, written and electric cultures has significantly restructured modernity. In assuming this standpoint, the shifting of time and space achievable through technical media became significant mechanisms by which human experience could be both unified and fragmented. Each time we turn on the television we are caught up with expert cultures and the life-worlds of others who are all distant from the places in which we live. Media forms both compress the world while rapidly expanding the amount of information regularly made available, thereby emphasising the significance of individual choice. Again, we could argue, despite the fact that many who have worked within this paradigm remain indifferent or even hostile to ethical considerations, that such dimensions have a normative relevance. That human beings are continuing to develop ever new and more sophisticated means of communicating with one another alters the moral boundaries of our world. That we are informed as to democratic movements in Burma, genocide in Rwanda and war in Bosnia presumably opens new moral and ethical dilemmas for modern subjects. Further, we could also ask, how the development of new communication media could become subject to ethical rather than instrumental criteria? Yet while I have dealt more fully with the complexity of these different traditions elsewhere, what is obvious, to me at least, is the subordinate nature of moral and ethical problems when it comes to discussing the media of mass communication.[1] We should not forego more concerted attempts to link the domains of media practice, morality and ethics. It is obvious then that what is really at issue in considering the kinds of mass communications environments we wish to foster are questions which are of an ethical and moral nature. This is, if you like, where I start.

So far I have perhaps painted an overly pessimistic picture of the current state of media theory as there remain considerable resources to call upon in addressing questions of media and morality. First, I shall consider the contributions of Jurgen Habermas who attempts to link a moral and ethical theory of communication to a substantive model of the public sphere. While many of the arguments presented here are well known, I want to concentrate more generally on the idea of discourse ethics. In this respect, I will show how such a position is linked to certain universalistic assumptions concerning the moral development of the subject. The problem with most contemporary discussions of Habermas and the media, and here I include my own, is that they fail to link such concerns to his more recent writing. In this the argument will propose that the figures of both Kohlberg and Mead have been central to the development of communicative ethics, while demonstrating how such concerns continue to impinge upon modern media cultures. Secondly, and more briefly, I will look to Raymond Williams's attempt to formulate a cultural materialist basis to ethical questions related to mass communication structures. Again I am aware that most discussions of Williams's work on communications fail to make this vital link. In respect of both Habermas and Williams, I shall also relate their concerns to feminist arguments related to an ethic of care and the deconstruction of the masculine subject. Finally, it could be argued, that both Habermas's and Williams's universalistic concerns are misplaced in current post-modern conditions. The argument here will question the relevance of the forms of universalistic thinking that were developed by modernity in favour of a more ambivalent linkage between the subject and structures of communication.

The public sphere: from refeudalisation to colonisation and juridification

The idea of discourse ethics is based upon the notion that the rightness or the justness of the norms we uphold can only be secured by our ability to give good reasons. In turn, these norms are considered valid if they gain the consent of others within a shared community. The moral principles that we uphold must be more than the prejudices of the particular group to which we happen to belong. Such collectively held norms can only be considered valid if they are judged impartially. In this sense, our ethical claims can be said to be deontological in that their rightness can not be secured by social conventions or appeals to tradition (Habermas, 1990a). The achievement of a universal ethical stance, therefore, requires that participants in practical discourse transcend their own egoistic position in order to negotiate with the horizons of other cultures and perspectives. A norm can only be considered valid if it would be freely accepted by all those it would potentially affect. These remarks, as should be clear, represent a radical reworking of the universalistic thinking of Kant, and a forcible rejection of relativistic standpoints.

In making these claims, however, Habermas is clear that we need to separate moral questions from ethical reflections that are related to the good life. This is especially necessary in modern multicultural societies that juxtapose and mix different cultural traditions and orientations. For example, we are unlikely to be able to reach universal agreement on questions such as to which particular communities we owe loyalty. We might have obligations to a particular region, football team, nation, religious group or family members. These networks of identity sustaining connection are likely to inform collective and individual forms of self-understanding. Habermas argues that such questions are best described as ethical rather than moral, and are largely driven by the issue as to 'what is right for me'. On the other hand, moral concerns are more properly associated with whether or not particular maxims are appropriate for the whole community. Thus whereas participants in processes of self-clarification inevitably remain tied to their communities and identities, moral questions require that we break and distance ourselves from our immediate ties to consider questions of universal rightness and justice (Habermas, 1993a). The distinction between morality and ethics could be said to apply to television. The programmes that I decide to watch obviously have a bearing on my social identity given the implications they might have for my communally negotiated view of the good life. However, such questions are radically distinct from finding agreement with others on the moral principles that should regulate television content and production. For instance, my favourite television soap opera is *EastEnders*, and I'm sure some of the reasons I watch regularly are connected with the feelings of community and the participation in 'ordinary' national life that it generates. These sentiments, however, are radically distinct from the principles of quality and difference which should arguably govern the institutional organisation of television.

These reflections bring us onto one of Habermas's central ideas, namely communicative action. For Habermas there are basically two types of action; they are instrumental forms of action which depend upon egocentric forms of calculation and strategy, and communicative action where actors are prepared to commit themselves to norms which are the outcome of rational agreement. Communicative action holds out the possibility of coming to agreement over (1) the objective world; (2) the social world of institutions, traditions and values; and (3) our own subjective worlds. We are able to reach an understanding of these three interrelated worlds due to the fact that human beings are part of an intersubjective linguistic community. For Habermas (1981) the very fact that we are language users means that we are communicatively able to reach an understanding of one another. Habermas argues that in every act of speech we are capable of immanently raising three validity claims in connection with what is said. These three validity claims, he adds, constitute a background consensus of normal everyday language use in Western society. The three claims – that are used by agents to test the validity of speech – could be characterised as: propositional truth claims, normative claims related to appropriateness, as well as claims connected to sincerity. These claims notably map onto the objective, social and subjective worlds mentioned above, and allows us intersubjectively to investigate questions of truth, justice and taste.

Habermas's (1989a) only complete work to date on the public is a historical account of the rise and fall of the bourgeois public sphere. Habermas tells how the bourgeois public sphere developed out of a feudal system that denied the principle of open public discussion on matters of universal interest. Although there had existed a public sphere in classical Greece, it is not until seventeenth- and eighteenth-century Europe that along with the development of capitalism it assumed a more distinctive form. The state, in this period, became the sphere of public authority that had a legitimate claim to the use of violence. The modern state could be clearly separated from civil society both judicially and institutionally. Civil society, as distinct from the state, comprised the domain of commodity production and exchange, as well as the 'private' family. Between the realm of public authority and civil society there emerged the critical domain of the public sphere. The purpose of the public sphere was to enable the people to reflect critically upon themselves and the practices of the state. The public sphere developed initially out of coffee houses and salons where male members of the bourgeoisie, nobles and intellectuals met to discuss works of literature.

While these open-ended conversations were always based upon practices of exclusion, they retain a certain immanence. The critical potential of these on-going conversations is secured through three main reasons. First, the social intercourse that eventually shifted from literary to political critique, opened up a social space where the authority of the better argument could be asserted against the established status quo. Secondly, areas of social debate that had been sealed off under feudalism, once they had lost the 'aura' that had been provided by the church and the court, became increasingly problematised through conversation that disregarded the status of the participants. And finally, Habermas wants to argue, the meetings that took place across Europe in salons and coffee houses, mainly between 1680 and 1730, were both inclusive as well as exclusive. While the qualifications for taking an active part in dialogue remained overtly restrictive, the claim that was being made was that this activity constituted a mouthpiece for the public. Habermas senses that while the 'public' remained small, the principle of universality was beginning to be accepted. This can be asserted as those who met the qualificatory criteria of being rational, male and propertied could avail themselves through active participation in the public sphere. Through the principle of publicity, he claims, it was established that the public use of reason was superior to its private utilisation. The pursuit of truth through an intersubjective dimension that reflected upon both civil society and the state, Habermas maintains, held out distinct possibilities for the reformation of asymmetrical relations of force. Thus the dominant male capitalist class, both maintained its hegemonic position through practices of exclusion, while simultaneously providing the cultural grounds for critique.

The tragedy of the bourgeois public sphere however was that the very social forces that brought it into being would eventually lead to its decline and destruction. The instituted dialogue of the salons and coffee houses would give way as communication became increasingly organised through large commercial concerns. The progressive institutional elimination of private communicative individuals coming into conversation in the public sphere, emphasised an increasing separation between public and private life. From this point on commercial culture was consumed in private requiring no further debate or discussion. Unlike the print culture of the discursive bourgeois salons, much of the new media (television, film and radio) disallows the possibility of talking back and taking part. Just as modern mass culture is received in atomised contexts, so the technical development of new cultural forms promoted privatism. Along with the 'privatisation' of culture, Habermas adds, there has also been a corresponding trivialisation of cultural products in order to gain a large share of the market. For Habermas, the operation of the market is best seen as a dual and contradictory process that has both emancipatory and dominatory effects and implications. For example, the video market provides a small strata of readers access to high quality films. However, the lowering of entrance requirements has meant that film has had to be accommodated to a mass leisure culture, that encourages passive relaxation and ease of reception. Modern cultural forms integrate subjects into a depoliticised culture, which bypasses the public sphere where claims related to rightness could be discussed. This has led to what Habermas has called the refeudalisation of the public sphere. By this he means that notions of 'aura' have been reintroduced into public dialogue by converting politicians into media stars and, I might also add, by utilising 'personalities' in issues of public importance. For instance, in the promotion of popular awareness concerning AIDS the issue has been demonised (by the homophobia of certain media), marginalised (the lack of a thorough wide-ranging discussion after an initial media blitz) and trivialised (through the use of kitsch and personalities) (Alcorn, 1989).

Modern media cultures in short have become progressively colonised by instrumental reason and public power. The cultural transformations and processes outlined above, if we follow Habermas, has led to the emptying out of meaningful social practices by expert systems. Whereas once publicity meant the exposure of domination through the use of reason, the public sphere is now subsumed under a stage managed political theatre.

The public sphere which had previously fostered rational debate amongst a male propertied elite had been replaced by new mechanisms of communication that depended upon privatised forms of reception and the promotion of politicians as media stars. For Habermas, such concerns can never be far away from the surface. Indeed more recently he seems to have replaced questions of refeudalisation with those that address the colonisation of the life-world and processes of juridification. Such notions are intended to supplement and update his earlier reflections.

Habermas explains the internal colonisation of the life-world through what he perceives as the 'indissoluble' tension that exists between capitalism and democracy. Democracy holds out the principle that institutions should be subordinable to discursive forms of argument and consensus seeking, whereas capitalism presumes a system of profit maximisation irrespective of normative concerns. These two basic principles mean that the formation of public opinion through mediated public debate is articulated differently by these dual perspectives. The key area of antagonism between these two principles, however, is not the media of mass communication but the welfare state. Following Offe (1984), Habermas argues that the material separation between the economy and the state displaces the centrality of class conflict in modern societies. The contradictory development of the welfare state has meant that it has been asked to perform paradoxical social functions. The welfare state is dependent on the successful workings of the economy for revenue, while being asked to compensate for the disruptive and disorganising consequences of capital. Habermas is clear that the compromise between capital and labour is bought at the price of a de-politicised political sphere and the enhancement of consumerism. Democratic, or what Habermas calls 'life-world' initiatives, become predefined around the systemic importance of the reproduction of consumptive lifestyles and the role of the welfare client. Through these processes the life-world (the realm of intersubjectively shared knowledge) becomes robbed of its capacity to form coherent political ideologies giving way to cynicism and fragmented forms of consciousness. The media of mass communication, if this argument is followed, becomes increasingly orientated around large-scale conglomerates and the structural requirement of the state to impose mass loyalty. Media therefore must obey the structural necessity of securing a profit or of legitimating the political order of modern society. Further, a point Habermas mostly ignores, publicly instituted media are subject to similar pressures to those most evident in welfare services. As Habermas (1989b) is aware the New Right sought to solve the crisis of legitimation currently being experienced by welfare regimes by privatisation measures, tax reductions and supply-side economics. This has meant that public as opposed to commercial systems of communication have been progressively deregulated during the 1980s and 1990s. Thus the relations between the system and the 'life-world' have not only had impacts upon social welfare, but have also greatly impoverished the economic and political base of public forms of communication.

At this point, it is important to introduce the concept of juridification. Generally speaking, by this Habermas means the increasing tendency of diverse areas of social life to fall under the guise of the law. The historical development of 'individual' civil, political and social rights both formally guarantees certain freedoms, while increasing the involvement of the state in social life more generally. Citizenship rights that have been won through civil, political and social struggles that both serve to bureaucratise everyday life, while providing certain individual entitlements protected by the law. Viewed in terms of the public sphere, rights to free speech can be said to have a regulative rather than a constitutive power. This perhaps allows Habermas to develop a more fully dialectical view of the public sphere than was previously evident. The public sphere can be said to be subject to countervailing pressures and demands that are not adequately captured by notions of refeudalisation. The idea of a collectively shared democratic public space is built at the point between system and life-world. It is systemically regulated by certain formal rights and the pressures of money and power, while maintaining its dependence upon the more communicative social matrix of the life-world. Habermas (1981: 389–391) in this sense articulates a more complex and ambivalent view of media cultures. Some of these features will be briefly considered here.

First, mass communication is important for communicative ethics as it detaches viewpoints and perspectives from 'provincial' perspectives and makes them widely available in space and time. In this respect, the media has the capacity simultaneously to hierarchise (by only including certain voices) and democratise (making views widely available) political views and perspectives. Secondly, mediums of mass communication, at present, are largely centralised structures which are based on one-way forms of communication, flowing from centre to periphery. This enhances forms of social control by reproducing a division of labour between the producers of media messages and their consumers. One the other hand, the capacity to transport images in time and space making them publicly visible also potentially opens them to validity claims in a variety of social contexts. Finally, Habermas (1989b) is aware that the public sphere is being reshaped through the emergence of 'life-world' movements such as ecological and feminist groups. These groups have both a more reciprocal relationship with the 'life-world' and have helped carve out more autonomous public spaces in such a way that openly resists ideological forms of incorporation in a way that is not reflected in mainstream political parties. Hence these developments in Habermas's thinking, position the media of mass communication as caught between systemic imperatives and the democratic considerations of communicative action. This leaves the media of mass communications torn between democracy and colonisation, discussion and profit, and freedom and silence. These spheres Habermas contends can only be reformulated by socially containing the expression of money and power through the application of discourse ethics. This would make the restructuring of social life the responsibility of the whole community rather than groups of self-selected experts. In complex mediated societies like our own, therefore, discourse ethics would have to be applied not only to media structures but also styles of media presentation and reporting. Only then would the whole community be in a position to be able discursively to rethink its currently perceived interests in respect of relations between culture and society.

The public sphere and moral progress

It is impossible to read Habermas without a clear notion that the democratic foundations of everyday life remain underdeveloped in modernity. Habermas's preoccupation with discourse ethics is nothing if it is not an argument for a more emancipated and less-reified social order. While Habermas resolutely argues that the application of the moral principles agreed upon in dialogic negotiations are not properly the concern of the philosopher, we are left in little doubt that certain material preconditions would have to be satisfied if the democratic possibilities of modern culture are ever to be reawakened. These would include the attainment of certain levels of education, an egalitarian distribution of wealth and of course the maintenance of a democratic, electronically mediated public space. Of the other preconditions, Habermas has spent a considerable amount of effort in outlining how discourse ethics is dependent upon a particular view of the subject. To put matters differently, there would be little point in Habermas championing the cause of communicative action, unless social subjects are endowed with the cognitive capacity to construct universally binding norms.

This leads Habermas away from the macro dimensions of money and power into an investigation, primarily through Kohlberg and Mead, into the moral development of the self.

In seeking to develop these arguments, I shall show how Habermas's view of a rational, plural and inclusive public sphere presupposes certain views regarding subjective development. Habermas (1979) argues that a fully emancipated society is dependent upon the ego development achievable by its citizens. Our ability to form an understanding of our unconscious desires and our cognitive capacity to embrace a universal morality contributes significantly to the cultural development of a mature citizenship. The growth in our common capacity to become fully cognitive human beings is therefore dependent upon the moral evolution of the ego. In this, Habermas follows Kohlberg, by highlighting six developmental stages which are necessary for the emergence of the universal principles that become attached to rights, reciprocity and justice. Habermas and Kohlberg, by outlining the stages of moral–cognitive development, are seeking to understand how an initially biologically and socially dependent human being becomes capable of a post-conventional morality. The argument, common to much ego psychology, charts the separation of the mature ego from the initial bonds of the early socialisation process eventually becoming a fully independent member of the community. In order for this stage to be reached the role identity formed within the family has to be weakened to allow for an ego identity to be based upon city, state and more global forms of identification. Both Kohlberg and Habermas posit an idea of the mature individual who is able to evaluate moral norms from the standpoint of the community, rather than the particular concerns of her family or social group. To illustrate this case, Habermas draws a homology between the moral and ethical development of human society and individual self-identity. Just as human societies have sought to question the binding power of tradition, so a post-conventional morality would hold that moral maxims and particular orientations should seek justification through universal ethics. As the social world loses its capacity, once and for all, to fix moral hierarchies through tradition this opens the cosmos to differing value ideas related to personal fulfilment. The fully developed ego therefore should in principle be capable of questioning the authority of previously held identities within the private sphere, as well as communally transmitted norms and values. Habermas invites us in our most intimate personal relations and public affiliations to subject ourselves to the reasoned discourse of others. We would, if these reflections are accurate, have to learn to live without the ontological or metaphysical guarantees that we are currently living within truth. Such a view of human beings most obviously has implications for the maintenance of an open, pluralistic and noisy public sphere that is able to reveal to us the fragility of our current practices and beliefs.

Nowhere is the notion that the formation of our identities are dependent upon intersubjective forms of recognition and moral notions of community better developed than within Mead. Habermas (1981, 1992) himself clearly realises the historical importance of Mead in developing notions of inter-subjectivity and an ethical understanding of the subject. For Mead (1934) the self emerges through a three-way conversation between the I, Me and generalised Other. Mead produces a theory of self-development similar to Kohlberg in that we can only understand the self by radically decentring monadic notions of consciousness. In this, Mead clearly states that 'the individual is not a self in the reflexive sense unless he is an object to himself' (Mead, 1934: 142). Human selfhood can be said to develop out of our capacity to view ourselves from the particular and general attitudes of other people. Until the individual is capable of viewing herself from the concrete and generalised standpoint of others we can not be said to have developed a personality. It is in 'taking the attitude of the other' that the 'me' learns to control actions, attitudes and social expressions. A subject only gains consciousness of itself to the extent to which it is able to perceive its own actions through the lens of the other. Mead distinguishes in this regard the 'I' – the spontaneous, creative response of personhood to others – from the 'me' – the organised set of attitudes of the other which we take as our own. The 'I' then is the acting ego, and the 'me' is the attitude of others which have been assumed as our own. If we take this ongoing conversation together it constitutes our personality.These features, according to Mead, allow us to talk to ourselves, and grant human beings with a shared capacity for inner dialogue and reflection. The self is caught in the constant ebb and flow of conversation between ourselves and others. For Mead these features crucially form the basis for self-understanding, as well as self-regard and self-respect. We are able to develop a feeling of trust in our own capacities the extent to which we are able reciprocally to negotiate mutual reciprocity and obligations through an intersubjective dimension (Honneth, 1995).

The final part in the dialogic puzzle of self-formation is provided by the 'generalised other'. For Mead mature selfhood can only arise once we learn to take the 'attitude of the other' in a wider communal sense. This is not a description of moral conformity, but a recognition, by Mead, that the 'self regarding self' can only handle community disapproval by setting up higher moral standards which 'out-vote' presently held societal norms (Mead, 1934: 168). When there is a conflict between the individual and the community, the self is thrown back into a reflective attitude examining whether the values and norms that are currently held are in need of revision. The necessity of the individual bringing her values to bear upon the community opens out a universalistic morality and lifts us out of our more concrete ties. The individual can be required to come into conflict with their community over the defence of a universalistic morality. Moral and ethical universality is only possible, according to Mead, because individuals have the capacity to take the role of the other. To live in a democratic order has as many implications for identity formations as it does for societal structures. Hence in Habermasian terms the shared moral worth of ourselves as human beings is dependent upon the constant conversational revision of our identities, and by an institutional openness to change through procedures of rational communication (Jonas, 1985). Habermas (1992: 186) himself best sums up this point, when he says that Mead consistently represents 'individualism as the flipside of universalism'.[2]

Habermas (1981) remains sympathetic to the overall direction of Mead's project, but offers a number of detailed criticisms. There is not the space to replay all of these arguments, so here is a brief outline of three of them. First, in Mead's terms collective identities would have to be the direct outcome of the negotiation between the 'I' and the 'me'. This seemingly ignores the prehistory of collective symbols and their ability to reinforce relations of authority prior to questions related to their normative validity. For instance, Habermas might, although it is not clear, have in mind national forms of consciousness that have been historically imposed by the nation-state. Here symbolic mechanisms are employed in order to sanction national hierarchies, relations between generations and feelings of in-group loyalty that are not merely the result of dialogic processes. Next, as we have outlined above, Mead fails to make a clear distinction between specifically moral and ethical questions. As Habermas makes clear the cultural uniformity necessary for agreement on ethical questions is no longer evident in the modern world. These changes, as we saw, necessitate the division between properly ethical and moral questions. Finally, the functional material reproduction of the social order is almost entirely neglected by Mead. Mead's analysis of modern society seemingly neglects wider questions of power and ideology. Habermas consistently makes the case, in respect of this criticism, that communicative action, and societies' moral development generally, would have to operate within empirical limits imposed by certain functional requirements. The social order for Habermas is not subordinable to the complex interplay of self and other. To argue that this is the case would merge questions of system (dependent upon material reproduction) and social integration (dependent upon cultural traditions and socialisation processes). Indeed in modernity the functioning of the systems of economy and state have become increasingly detached from questions of social integration. The regulation of society by money and power brings us back to Habermas's main political point that such domains need to become remoralised rather than collectively owned. A radical politics can no longer be characterised through particular demands, but would focus on a redistribution of power and an opening up of communicative social processes. The struggle to remoralise social conflicts in an age which has seen the increasing polarisation of social groups could only appear if the public-sphere is communicatively redrawn (Habermas, 1990b).

This is not the place to assess the validity of Habermas's criticisms of Mead, especially as this has already been done elsewhere (Crossley, 1996). What is more pertinent for our concerns is that Habermas, through the work of Mead and Kohlberg, upholds a normative conception of the mature citizen.

This is an extremely bold move given certain aspects within social theory that would either take the Foucaultian position and warn against the deep dangers of setting up normative hierarchies, or move with the Baudrillardian current arguing that the moral self is a mere fiction of enlightenment nostalgia. My own sense is however that, while we might be able to explore the limitations of Habermas's attempts to rejoin subjective processes to universal concerns through a number of perspectives, contemporary feminism asks the most difficult questions. Rather than dismissing Habermas's concerns with morality and ethics as being part of an outmoded rationalist culture, many currents within contemporary feminism have sought to engage with Habermas precisely because he takes these domains seriously. Habermas then is important because he recognises that the development of the self is not merely a matter of power or discourse, but has ethical and moral implications. If a more democratic public sphere is to be envisaged in a future society it will be because we think of ourselves as having something to offer beyond the recidivism of cynical reason. The reinvigoration of the public sphere will only be possible if we are able to link the concerns of dialogue to those of morality and ethics as Habermas is well aware.

Feminism, the subject and an ethic of care

Some feminist theorists have begun to argue that child-rearing arrangements are central elements in the construction of gender identity, and help maintain male dominance. Further, they argue that the consequences of these cultural practices can be extended widely into almost every domain of social life, deeply shaping the nature of power, knowledge and ethics. In terms of moral reasoning, it has been the work of Carole Gilligan that has posed the most difficulties for universalists such as Habermas. Gilligan's (1982) 'big idea' is that moral development leads to a consideration of universal rights and justice takes masculinity as the norm. According to Gilligan, such thinking presupposes a universal disembodied subject who has no concrete ties and obligations towards others. Women, therefore, are less likely to satisfy the requirements of the fully mature subject due to different patterns of socialisation. Further universalistic models of development actually repress the 'difference' of women. Much of the work done within feminist psychoanalysis, for example, has heightened our understanding that for men to imagine themselves as rational autonomous egos in search of universal principles they must first repress powerful unconscious feelings of dependency. They are able to do this as men's primary role continues to be sought within the public, rather than the private sphere. It is more commonly men's experience to become progressively detached from early feelings of relatedness and care, than that of women's. In Habermas's notion of the mature public 'man' who has a well-developed capacity to reason universally, it is not clear what status the capacity to feel empathy, benevolence and care actually has. To put the point in more overtly psycho-analytic terms, the development of the kind of moral reasoning Habermas describes not only more fully encompasses masculine development, but is, of itself, born of psychic repression. Men are only able to conceive of them-selves as universal subjects the extent to which they are able to deny the infantile experience of dependency, and the concrete ties that bind.[3]

These are powerful charges. Habermas (1990c) has however sought to reply to these and similar arguments made in accordance with Gilligan's views. The claims of Gilligan, charges Habermas, are more properly con-cerned with the application of norms than with questions of universal justi-fication. The rightness of moral questions can only be decided through a wide-ranging communal conversation not, it seems, from the particularity of our ethical attachments. Notions of care and sensitivity only come into play when we are seeking to relate universal norms in a context-sensitive manner. Similar to the critique he makes of communitarians, and indeed Mead, feminists who raise questions connected with an ethic of care are confusing ethical and moral questions.

This reply seems unsatisfactory for a number of reasons. The first is that Habermas is not properly attentive to the feminist argument that to become a mature self we should have the capacity to experience autonomy as well as dependency. Jessica Benjamin (1992) has argued that a critical feminist politics should attempt to deconstruct masculine and feminine identities and the principles of public autonomy and private care that have been historically associated with them. To problematise the realms of masculine and feminine, as well as public and private, would introduce nurture into the public realm and questions of autonomy into the private sphere. This would seemingly threaten a masculine identity whose presumed autonomy is based upon the exclusion of affective feelings from an instrumentally defined public. Such a bold move could also inform the argument that universalism and an ethic of care might be reconcilable. As Benhabib (1992) has argued it is not clear what purposes are being served to counterpoise the personal and the moral. This view might be able to remoralise public conflicts, but leaves questions of sexual morality, personal integrity, child care and domestic responsibility outside the moral domain. Again we are brought back to the argument that the mature human subject should be capable of formulating problems in terms of universal rights and justice, as well as hav-ing the capacity to feel sympathy and empathy. Indeed Habermas himself, more recently, has begun to be persuaded by the logic of this view. This is evident when he writes that moral reasoning must reconcile two aspects:

> The first postulates equal respect and equal rights for the individual, whereas the second postulates empathy and concern for the well-being of one's neighbour. Justice in the modern sense of the term refers to the subjective realm of inalienable individuality. Solidarity refers to the well-being of associated members of a com-munity who intersubjectively share the same life-world. (Habermas, 1990a: 200)

This brings me on to a second related argument: communitarian writers have consistently argued, with some justification, that Habermas's moral minimalism presupposes more than he realises. That is, for wide forms of discussion to take place we must have equal respect, free speech and the redistribution of social resources. Habermas presupposes a particular political community, which is exactly what he says he wants to avoid (Walzer, 1994). The argument here, put more robustly, is that while Habermas claims to be upholding a politics of process over specific aims he actually presupposes a radicalised version of social democracy. For communitarians, like Walzer, Habermas's discourse ethics is more properly understood as the radicalisation of principles that are already held within the political community. What is missing in his universalism, therefore, is not only his lack of concern for the gendered nature of moral questions, but how they, in complex global societies, are likely to be worked through differently by diverse cultural communities. Habermas therefore is not only masculinist but ethnocentric as well.

However, even communitarians like Walzer, reversing previously held perspectives, now believe in the need for a globally shared moral minimalism. Otherwise how are we to criticise other cultures different from our own who refuse to respect basic human rights? If we only have a contextual morality then how are we to object to cultures which attempt to ethnically cleanse shared public spaces? As with the feminist argument regarding care, what is required, in my view, is a more reciprocal relation being drawn between social context and morality. This would point to the interconnections between how our needs, specific identities and normative concerns can be said to interconnect. The problem with Habermas's extreme formalism is that questions of ethics and morality are very neatly separated. Both feminist and communitarian critics would argue that the kinds of moral claims we make would be informed by our current identities, affective ties and communal obligations. However, the critical point that Habermas makes in reply is that our immediate commitments should not be allowed to override more universalistic criteria. My argument is that instead of rigidly separating the moral and the universal from the ethical and particular we should seek to appreciate how these domains intercut one another. What implications, if any, do these arguments have for a mediated public sphere? Arguably they are twofold: (1) the regulation of global media cultures should indeed be subject to universal moral principles; and (2) we must make sure that the importance of achieving a more participatory public culture is not allowed to overshadow the ways in which moral self-development is underwritten by private domains.

1   The first point is to accept the critical point opened by Habermas that we can indeed make a connection between the moral development of society and the subject. This allows us to make the case for a plural public space where opinions and identities can be revealed, tested and scrutinised.

Globally however the actual shape of this communicative sphere will depend upon the cultural traditions and political practices that are already present. For instance, in Western Europe it is likely that the principles of public service broadcasting will remain important, whereas in many African societies any future public sphere is likely to be developed around radio rather than television. The relationship between different political and cultural traditions and a universal morality is better represented dialectically than being abstractly riven apart. The principles of process rather than outcome should be regarded as informing universal human rights to which all have access. Such a demand is built upon the recognition that when plural public cultures are deformed by money and power they do great violence to the fragile domain of mutual recognition.

2   The second point concerns questions of moral development in relation to both public and private spheres. The feminist argument that moral development is only partially dependent upon our ability to act in the public is an important insight. Our shared capacity to write letters to newspapers, participate in radio talk shows and make our own minds up about mediated public events are all related to questions of communicative ethics. These interventions into the public should both enlarge our horizons, build relations of mutual respect while being guided by perspectives we hold until defeated by a better argument. But, as the feminist critics well realise, our ability to be able to empathise with the problems of our neighbour also depend upon shared emotional resources which are not matters of rational discourse alone. Further, moral development can not be measured by our capacity to break free of our primary bonds, while misrecognising ourselves to be autonomous from related others. This points to a doubly differentiated understanding of moral development which crosses both public and private.

Raymond Williams: communications and materialist ethics

There is a strong temptation to stress the value of Raymond Williams because of the obvious parallels that can be drawn between himself and Habermas. The most obvious being their shared stance as public intellectuals and their involvement in the post-war New Left. If we wanted to continue this comparison we could also point to their shared orientations in the field of media and communications. Williams, more willing to offer detailed prescriptions than Habermas, argued that the media should be taken out of the control of commercial and paternal institutions, underwritten by capital and the state, and both democratised and decentralised. Once institutionally separate from the government and the market this would provide cultural contributors with the social context for free expression. Williams creatively imagines a mediated utopia of free speech which is built around the rights of contributors to authentic expression. Open democratic forms of 'talk' would have no necessary endpoint, given all of those who contribute must remain open 'to challenge and review' (Williams, 1962a: 134). The intention here is to promote what Williams called a 'culture in common' rather than a common culture, and strengthen communal bonds by including previously excluded perspectives. Williams's idea of a democratic community is complex and built upon difference rather than homogeneity. These differences however also have to be reconciled, as we shall see, with what human beings have in common. And yet for Williams this was not a conversation that could begin unless democratic and civil spaces were opened up free from the pressures of the capitalist economy and the state. Again similarly with Habermas, Williams explains that the capitalist economy and nation-state serve hegemonically to shape social needs in the interests of power rather than the community as a whole.[4]

However, if the theory of communicative action takes a linguistic turn in philosophical thinking, Williams's later work on media and culture takes a more overtly material twist. Through the development of cultural materialism, Williams sought to counter the evident strains within Marxism and post-structuralism. First, Marxism in its many guises had failed to represent cultural practices as being properly material. For Williams the activity of listening to the Beatles is no less material than working in a car plant. He suggests that in making a cultural practice superstructural Marxists were claiming that 'intellectual' activities were either a reflection of the economic base, or were somehow less real. Such a view mistakenly disallows the ontology of culture, and the relative autonomy of political and cultural spheres from the economic base. The other strand within contemporary theory that Williams sought to criticise was the prioritisation, amongst post-structuralists such as Althusser, of the structural features of language, over language as a human praxis performed in social contexts (Williams, 1979). Cultural practices, therefore, were both material as well as being significatory, while being dependent upon human creativity, rather than the grinding out of social structures.

These critical elements are noticeable in Williams's (1980a) reconsideration of the media as a productive activity. By discussing the mass media as a means of cultural production he emphasises a sustained historical analysis of the ways in which communicative actions are organised into socially contingent social relations. Communicative relations of exclusion are both historically mediated and overlain by technology rather than directly caused by it. A fundamental division of labour exists within communicative relations at two levels. The first is that social communication is regulated by large media conglomerates and the nation-state which subject cultural production to the general conditions of political and economic organisation. The other main division of labour being between those who are 'authorised' to speak and those who are not. Williams points that there is a basic material division between leaders, personalities and celebrities whose actions and voices are worthy of note, and a more passively defined public.

In understanding the social organisation and regulation of communication we should investigate the ways in which communications have been transformed by social labour. These would include what Williams terms amplificatory, durative and alternative means of transformation. The invention of human technologies such as radio, television and the telephone has meant that voices and perspectives can be amplified thereby projecting them across huge social distances. Further the invention of writing and other media technologies has made human cultures durative. By this Williams means that representations can be stored across time and space, disassociating cultural production from their original context. Finally, Williams argues that the history of human communications has revealed that human societies are continually inventing alternative mediums of communication. These have had transformative impacts upon the way we currently live. However new technologies have to be fitted into the overwhelmingly capitalist division of labour. In this respect, a materialist analysis of the media would seek to develop a historical understanding of the media, an appreciation of the social divisions that it marks, and a consideration of how technology (dead labour) has transformed communicative practice. Williams's argument, therefore, is to treat communications like any other social practice, working out its relationship with the state and the economy, as well as mapping out its own specific trajectory. And yet Williams, as I have indicated, couples such concerns with more normative ethical considerations.

Williams's vision of a socialist response to communications differs substantively from that of Habermas. Radical politics would have to bring the organisation of societies' communicative structure into social rather than state or private ownership. The means of communication in this argument would be brought under the control of the community thereby abolishing the previously instituted divisions of labour (Williams, 1983). A properly socialist media would thereby seek to develop the communicative capabilities of the people and provide them with new opportunities to participate in public dialogue. As Williams writes:

> socialism is then not only the general 'recovery' of specifically alienated human capacities but is also, and much more decisively, the necessary institution of new and very complex communicative capacities and relationships. (Williams, 1980a: 62)

Williams, in conjuncture with his other writing on socialism, offers a view of a complex, participatory and planned society, where the means of production (cultural as well as economic) have been taken into common ownership. If Williams differs substantially from Habermas on what constitutes modern socialism, he shares the orientation that subjective processes of self-formation are implicated in any wider view of society. But whereas Habermas discusses questions of moral development that encompass both self and society, Williams prefers to talk in terms of human needs and nature. In this sense, Williams emphasises a sense of limits that recognises our common ecological vulnerability and interconnection with nature. Human beings are both within as well as outside of nature. We are caught up with the natural world while having developed distinctively human features, capacities and characteristics. Following Timparnaro, Williams claims that much of our experience as human beings can be appropriately termed passive whereby we are constituted through a common biological inheritance. From this recognition could spring a 'global materialist' ethics which sought to hold in check, as far as possible, the suffering that can be associated with old age, hunger, lack of shelter, disease and infant mortality. Williams calls such a project one of 'widening happiness'. Yet whether Williams is considering a shared material condition, creative linguistic praxis or the felt need for community it is our shared interconnection with other human beings that is never far from view or concern. Our communicative capacity to engage critically with one another, our biological sameness and wider communal identifications all point in the same direction.

The media of mass communication, therefore, are profoundly important not only because they potentially allow for wide forms of social participation, but that the functioning of the media regularly reminds us of our mutual interdependency. The most powerful arguments for global socialism remain the lack of opportunities for participation in discursively shaping societies institutions, and the failure to meet common social needs through an egalitarian distribution of resources. That we have common interests in securing human flourishing and material security is however often obscured by the actual content of the media. What Williams (1989a) called the 'culture of distance' seeks either to naturalise social relations or obscure the connections that exist between human beings. The professional practices of the media will seek to represent global human tragedies by maintaining a safe distance between ourselves and others. This can be achieved by banishing images of the unemployed from our screen, representing the victims of wars and famines through an unthinking racism, or, as in the case of the Gulf War, consistently denying the home population of any real knowledge of the suffering being experienced as the result of bombing campaigns. In such cases, for Williams, what is required is a diverse range of perspectives that continually remind us of our shared human condition. And yet the dialectical fecundity of Williams's arguments, acknowledging the complexities of mediated human societies, also points to the necessity of global media orders in helping make such identifications possible. Like Habermas, Williams represents mediated social practices as containing an emancipatory kernel that would find a fuller expression in a different social order.

Habermas and Williams in post-modernity

At first glance both Habermas and Williams come to a similar position by very different routes. Both would argue that the need for a globally pluralist media is connected with the capacities of the human subject. Further, as should be obvious, while Williams is willing to be more prescriptive, they mutually offer the view that a democratic society is characterised by the capacity of civil society to uphold a reflexive and participatory culture. While there is much that could be said on the similarities and differences between Habermas and Williams, here I want to concentrate on two aspects: that is, the difference between discourse and materialist ethics, and the relevance of these arguments in post-modern mediated contexts.

The most basic difference between Habermas and Williams seems to lie in their disposition towards morality and ethics. For Habermas we are able to use reason due to the breakdown of tradition, the rationalising impulse of modernity and because of our intersubjective capacity as language users. A materialist ethics, in Habermas's view, could become an important voice within the conversation, but would have a similar status to that of an ethic of care, and might more properly be thought of as a discourse of application. Further, he might also claim, Williams's materialist thesis disguises the differences between instrumental and communicative practices, and dangerously reinvents metaphysical thinking by suggesting that ethical truths can be derived from human beings' ontological condition.

The first point can be treated in a similar way to Habermas's arguments in respect of an ethic of care. Just as an ethic of care can be balanced against discourse ethics, so might a materialist ethics. That human beings continue to feel sympathy and concern for others due to their shared material condition is related to shared experiences of solidarity and concern for others in respect of bodily suffering. Both a materialist ethics, as well as an ethic of care, would emphasise human beings' shared vulnerability and dependence upon others. Again this reminds us that maturity is not only achieved through the development of our dialogic capacities soberly to reason with others, but also through our ability to *experience* the others' pain. The advantage that a materialist ethics has over an ethic of care, however, is that it must be universal rather than particular in orientation. Whereas an ethic of care is orientated to specific family members, materialist identifications would have to cut across all social divisions. A materialist ethics, as Terry Eagleton (1990) has commented, recognises that all human beings are both frail and mortal, indicating a trans-historical domain worthy of human ethical concern. The problem with discourse ethics is that they are so deontological that they miss the connection between certain facts about human existence and the values that we currently hold. A materialist ethics could provide grounds for solidarity with others irrespective of the cultural differences that are revealed within the conversation. However, these remarks do not mean, to repeat, we have to make a choice between discourse ethics and more materialist concerns. As we have seen, Williams understood that human reciprocity, communication and understanding was a necessary pre-condition to the realisation of our common natures. Indeed, it is probably true to say that on questions of morality, both Habermas and Williams view such questions in terms of the material movement towards a more humane society. Before, if you like, we are able to enter into extended conversations with one another certain basic human needs would have to be met. In this way, both materialist and discourse ethics ask troubling questions of the dominant capitalist order.

Where I think Habermas does score over Williams is his resistance to the idea that the development of societies' capacity to learn can not be seen in strictly material terms. As is well known, Habermas's attempts to recon-struct historical materialism by linking the overtly material processes of production to societies' cultural institutions which monitor moral insight and consensual forms of understanding. To treat the cultural domain as being as material as the economic obscures the application of the different rationalities that have accompanied their development. Habermas's earlier distinction between work and interaction sought to point out that society was driven by the economy as well as by cultural traditions, political means that sought consensus and practical knowledge. Yet given Williams's cul-tural Marxism this is unlikely to have been a conclusion with which he would have been out of sympathy. Williams, unlike many in the Marxist tradition, clearly perceived that 'actually existing' models of socialism had much to learn from more formally democratic traditions of thinking. Further Williams's central concept of the long revolution had precisely the social creation of a learning and reflexive society as its ultimate aim. However, it should be said, by making culture overly material, Williams does begin to threaten these more hermeneutic insights.

Post-modern ethics, democracy and the media

Perhaps the main problem with such reflections is that they are currently deeply unfashionable in many of the dialogues taking place within the academy. One of the many reasons for this is that they seem unpracticable and riven away from the ways most people live their lives. J. B. Thompson (1995) has argued, with Habermas in mind, that it is no longer clear what practical relevance discourse ethics has for global media cultures. Practic-ally, discourse ethics seems to apply to those who share a common social location and who are able to dialogue directly with one another. But under global conditions where the media is able to recontextualise imagery into local contexts, what would an all-inclusive conversation look like? For example, our common fate at present is pressed by issues of nuclear pro-liferation, global warming and the spread of the HIV virus. How could the millions of spatially diverse people whom these issues affect make their voices heard? Further, it is likely that many of those who would be affected by such issues will be future generations, but again to build a morality out of reciprocity avoids rather than confronts these issues. In these and other respects, discourse ethics has failed to develop along with the changing contours of modernity. Rather than an ethics of co-presence constructed around our ability to dialogue with the others, Thompson advocates the renewal of moral–practical thinking based on responsibility. The emergence of a global media has reminded us of the interconnectedness of humanity and of the necessity of breaking questions of responsibility away from more traditional spatial and temporal coordinates.

These sentiments probably find their most coherent expression in the recent social theory of Zygmunt Bauman. Bauman has sought to define a post-modern response to some of the ethical and moral problems raised by our current age. He defines post-modern sensibility as being aware that there are human problems with no really good solutions. For Bauman post-modernity is modernity without illusions. Modernity offered an ethical discourse of experts who sought to legislate codified ethical responses through a universal law. This created a special cast of people whose job it was to issue binding and authoritative rules. The legislators of morality gave existential comfort in a society that was replacing the law of the divine with a human order. Unlike Habermas, Bauman argues that such attempts to ensure moral progress through law-like codes has been disastrous and has actually sapped autonomous moral abilities. There are, according to Bauman (1993: 29), two main sources that have undermined the West's confidence in its own ethical mission. The first is the link between the most morally troubling events of the twentieth century such as Auschwitz and the Bosnian death camps and the growth of rational bureaucratic control. These were the legitimate products of the law like decrees of experts which sought to substitute individual moral feelings with bureaucratic codes. The other is the doubt that modernity is a civilisation which is fit for global application. It has been the trail set by modernity that has fostered a world of economic polarisation, ecological degradation, nuclear proliferation and consumptive irresponsibility. These insights, for Bauman, remove the veil from the lie that modernity has been a story of moral progress. On the contrary, the narrative told by modernity is one of history that is written from the standpoint of the victorious and the powerful. Or as Bauman (1993: 228) puts it: 'superior morality is always the morality of the superior'.

These bleak remarks, however, could become the source of a considerable opportunity. The waning of the self-confidence of modernity and the detraditionalisation of society generally beckons new opportunities for a morality without ethics. Rather than investing our faith in ethical experts or bureaucratic systems, Bauman reasons we should return to questions of individual responsibility and obligation. Against communitarian and universalistic commitments, Bauman contends that the moral impulse can not be contained through accordance with community norms or universal laws, but can only be revived if we take the individual as its core. Moral responsibility must be personally owned and can not be shrugged off onto abstract laws, community rules or traditions. We are moral to the extent to which we are able personally to own our obligations towards the other. Bauman writes:

> The readiness to sacrifice for the sake of the other burdens me with the responsibility which is *moral* precisely for my acceptance that the command to sacrifice applies to me and me only, that the sacrifice is not a matter of exchange or reciprocation of services, that the command is *not universalizable* and thus cannot be shrugged off my shoulders so that it falls on someone else's. Being a moral person means that I *am* my brother's keeper. (Bauman, 1993: 51)

Bauman goes on that not only has modernity's universal pretensions run their course, but that the social conditions within which moral selves operate have also fundamentally altered. The impact of new technology, such as the mass media, has meant that we are now aware of moral problems that are far removed from the places we inhabit. Echoing many of Thompson's concerns above, Bauman contends the mass media regularly make us aware of issues which are both worthy of our moral concern and resist technical fixes or easy solutions. The uncertain risky environment of late modernity will often mean that it is better to do nothing than to act. Indeed, first and foremost, what is required is an ethics of self-limitation. By this Bauman means we need to become aware of the long-range and potentially long-term effects that our current actions may have for future or related communities. If modernity was about discovering with certitude an ethical order through the use of reason, post-modernity refuses any relation to the law, but insists that we care for one another.

There is obviously much that is persuasive in these debates. Bauman's more concerted concern to focus on questions of individual responsibility is welcome in an age which has seen these questions either displaced onto the functioning of modern bureaucracies, or the operation of market economies. But what is missing is Habermas's and Williams's sense that what is important is the linkage of moral and ethical questions to the provision of a pluralistic public sphere and the community in general. Habermas may indeed be mistaken, in the light of the horrors of the twentieth century, that we can talk of moral progress. Yet lacking from Bauman's reflections is the understanding that unless we find new enabling ways of talking with one another then many of the questions he opens out are likely to remain marginal. It is only through the provision of a pluralistic public sphere that the voice of the 'other' is likely to be heard. Unless, as Habermas and Williams insist, we are open to the respectful challenge and criticism of others through open-ended forms of dialogue we will be unable to decide what our *collective* obligations towards others should be. That is, moral questions are as much about personal responsibility as they are about communal provision. My concern is that Bauman detaches the moral sense of the individual from that of the community. The interdependence of the individual and the community provides the grounds for rights and responsibilities in an increasingly fragile world. This again makes essential for our survival public domains where the voices of ourselves and others can gently, but yet insistently, interrogate one another. Of course in a globally mediated age this is likely to take place in a multitude of contexts including the places we work, care for others and rest. However, we remain dependent upon a diversity of public spheres connecting the local and the global insistently offering different perspectives from the ones we currently hold. As Habermas writes:

> persons understood as mutually respecting individuals, are morally obliged in precisely the same way as persons understood as members of a community engaged in the activity of realising collective goals. (Habermas, 1993b: 34)

To maintain that the development of the individual is the flipside for the development of the community insists upon the political importance of continuing the conversation. That this can only be achieved in shared spaces carved out by institutions and maintained by personal qualities is a line worth holding. This is indeed an as of yet unrealised ambition of modernity that is also a global necessity. To suggest that everything is the fault or responsibility of the community is a crude act of displacement; yet to reduce morality to the level of the individual is often to engage in the worst kind of moralism. Despite Bauman's pessimistic reading, modernity has been the sight where communal rights and obligations have both enabled and disabled individual and collective futures. The media, as Habermas and Williams maintain, exhibit critical possibilities despite and because of its entanglement within networks of social power. The idea of a cultural democracy whereby we can all stand in relations of mutual respect and tolerance seeking to forge relations of solidarity and hope is a continual thread that runs through modernity. That such dimensions will continue to recognise the interdependence of the personal and the political in the mediation of modern identities has much to say about the unrealised potential of the times we currently inhabit.

The problem with such proposals however is that they remain connected to an unbridled sociological optimism, the sources of which seem to lie in the notion that by more adequately satisfying people's communicative needs, this will of necessity lead to a more substantial form of cultural citizenship. Such a view could easily be countered by the more pessimistic view that the advance of fair, rational and democratic media would be met with indifference by most people. Keith Tester (1997) puts this view well:

> We watch and consume pictures or reports and perhaps feel that we ought to be moved by them; but in so far as we are also possessed of a quite blasé attitude in the face of the fleeting, we are not so moved. In fact, we are more likely to want to see more and more pictures of horror simply in order to discover how deeply and irredeemably blasé we might become. (Tester, 1997: 40)

Tester, building upon Simmel's (1950) observations that the blasé attitude is the psychological disposition of the city dweller who lives in a culture of over-stimulation, certainly seems to have a point. Images of distant wars, genocides and famines do not persuade most people to leap out of their armchairs and start organising campaigns for fundamental human rights. The barely remembered images from last night's television news are more likely to be forgotten than acted upon. However, if we follow Tester too far, we are likely to forget that responses from civil society are altogether more complex and unpredictable than his 'misanthropy' allows. While he emphasises an important feature of modernity, his analysis should be re-joined to less cynical formulations that could equally point to the operation of human rights and political agencies that seek to open out more overtly political concerns in respect of the televising of human suffering. My argument then is not that if the 'correct' information were given to people they would soon become good democratic citizens, enthusiastically debating the contours of their own society and its inevitable interconnection with others. Here I think that it is long overdue that we break with a certain Left moralism that supposes that the virtuous activity of the people is smothered by the illusions propagated by the media industry. This argument not only presumes that 'truth' is an uncontested category, but that we are 'perfect' political subjects with the time, energy and mental capacity to engage with all of the political and moral questions worthy of our attention, without this process raising questions of doubt and ambivalence. Rather I am arguing that the dynamic interrelation between civil society, state and more global connections are undermined rather than fostered by certain institutional and moral criteria. This, then, is a politics without guarantees. A politics of communicative needs is better placed within the context of doubtful questioning than more certain frames that seek assurance. Indeed it is the continued 'visibility' of many of the deeply troubling issues that we currently share that will contribute to the complexity rather than the simplicity of our common future.

CHAPTER 3

Global media and technological change: social justice, recognition and the meaningfulness of everyday life

One of the most striking features of modernity as we have seen has been the transformation of the media of mass communication. In traditional society communication was oral, cultural traditions were conservative and identities were largely locally based and formed. The community was defined through face-to-face interaction, and social life was based upon tradition, hierarchy and rank. The development of print technology that accompanied the spread of national patterns of identification allowed languages a fixity they were denied in oral cultures. Print not only enabled the formation of 'new imagined communities' but also fostered the growth of practices of critique. Free from the need to preserve tradition through community rituals, cultural knowledge could now be stored within books, newspapers and pamphlets. The fostering of a critical public sphere emerged through the coming together of capitalism, nationalism and print technology. New possibilities were offered to practices of critique by the social formation of the press, literary magazines, coffee houses and an educated public between 1680 and 1730. However, conversations for the most part of the seventeenth and eighteenth centuries were overtly nationally defined, restricted to members of social elites and dependent upon the granting of civil rights. The rise of labour and other radical movements in the eighteenth and nineteenth centuries sought to challenge the exclusiveness of these elite conversations.

The formation of the popular and radical press grew up around Jacobean societies, Chartist movements and early trade unions that sought to radicalise critique and extend the process of communication. Notably throughout the twentieth century the struggle for political and social rights amongst ethnic minorities, the working class, disability and feminist groups and other organisations has sought to provide alternative sources of mediated information, while seeking to challenge the ways in which the dominant hegemony constructed popular beliefs. These movements have campaigned to reformulate the national conversation, often through a discourse of rights, in order to widen the communicative community. The deeply felt desire amongst all communities to find their ways of life, critical voices and perspectives represented within a wider shared public culture has been a major impetus for social change within modernity.

The twentieth century, on the other hand, has also witnessed the development of a mass culture. This culture was based upon standardisation, mass consumption and predictability. The extension of civil, political and social rights that played such a major part in redefining webs of communication within society was also accompanied by the extension of mass markets created by capital. The development of mass forms of media cultures was emphasised by the structural dominance of the press and television in defining common cultures. The most important critics of mass culture, including writers such as Walter Benjamin (1973) and Raymond Williams (1965), always perceived its development as a source of ambivalence. The mass media offered new opportunities for capitalist expansion and ideological forms of control while simultaneously containing the kernel of a more democratic and participatory culture. These seeds of hope, however, would not be realised by the systemic imperatives of technology, state and economy that drove the media along, but were attached to democratic movements from below and informed intellectual criticism. Both Williams and Benjamin sought to capture the dialectical possibilities being opened out by the development of media cultures despite their overtly economic, instrumental, national and centralised character. Culture had to be both politicised and democratised if it was going to build upon widespread forms of participation that had been fostered by the mutual development of citizens' rights and capital's restless need to find new markets. The development of mass education, a liberal democratic culture, leisure time and opposition cultures all influenced the shape of media cultures. Yet viewed from the perspective of a post-national and post-liberal age like our own these views need to be redrawn to consider more fully global interconnections and communicative obligations. While rights to autonomous self-definition within a national community currently remain the central locus for cultural struggles, such dimensions need to be reorientated globally and in terms of duties. Further, if it is the job of critical social theory to understand media and culture within its broader social contexts, then we currently need to look beyond the so-called mass culture debate due to the changing nature of media cultures and current social environments.

The media of mass communication is currently undergoing a complete transformation the full consequences of which we can only glimpse at from our present point in history. Processes of technological development, globalisation and commodification have meant that there has been a rapid increase in the amount of information made available, the spatial compression of the 'knowable' world, the fragmentation of new consumptive communities and the general speeding up of our shared cultural world.

These developments have helped foster ideas of a global civil society, the decline of the national community and the regulatory powers of the state, information overload, an instantaneous 'three minute culture', and the destruction of a mass culture based upon conformity. Elite and popular national cultural traditions may still be preserved by nation-states, but they are also being joined by more spatially disorientated cultural flows. Arguably then, the ordered nature of modernity is being replaced or at least supplemented by more unpredictable information flows and cultural coordinates.

While the climate of public cultures is certainly changing it is a myth to claim that they do not remain heavily structurated by the dimensions of power and authority. Processes of instrumental reason, capitalist economics, world regional power and national cultures remain major forces. A notion of 'cultural political economy' should seek to unravel the new coordinates that are reshaping media landscapes in such a way that heralds the development of new identities along with the maintenance of cultural tradition and more permanent institutional features. However the globalisation and technological reorientation of the media may be driven by modernity, but this does not mean that many of its consequences can be derived from these features. Further, it also does not follow that the kind of culture that is being ushered in by such developments meets people's cultural needs or the demands of democratic and oppositional movements. We are not so much witnessing the evaporation of cultural power but its reformation and restructuration. The global village may be able to provide us with instantaneous images from 'distant' social conflicts as well as historical images of social worlds that have since been lost, but is it able to provide an informed communicative culture relevant to the needs of the modern world? This question, despite the enormous amount of writing currently being produced on this subject, it seems, is rarely asked. To reformulate my question somewhat: how far do image cultures go in meeting human needs for social justice, equal forms of recognition and meaning? These questions, for some readers of contemporary 'cultural' philosophy, might seem odd ones to measure against the media. The problem here has been that many of the debates regarding new media cultures have either been highjacked by either post-modernism optimism or Marxist pessimism. Neither of these traditions within media and cultural theory take seriously enough the substantive moral and ethical questions that are central to this volume. Notably we have hardly begun to think about what a socially just media might be like. We have of course many sustained discussions of ownership patterns that deform democratic processes, detailed outlines of conglomeration tendencies that are concentrating media power into the hands of large-scale transnational corporations, and critiques of privatisation which are promoting cultural divisions rather than a shared public culture, but not enough that articulates these changes in terms of more substantive criteria that can be associated with citizenship.

36

Media and cultural citizenship

The struggle for what I have termed social justice, equal recognition and a meaningful life are all social goods that go beyond the media. For instance, the need for a socially just media of mass communications can be linked to wider demands for a more fully inclusive society that cuts across areas related to work and employment, health care, education, nursery facilities as well as other social spheres. The problem has been that while the social sciences often talk of exclusion from housing or employment there has been much hesitation in using such terms to apply to culture and media. Reasons for this are obviously complex, but seem to rest in no small part with culture and media studies' literary heritage, and more recently upon some of the theoretical excesses of post-modern thinking. A number of prejudices seem to persist in these approaches that prevent a fuller appreciation of the more structured elements of public cultures. Whereas post-modernism often wants to consider the evaporation of the subject into the discordant flux of media simulations, more traditional literary criticism has sought to emphasise the development of individual taste and sensibility. The more subtle mediations between the individual and community are given up in these mutual exaggerations and evasions. As Raymond Williams (1989a) pointed out long ago, to argue that certain cultural practices and institutions are exclusionary is different from arguing that ordinary people are excluded from culture. He continually warned that such a view implies that the 'masses' were themselves living in ignorance outside of any recognisably cultural framework. Against such a notion, Williams spoke of the 'ordinariness' of culture. By this he meant that culture was a material process that had to be produced and reproduced in social relationships. Culture, following this view, remains an intersubjectively held phenomenon which is permanently caught between the mediations of individual and community. This being the case, it should be possible, in certain respects although not in others, to link 'cultures' circulation, as Williams suggested, to wider social questions.

Social justice and the media

The best-known account of social justice in the social sciences is provided by John Rawls. Rawls's (1972) classic defence of justice as fairness has made a tremendous impact across a wide range of disciplines since the 1970s. His basic argument is Kantian in that he argues that we should do what is equally good for all people. Rawls offers a theory of justice that aims to link a notion of the individual to publicly held principles of justice. The fairness of the principles of justice are ensured by parties entering into a thought experiment that prohibit people tailoring their principles to advantage themselves. In what Rawls terms the 'original position' people decide the principles of justice under a 'veil of ignorance' that prevents them from knowing their sex, ethnic group, social class, values, religion, physical abilities, etc. The principles of justice are those that would be accepted by free and equal individuals in order to ensure cooperation among members of society. In this view, the original position helps us to formulate publicly held principles of justice. As is well known, Rawls represents these two principles as: (1) rights to basic liberties as long as these do not infringe upon other people's basic liberties and (2) equality of opportunity for all and a fair distribution of resources that derives the greatest benefit to the least advantaged members of society. These arrangements seek to combine the principles of liberty and equality that can be derived from the Western political tradition, and takes as its basic idea the insurance of a fair society that can maintain cooperation over the generations.

More recently Rawls (1996) has sought to rework these arguments by asking how is it possible for a just and stable society to be maintained in the face of persons who remain divided over their fundamental values? Rawls admits that in the previous volume he tended to take for granted a consensual society thereby not fully appreciating the inevitably multi-cultural makeup of modern society. Political liberalism, in this context, is best understood as the search for a society that can gain the support of an overlapping consensus of principles that can be endorsed whatever the individual's respective orientation. Rawls argues that it is basically illiberal to expect a society to be based upon a comprehensive moral or philosophical standpoint. The basic point being articulated is that a stable and just society must be able to contain within it a plurality of perspectives and value positions. Modern societies are irrevocably pluralistic and contain people of different sexualities, religious convictions, class loyalties, ethnicities, political persuasions and so on. For a society to cohere, Rawls argues that it must gain the support of what he calls 'reasonable and rational agents'. This term is intended to apply to those who are prepared to search for ways in which all people can co-exist and cooperate with those who hold different values and perspectives within the community. On the other hand, people can be said to be 'unreasonable' if they are unwilling to accept any general principles that might govern the terms under which free and equal citizens cooperate with one another. Citizens then are persons who are able to accept responsibility for their actions and act in accordance with others. Under political and social conditions secured by basic rights and liberties one would expect irreconcilable and conflicting doctrines to flourish. While Rawls wants to remain agnostic as to the truth or validity of different versions of the good that people hold, he does argue that it is unreasonable under conditions of political liberalism to use public power to enforce comprehensive doctrines. Through the use of virtues such as tolerance and respect the aim of political liberalism is the achievement of an overlapping consensus among those who accept the fact of reasonable pluralism. This process should then lead to what Rawls calls a stable constitutional consensus. By this he means that liberal principles become fixed, once and for all, into the constitution. Rawls is clear however that once these principles are in place those who share the consensus should continue to engage with those groups who do not wish to be part of the doctrine. Justice as fairness therefore does not attempt to cultivate any distinctive version of the good life, instead it honours, as far as it can, the distinctive ways of life of others, providing they act in accordance with reasonable versions of citizenship. Political liberalism thereby abandons the idea that political society will ever be united through a comprehensive moral doctrine. This of course does not mean that individual citizens do not have their own idea of the good, but that these must be tailored to fit a political conception of justice. The priority of the right over the good entails that the collectively held principles of justice are allowed to place limits on the freedoms enjoyed by citizens.

Crucially for our concerns political liberalism remains dependent upon what Rawls refers to as 'public reason'. Public reason concerns matters of public importance which are made widely available to citizens within the community. Politically liberal debates are orientated in terms of the good of the public and conform to the ideals of justice as fairness. Again different political, religious and philosophical doctrines properly play a role, but they must be governed by the overlapping consensus achieved by the constitution. A Rawlsian model of the public sphere, therefore, grants people basic rights and liberties and the opportunities and means to make use of public reason. The public sphere is protected in terms of basic rights from attempts by governing bodies to censor debate, provide people with chances to enter into reasoned argument and materially ensure that all have the opportunity to take part in democratic exchange. In questions of dispute, public reason comes to the fore in that reasonable citizens will want to persuade others that their demands or arguments are actually derived from or are compatible with the constitution. Rawls (1996: 248) offers the example of diverse religious groups who oppose one another on matters of education, with one group favouring government support for public education alone, and the other hoping for help with church schools as well. A way out of this dilemma, according to Rawls, would be to allow the representatives of each group to attend a public forum, and then argue how their particular versions of the good affirm the rightness, or otherwise, of the constitution.

If these arguments, as they would surely have to be, were applied to the media of mass communication they would ensure a publicly accountable system of communication that both guarantees certain rights, provides fair opportunities for different viewpoints to be heard, and makes sure that everyone had the cultural technology capable of transmitting the debates in question. The media would have to remain agnostic as to the substantive positions of those involved in media debate, but would have to be seen to be loyal to the constitution. For example, the question as to whether or not publicly to transmit the views of a racist political party could be viewed in these terms. First, such a grouping would fail the test of reasonableness in that they are unprepared to accept the rights and liberties of other members of a multi-cultural community. A clear case then could be made for excluding such organisations from operating in public on an equal footing with groups who sought to maintain the overlapping consensus. The public media would also have a duty to inform the community of the practices of such groups and continue a dialogue with them, in accordance with notions of public reason, in order to persuade them to alter their standpoint. For Rawls such debates not only affirm public trust and confidence, but also provide strong incentives for citizens to act in accordance with the constitution.

Such arguments have an obvious importance for the regulation of public systems of communication. However, we may also doubt the extent to which constitutional guarantees are likely to ensure high-quality forms of public communication and open forms of discussion. We may be able to ensure that people have rights to communication, certain opportunities to participate and equal access, but still have a communications structure that is largely governed by and run in the interests of large-scale media conglomerates. As Jean Seaton (1995) has argued, regardless of constitutional guarantees using the courts to protect freedom of speech is always easier for the rich than the poor, constitutional provisions will be largely ineffective unless corporations perceive them to be in their interests, and it is noticeable that while constitutions outline general principles they can rarely cover the specificity of the threats to media freedom. Constitutional attempts to regulate information flow within a society assumes that the main issue concerning the democratic operation of the media is a lack of rights. This is not of course to argue that within many nations, whether this is through ethnic nationalism, despotism or other forms of ideological closure, certain communicative rights would indeed be an important advance. However a socially just media can not be delivered by constitutional packages alone, but of necessity involve the examination of relations of ownership and control. In this respect, Rupert Murdock's growing media empire could be considered unjust because of the amount of political influence it is able to wield, the increasingly commercial definitions that are becoming attached to media flow, his ability to avoid paying social insurance into the public purse and the amount of market influence he is able to exert. Social justice, therefore, within the media actually requires publicly regulated and accountable media institutions and structures that are not allowed to become increasingly concentrated into the hands of private magnates.

One of the key defenders of an open and pluralistic media in contemporary social and cultural theory as we have seen is Jurgen Habermas. Habermas's model of the public sphere while being more precisely connected to changes within the media shares a great deal with Rawls. The difference is that Habermas, given the tradition of critical theory within which he works, has a more explicit concern with the connection between social and ideological power and public spaces than seems evident in Rawls. For

Habermas the political expression of democratic communicative relations is distorted by the operation of money and power. More explicitly, Habermas (1995) argues that while sympathetic to Rawls's project he believes that it is misconceived in a number of respects. The first of these is that the notion of an 'original position' assumes an individualistic rational choice perspective that remains inadequately grounded in an intersubjective framework. Rawls overly presumes what we would all will and thereby 'neutralises the multiplicity of particular interpretative perspectives from the outset' (Habermas, 1995: 117). Whereas the original position asks us to consider justice from a monological perspective discourse ethics holds that a comprehensive view can only arise if we take on the position of the other. A point following on from this view is that Rawls oversteps the mark between a critic who is seeking to provide the democratic conditions so that we might find out what the good society is like, and the role of the expert who feels *himself* to be in the position of legislating for change. Further, Habermas, as one might expect from someone who argues that the enlightenment is an unfinished project, has problems with Rawls's argument that reasonable pluralism should be agnostic as regards truth claims. For Habermas this actually undermines the normative binding force of the conception of justice being offered by Rawls. Unless Rawls thinks his notion of justice is more truthful than other accounts why should we decide to resolve the problems of living together in such a way? Finally, Habermas is concerned that the monological 'original position' logically leads to the drawing up of a constitution that is placed beyond the formulations and renewed insights of the community. This would, according to Habermas, prevent the citizens who make up the community from seeking to radicalise and deepen the constitution within a shared life world.

Rawls (1996), in reply to Habermas, seeks to defend his conception of justice against these objections. He argues that the main difference between himself and Habermas is that whereas the theory of communicative action is a substantive doctrine, Rawls's own conception of political liberalism leaves philosophy as it is. By this he means that political liberalism presupposes that each individual is responsible for their own notion of the good, and if these are to be considered reasonable then they must allow for the fair cooperation of others within the community. Conversely Habermas, argues Rawls, offers a more substantive view than he thinks, seeking to defend a specific theory of communication, rejecting religious and metaphysical thinking out of hand, and a general account of meaning and truth. In comparison Rawls argues his own claims are both more modest and in keeping with the liberties required of a just society. Here Rawls's arguments bare a marked similarity to many of the objections that have been levelled at both himself and Habermas by their communitarian critics. Both Charles Taylor (1989) and Michael Walzer (1994) have argued that Habermas's moral minimalism already presupposes a social democratic community. That is, for wide forms of discussion to take place we must have equal respect, free speech and the redistribution of social resources. Habermas, therefore, presupposes a particular political community, which is exactly what he says he wants to avoid. A slightly different, if related objection, is proposed by Parekh (1993), when he argues that the liberalism of writers like Habermas and Rawls is drawn from certain intersubjective understandings that are derived from individualistic societies, rather than those that are defined in more strongly communal terms. In this view, both Rawls and Habermas are seeking to provide a morally 'thin' view of liberal notions of justice, while actually presupposing dominant conceptions that are derived from the political communities and thought systems of Western liberalism. There would certainly seem to be a problem of this order underlying the thought of both Habermas and Rawls. Yet if such arguments were taken to their logical conclusion it would cancel the search for a just society that is based upon principles other than those that could be derived from local forms of life. Both Habermas and Rawls hold that questions of justice involve the search for norms that have both a universal purchase, and that when they are applied to local situations can offer a form of critique. Indeed, if anything, the globalisation of the media revitalises such questions; that is, how might we discover ways of living together that fosters a culture of critique without simply insisting on the values which happen to be closest to hand? The increasing intensification of cultural interconnection has given new imperatives to such questions. The search for what Rawls calls a 'well ordered society' in this sense is inevitably a global as well as a national and a local project. Further, it is unlikely that we could have a discourse that sought to instigate conceptions of justice that did not draw upon certain background beliefs in respect of how a just society should indeed be ordered. The trick is, as Rawls and Habermas are well aware, to generate an inclusive overlapping consensus that is not repressive of cultural diversity, unless of course it is manifestly unjust. Theoretically this points towards an ongoing and constantly changing tension between universalistic conceptions and the substantive norms of particular forms of life.

Habermas's (1996) most recent writing on the public sphere has sought more to precisely define its dynamic and spatially complex nature. Habermas maintains his Meadian roots by continuing to link the cognitive capacity of the self and the institutional mechanisms of society in the promotion of a critical pluralistic culture. The distinction between ethics (questions of what's right for me) and morality (questions of what's right for the community) means that the public sphere is continually involved in a process of deciding what can reasonably be decided by the community and what can not. The decidability of such questions presupposes a participatory democratic culture that is able to couple the increasing individualism evident in ethical decisions and dilemmas with a need for a moral discourse at the level of the community. The primary task of the public sphere, therefore, is the detection and identification of public problems that need to be fed into the procedures of parliament and the state. The public sphere in the modern media

age operates as a signalling device highlighting matters of public importance that have to be decided upon by the structures of representative democracy. Public opinion, in this respect, is not so much the result of opinion
polls (although these are a contributing factor) but proceeds a period of
proper focused debate. Referring back to more familiar themes that can be
associated with Habermas's notion of the public sphere, he argues that
agreement can only emerge after a period of what he calls 'exhaustive con-
troversy' (Habermas, 1996: 362). However, Habermas is clear that such widespread discussions only become converted into communicative power once
they pass through the institutional matrix of democratic will formation.
Proceeding this we can say that public opinion has been activated once the
various interactive agencies of state and civil society have become focused
on a particular problem. An informed public culture, in this respect, is built
upon the complex interaction of a number of different public realms and
arenas. Habermas (1996: 374) writes:

> the public sphere is differentiated into levels according to the density of commun-
> ication, organisational complexity, and range – from the episodic publics found in
> taverns, coffee houses, or on the streets; through the *occasional* or 'arranged' publics
> of particular presentations and events, such as theatre performances, rock concerts,
> party assemblies, or church congresses; up to the *abstract* public sphere of isolated
> readers, listeners, and viewers scattered across large geographic areas, or even
> around the globe, and brought together only through the mass media.

The relationship between systemic sources of social power and civil society
are crucial in determining public opinion. Habermas argues that the profes-
sionalisation of opinion management through an array of spin doctors, poll-
sters, spokespeople for powerful vested interests unequally distribute the
opportunities for exerting a powerful influence on public opinion. The 'man-
agers' of public opinion however have to work within certain constraints
in that once an interpretation or perception appears within the public it
is open to questions of public scrutiny and legitimacy.[1] The other domain,
which I have already mentioned, which disrupts and critically questions the
carefully packaged representations of the powerful, is civil society. Habermas
(1996: 366–367) carefully describes civil society as:

> nongovernmental and noneconomic connections and voluntary associations that
> anchor the communication structures of the public sphere in the society compon-
> ent of the life world.

The domain of civil society, then, is much more than a well-scripted public
relations exercise, but crucially involves the direct intervention of ethical communities, feminist campaigners, green networks, religious denominations,
trade unions, ethnic organisations and parents groups. A societal-wide conversation is dependent upon the emergence of an 'energetic civil society'
which is able to force issues and perspectives onto a public agenda. If we

take a range of activities from road protests to public sector strikes, and from feminist campaigns against male violence to protests against the arms trade, then all of these movements based within civil society are attempting to influence and form public opinion. A robust civil society ensures that the communicative basis of the life-world never becomes completely colonised by agencies of money and power. For example, in 1998 England football star Paul Gascoigne was publicly shamed by much of the tabloid press in that they carried pictures of his wife after having been horribly beaten by the player. The footballing authorities attempted to dismiss the incident as a 'private' matter having little to do with Gascoigne's public role, but arguably the pictures themselves and the protests of feminist groups breached the 'wall' between public and private. Both the publishing of the pictures and the activities of women's groups radically questioned any simple distinction between private conduct and public accountability. Yet this matter is further complicated if we also insist that the public sphere has a 'private' basis in that the exchange of letters, conversation and e-mails is rooted in personal integrity. The public sphere is therefore ensured by certain publicly held rights and by the protection of private realms that need to be insulated from the panopticon-like gaze of the state. Unlike much mainstream liberal thought Habermas views the domains of public and private as distinct if ultimately overlapping arenas that need to be preserved in order to ensure the operation of an effective civil society. Civil society then, under certain circumstances, is able to convert itself into communicative power through the channels of public communication and the activation of public normative sentiment. A recent example of this in Britain has undoubtedly been the public reaction to questions of gun control after the Dunblane massacre. After the widely felt public outrage connected with the killing of 'ordinary' school children the residents and parents in the local community organised a campaign to ban handguns. The 'Snowdrop' group managed to build a nationwide consensus isolating the gun lobby and certain members of the ruling Conservative Party.[2] These examples, I think, bare out a more dynamic and interactive conception of the public sphere than might have been conceived had the debate become overly concerned with 'top–down' questions of power and ideology. For the public sphere to be socially just it must both prevent the manipulation of the public by forces with vested interests in social control and pull together an otherwise fragmented public. A widespread publicly inclusive conversation therefore would shatter attempts at 'information processing strategies' and substitute them with genuinely communicative interests and passions.

Here, perhaps, the major point of difference between Habermas and Rawls seems to emerge; that is, while Rawls defends the public sphere in terms of certain rights, with Habermas one has a much greater appreciation of the duty to participate. That he rarely makes this explicit is both due to Habermas's proceedualism and the concern that any obligation to participate could conceivably become an illiberal imperative. Notably, however,

Habermas's view of a discursive democracy is based much more on rights than corresponding questions of obligation. Arguably without such a communally shared moral imperative, as Habermas would probably agree, the everyday electricity of civil society is likely to remain undercharged. As Etzioni (1996) has pointed out, liberals such as Rawls and Habermas prefer to leave the definition of the good to individuals rather than society. Communitarians, on the other hand, argue that neutrality on such questions actually privileges one side of the debate. Thus without building an ethic of participation into the foundations of modern societies, the state is actually signalling that it would prefer a depoliticised more easily manipulable civil society to the one advocated by Habermas. Communitarians would argue that if society wishes to foster a rich tapestry of civil associations this could not be sustained through thin versions of the good. The state would need to ensure that, while individual liberties were defended, the media was democratically controlled, citizens were educated as to their responsibilities and republican sentiments are widely held. While Etzoni and some of the other communitarian writers seem to think that such virtues are handed down from on high rather than arising through the complex mediation of experience, experiment and moral and ethical reasoning, they seem to have a point. While a democratic civil society generally supposes that the community has access to the necessary resources to make political participation a realistic possibility, unless this is matched by a normative attachment to a participatory citizenship the institutions of a shared civil world are likely to fall into disrepair. The Habermasian response would be that such responsibilities could never be fixed in stone, but should be open to proper review by the members of the community.

Under the conditions of a just civil society then citizens should not only be encouraged to participate, but they should also accept that they have not only a right to be heard but a responsibility to listen and to respond to others. To understand the other we have to be prepared to attend to what is said as well as the intersubjective background and social context that informs the meaning of speech. As Gurevitch (1990) argues, understanding often requires that we listen in such a way that we recognise the limits of our ability to understand, in that we have respect for the other's otherness. This can become obscured if understanding is merely assumed rather than hermenetically problematised. The right to be heard then and the obligation to listen are two sides of the same coin. A just media and civil society is dependent upon the interconnection between formalised rights and duties and the self-regulating structures of the 'life-world'. Through Rawls's and Habermas's competition to out-manoeuvre one another in a minimal definition of political community the language of rights rather than duties has become overly developed.

Similarly, Charles Taylor (1995) has recently argued that a more communitarian emphasis on questions of belonging and obligation to a particular community is important if social cohesion is to be maintained. Kantian liberals for Taylor underrate the notion that 'hearing' the other is not only dependent upon a particular interchange and access to rights, but on the quality and type of social relationship. Centralised bureaucracies, rifts in the political community and a wider sense of fragmentation all seek to promote instrumental rather than sympathetic bonds in the community. The overall sense of identification that people have within a society is thereby fostered by whether or not there exists a basic sense of identification, and feelings of trust in democratic procedures. An interlocking public sphere that regularly moves issues between the local, national and global has an 'openness' to the concerns of its citizens and is more likely to foster feelings of solidarity. On the other hand, an overly formal stress upon the rights of the individual in current contexts would further atomise modern communities, thereby weakening common loyalties. The question that seemingly neither Habermas nor Rawls adequately face is how communal solidarities are to be promoted through an increasing concern with the rights of individuals. The media, for example, must be the place of dialogic interchange as well as the sphere that trades upon common symbols and bonds that reinforce a sense of obligation to the community as a whole. The media in this view is as much about difference and conflict as it is about building common solidarities and loyalties. A socially cohesive society therefore requires not only justice but a shared capacity to recognise where 'we' differ and what 'we' share together.

A socially just media of mass communication then will need to be open to a diversity of perspectives while simultaneously promoting an ethic of participation amongst its citizens. This suggests both extra-media and media-centric strategies on behalf of questions of cultural citizenship. First, access to material resources, cultural capital, emotional resources and self-respect necessary to participate within media debates depends upon a range of institutions from the economy to the family and from the education system to more individual capabilities. Outside of a society that stressed the importance in particpating in media public debates by joining pressure groups, writing letters to newspapers and monitoring television output it is difficult to see how the connection between the media and citizenship would not become a wholey passive affair. Secondly, a socially just media would need to be driven more by communicative questions than those of money and power. To put the point more practically, the desire to contribute to public debate, experiment aesthetically and open out original perspectives should all hold sway over the state's attempt to impose mass loyalty or capital's need to make a fast buck. A socially just media therefore would require a cultural politics that moved on these two fronts simultaneously.

Yet Habermasian and Rawlsian approaches to the media might also be dismissed as outmoded given their preoccupation with a binary that views the media as either promoting freedom or domination. More post-modern perspectives, such as those offered by McLuhan (1994), Baudrillard (1993) and Poster (1995), suggest a reorientation of concern away from whether or not media contribute or detract from autonomous social relations and open out a broader inquiry into the way cultural shifts are reconfiguring social identities. Whereas modernity articulates a linear 'bookish' subject which is propelled to search for truth behind illusion, post-modernity elicits identities that are 'televisual' in that they are decentred, multiple and unstable. Whether we are talking about the transition from written to electric cultures (McLuhan), from serial to simulated cultures (Baudrillard), or from the first to the second media age (Poster), these concepts point to a notion of the media that outstrips its function as a feature of liberal democracy. The emergence of the internet, hand-held video cameras, virtual reality and other media forms herald a new age of soft interconnectivity, fluid communities and shifting attentions. For instance, virtual reality enables the participant to move beyond the distinctions between 'truth' and 'falsity' into a realm that is intimately concerned with questions of identity and self-construction. Virtual reality therefore is more centrally connected with questions as to who we are and what we might become than normative questions of justice.

Despite the validity of these projections we might equally link new media forms into wider questions of social justice. Who has access to the new media? How might social movements utilise the evident potentials within these new forms in order to subvert symbolic hierarchies and introduce new discourses into communal patterns of identification? These questions, while undoubtedly modernist in formulation, remain as relevant now as they were at the turn of the century. The difference remains, as we shall see, that while notions of identity and justice remain interconnected they are ultimately separable questions.

Recognition and the media

Human needs for personal feelings of self-regard and respect from the wider community is a theme that can be traced back to the theories of Hegel, Mead and beyond. Building upon this tradition, Axel Honneth (1995) has argued that both Hegel and Mead uphold the notion that we can only come to see ourselves as bearers of rights once we are able to take the position of the 'generalised other', thereby accepting that such claims apply equally within the community. This form of respect ushered in by rights is cognitive, and should be detached from personal feelings of liking. Yet intersubjective feelings of self-regard in the private realm and self-respect in the community remain related through a moral dimension which seeks recognition from specific and generalised other(s). Just as human infants require the love of their primary carers to attain basic self-confidence, so the granting of rights within the community helps foster a sense of self-respect. This parallel can be taken further if we consider the intersubjective dimensions of love relationships which seek to balance autonomy and dependence, and attempt to gain the recognition of the community through symbolic struggles at the level of the public sphere. The mobilisation of those seeking to raise their social worth must first gain the attention of the community through the public sphere, and hold together their own movement by providing a shared language which enables participants to 'bridge' their own feelings of harm and the development of a collective identity. The claims for recognition and respect are moral and introduce a normative dimension into identity politics. In this instance, Honneth links the needs for love and respect which correspond to the struggle for recognition at the personal and collective levels to notions of self-esteem though the experience of solidarity with others. That is, while interpersonal relations are able to secure feelings of trust in relation to the self and the granting of legal rights enable basic notions of self-respect, it is through feelings of solidarity that people achieve social esteem. Basic notions of esteem in a post-conventional society can no longer be assumed to overlap with hierarchy and rank in any unproblematic way. The achievement of esteem, unlike that of rights, is characterised through what makes people different rather than what they share. Esteem in a society that has witnessed the rapid individualisation of achievement and the decline of tradition is inevitably pluralistic and open to competing symbolic definitions. The negotiation of social worth, rights and love form an interconnected intersubjective dimension that goes some way toward explaining why the achievement of recognition is never wholly symbolic, but moral as well. The holy trinity of love, rights and solidarity being general patterns of behaviour that provide the conditions for both internal and external freedom.[3]

The struggle for recognition is then different from, although overlapping with, that of justice. Justice, in terms of the media, is concerned with the distribution of opportunities to be seen and to be heard. In the case of recognition we are concerned with persons having opportunities to participate while maintaining a sense of personal integrity and being respected by the wider community. Questions of justice and recognition then are interrelated if analytically separate. Individual and collective social respect can not be generated by policy criteria but must be demanded, negotiated and sometimes denied.

Nancy Fraser (1995) has similarly argued that post-socialist notions of justice require a dual strategy of redistribution and recognition. This should, she argues, lead on to an attempt to think about the ways in which economic disadvantage and cultural disrespect are interrelated. In other words, our integrity as human beings does not simply flow from our access to material resources, but is also dependent upon processes of cultural domination (being interpreted as culturally inferior), non-recognition (being excluded from the dominant imagery of one's culture in society) and disrespect (being continually portrayed in a negative or stereotypical way). For instance, gays and lesbians are not only discriminated against in the employment field, but are also culturally marginalised through the cultural construction of heterosexual norms. The remedy for these forms of injustice is the recognition of lesbian and gay similarities and differences between themselves and the 'dominant culture', as well as economic redistribution. The overcoming of heterosexism would require the deconstruction of dominant ideologies through an increasingly pluralistic public sphere and the renegotiation of respect and esteem. Unlike what Fraser terms mainstream multiculturalism that proposes revaluing marginalised groups, a more deconstructive approach would also have implications for the assumptions of the dominant culture itself. According to both Fraser and Honneth then the need for recognition is sharpened within modern multicultural societies and can be considered as fundamental in determining social struggles as the desire for more traditional forms of justice.

These aspects can be brought into sharper focus if we consider the struggle for black citizenship, identity and recognition within the United States. In a marvellous book Henry Louis Gates Jr (1994) describes the importance of television in establishing relations of recognition in the racially segregated town of Piedmont during the 1950s. Gates describes in some detail how, given the absence of white people in his life, he came to know them through popular shows on television like *Topper*, *Robin Hood* and *Lassie*. Television in America however was completely dominated by images of white middle-class people, but Gate's moving account describes the sense of excitement felt within black communities at the initial appearance of *coloured people* in the mass media. In the 1950s in America this was such a rare event that a black face on the television would send ripples of pleasure through tightly knit black communities. Gates (1994: 22) writes:

> Lord knows, we weren't going to learn how to be coloured by watching television. Seeing someone coloured on TV was an event.
>
> 'Coloured, coloured, on Channel Two', you'd hear someone shout. Someone else would run to the phone, while yet another hit the front porch, telling the neighbours where to see it.

Before questions related to the way black people are represented within the dominant image culture can be discussed, there is perhaps an even more fundamental demand that they should have a presence within the culture. The basic right to find representations of one's own presence and cultural relations within the dominant culture has to come logically before questions of representation can be raised. As Honneth (1995) argued above we might align questions of basic self-respect with a general sense of legal entitlement that could be linked into the idea that we share a right to be represented, while connecting the need for social esteem to questions of how black people are actually coded and decoded within the dominant culture. Questions of recognition are important because they can be linked to a basic moral requirement that we share for rights and solidarity with others. The media of mass communication therefore has a responsibility to represent social groups in such a way that promotes social esteem and does not encroach upon what these groups feel to be their basic rights. In a globalised media the spatial context within which these demands and needs arise can vary from the protests of local residents groups seeking to change the practices of the local authority, to human rights organisations who are trying to gain the world's attention regarding human violations.

Cornel West (1994) has argued with reference to contemporary black American popular culture that questions of social respect and esteem go much further than the conversation has allowed so far. West provocatively argues that recent discussions among liberals and conservatives concerning the plight of African-Americans have become overly polarised forcing participants to choose between structural and behavioural impediments to black upward mobility. The main problem with this debate, argues West, is that culture is as much about structure as it is about identity, and that these two elements are intrinsically tied together. The interconnection between structure and identity is perhaps most marked through the emergence of what West describes as black nihilism. By this he means that the combination of economic deprivation, political marginalisation and cultural disrespect has produced a life of 'horrifying meaninglessness, hopelessness, and (most important) lovelessness' (West, 1994: 23). Previously black struggles had sought to provide a powerful counter culture to equip black people with a strong sense of self based upon self-love, self-respect and self-esteem. While these were not available from the wider society, black communities, through religion, familial networks and the civil rights movement, were able to sustain a disciplined yet emotionally supportive culture. However, the cultural structures of black civil society are currently in a state of collapse having been eroded by the structures and identities fostered by market capitalism. Mainstream media promote a culture of responsibility-free consumption. Decontextualised images of sexual gratification, easy solutions to existential problems and unbridled hedonism have a pervasive presence in America's commodified media culture. West comments:

> Like all Americans, African-Americans are influenced greatly by the images of comfort, convenience, machismo, femininity, violence, and sexual stimulation that bombard consumers. These seductive images contribute to the predominance of the market-inspired way of life over all others and thereby edge out non market values – love, care, service to others – handed down by preceding generations. The predominance of this way of life among those living in poverty-ridden conditions, with a limited capacity to ward off self-contempt and self-hatred, results in the possible triumph of the nihilistic threat in black America. (West, 1994: 27)

The economic penetration of civil society then has produced feelings of meaninglessness and undermined a sense of respectful recognition which had been constructed in the process of struggle by black communities. These processes can only be countered by what West calls a 'politics of conversion' whose strategy is to regain hope and give modern life a sense of purpose.

This is a politics which links a sense of justice with the need to love one's self and have respect for other members in the community. West advocates a local politics of love and respect that seeks to meet the challenge of nihilism head on. Implicit in West's argument would be the need to promote counter-images of black people who are worthy of love and respect and who can be seen to exemplify moral integrity. These have been strikingly absent from the recent media event that revolved around the trial of O. J. Simpson, and charges of sexual harassment levelled at Judge Clarence Thomas. The attempt to regenerate civil society should be based not only upon questions of justice, but the desire to promote responsibility and respect in society's institutions.

A politics which seeks recognition therefore can be linked to that of justice. As both Gates and West remind us, in a mediated age these symbolic struggles are likely to have even greater pertinence in the future. Despite many of the problems that might be levelled at such arguments it is important to note that a revitalised cultural citizenship is intrinsically moral and bound up with questions of recognition and the remaking of identity. While the decline of a well-ordered black civil society has been viewed more ambivalently by black feminist critics, the need to renegotiate basic relations of recognition can also be seen as a long-standing demand of the feminist movement (Hooks, 1992). Similarly, with the demand for justice the achievement of a media culture which secures a basic sense of recognition for the whole community depends upon the interlocking structures and practices of state and civil society.

Meaningfulness, everyday life and the media

Globalisation, as we shall see, will increasingly come to mean that certain world regions are likely to become overloaded with mediated information. The development of information superhighways in Europe, North America and South East Asia will provide a sharp contrast with the more traditional systems of communication that are still likely to characterise the Earth's poorer regions. How, though, might we view the rapid technological development of different mediums of communication in terms of its impact upon the structures of everyday life? In this context, I am particularly interested in the impact that the technological development of the media will have on the already media saturated cultures of the world's most dynamic economic regions. To unravel these questions, which are of course related to the previous two sections, I want to look through the philosophical lens of critical hermeneutics. My argument here is that the rapid technological development of the media should be viewed dialectically. Ricoeur (1978) argues that the task of hermeneutics is both to restore and destroy meaningfulness. Hermeneutics works within a framework that struggles against falsehood, oppressive ideologies and the securing of harmful illusion.

On the other hand, hermeneutics' more positive aspect seeks to recover meaning through interpretative work, recollection and respectful listening. Hermeneutics, therefore, is uniquely positioned to be able to reveal the extent to which the transformation of media cultures is likely to deliver a dominatory and nihilistic culture that robs the present of its capacity to be both critical and meaningful.

The crucial place to start in this respect is with Habermas's distinction between technical rules that are dependent upon the direct calculation of means and ends in order to reach certain goals, and normative rules which are both shared and contextual to everyday life. Democracy, for example, is best seen as a contextual norm. If we uphold the norms of democracy (e.g. rule by the people) it will give us a strong impetus to go out and vote. However, if we were to look at purely calculative voting we would probably never bother as it is unlikely that our single vote will make a difference to the outcome of an election. For Habermas the distinction between technical rules and normative rules gives rise to two distinct forms of rationality. They are instrumental rationality, which embodies a form of reasoning that is goal directed and measured by efficiency criteria, and communicative rationality, which is interpretively orientated towards understanding the interconnections between the external world, the community with whom we share an intersubjective life-world and the self. Habermas (1971) argues that the balance between these two spheres of social practice have become progressively deformed by the trajectory of modern capitalism. Along with the intervention of the state into the economy in order to avert social crises and the conversion of the natural sciences into the leading productive force, labour can no longer be assumed to be the supreme source of value. The displacement of Marx's theory of value (which is only appropriate for liberal capitalism) and the conversion of technology and science into the main ideological prop for late capitalism is characteristic of contemporary society. Ideologically the promotion of technical consciousness, which can be linked to the spread of technology and instrumental reason, seeks to convert social questions into technical problems to be solved through quick fixes. Problems of hunger are solved through media panics and hastily organised airlifts, prisoners' riots through the introduction of more sophisticated mechanisms of surveillance and the decaying underclass with the need to return to easily learned moral codes. Technocratic solutions then are often short term, cynical, deny any ethical orientation and deliberately elude any reference to the good life.[4]

In modernity then, legitimation comes much less through a 'belief' in certain principles, but through the fetishisation of scientific progress and rewards for privately defined needs. The unchecked progress of this particular logic will end in the replacement of communicative ethics by the frozen logic of scientific calculability. The domains of science and technology are cut away from a depoliticised population and are largely shaped by social interests that seek to reproduce the existing order of things. Examples of such phenomena abound, but we could ask what are the communicative reasons that lie behind the development of the multi-channel world of digital television? Will this ensure that citizens are better informed than ever before concerning the political and community questions that urgently need answering? To such questions we could only offer the most timid affirmation given that the new systems are likely to herald a commodified universe where choice is at an absolute premium, but where the older values of public service are likely to be increasingly undermined.

A further example of what Habermas means is provided by reports concerning the development of so-called 'immortality chips' (Millar and O'Neill, 1996). Scientists working on a project called Soul Catcher 2025 are devising computer chips that will eventually be able to record an entire human life after they have been inserted in the eye. This would, according to the upbeat scientists, provide a personal video diary for each of us stretching from cradle to grave. What is immediately noticeable about such futuristic speculations are that they are largely devoid of ethical considerations. What human purposes could such developments contribute towards? Would technological developments of this kind have 'social' uses other than 'entertainment'? How might certain limits be placed on such technology to prevent the infringement of personal dignity? Indeed what safeguards need to be utilised in order to ensure that the development of such technologies are not used for oppressive forms of surveillance and social control? Following Habermas it is notable that such considerations are entirely absent from the technological optimism of the scientists involved in the project. In Habermasian terms then (and running parallel to the development of internet cultures, super information highways and digital television), these developments are technologically and economically rather than ethically driven. It is as if ethical criteria with regard to human purposes can only be conceived of after the technology has been developed. Much media has had this sort of history with radio, television and the internet developing out of military uses and developments. That media technology can have unintended consequences is undeniable, however, it also shows, as Habermas has long maintained, that technological development is rarely subject to 'public' criteria. In hermeneutical terms, the flooding of the world with information, images and media spectacles defines the 'good life' in overtly instrumental terms.

Similarly Lorenzo Simpson (1995) argues technological processes have a strong connection with the development of certain post-modern features such as irony and play in that both are dependent upon a weightless world where commodities have become decontextualised from their original locations of production. For example, virtual reality (to pick up on an earlier discussion) is based upon the assumption that our actual physical limits can be transcended by offering us an experience we can both control and manipulate. Technology therefore offers us experience where we can displace the other, manufacture our history and transcend our bodily limits.

Again technocratic consciousness suggests that at the click of a switch we can become different people and resolve our difficulties without too much by way of cost in terms of our current identities. From the contemporary lifestyle magazines' obsession with 'how to' be successful in work and leisure to self-help books' endless checklists against which we can judge the perfectibility of our relationships, technocratic consciousness is a strong component of media cultures.

The speeding up of media cultures encourages the technocratic belief that what is important about information is that it is both up to the minute and that it can alert us to problems that require immediate solutions. Alternatively, a more communicative media culture would, in Raymond Williams's terms, suggest that in democratic exchange not only must the cultural space be available for multiple forms of dialogic exchange, but that sufficient time be allotted to this process. Williams (1989b) argues that if cultural producers in a democratic community do have obligations to one another it is the duty not to move on too quickly. Williams writes:

> I mean the temptation at those difficult points of working in language to fall into the habit of which Orwell described so well when he talked of many political speeches as simply arranging gummed strips of words which other people had put into order, gumming these strips together until you had something of sufficient length, the words falling into familiar patterns which appear to make a sense of a kind. In much important writing it is at that point, when the words can come too easily – when the words are, so to say, ready-made – it is that hesitation that is the crucial condition; a hesitation from which in the worst cases emerge, and from which I suppose no writer ever completely emerges, but a hesitation which is of great consequence to significant production in writing because at that moment something new is happening in the language itself. (Williams, 1989b: 94)

While Williams's remarks were undoubtedly aimed at writers they would seem to be equally applicable to a range of activities within the media and cultural industries generally. The hermeneutic and democratic requirement that public spaces be orientated around the requirements of peaceful and intelligent dialogic exchange rather than the imperatives of technological reason remains a crucial insight. To concern oneself overtly with the effectiveness and speed of information flow is already to allow what should be concerned with ambivalence, engagement and debate to be overly technologically defined.

Such arguments have much to commend them, but they remain inadequately dialectical. While the development of modern systems of communication can be connected with nihilistic and meaning-denying formations, viewed from a different perspective they have simultaneously flooded the world with meaning. Much of the work evident within critical theory and post-modernism has emphasised the sense of meaninglessness ushered in by modern communication flows. Ulrich Beck (1996), on the other hand, argues that the pervasive power of instrumental reason and technical control has actually given birth to a new form of politics he calls 'sub-politics'. The humanity-wide project of saving the environment has been brought about through the actual destruction of nature as well as the accompanying culture of risk and uncertainty that has become wrapped around human conceptions of well-being. The politicisation of issues involved in the application of science and technology is rapidly introducing an increasingly reflexive culture whereby politics and morality is gaining the upper hand over scientific experts. A shared environment of global risk enables the formation of a democratic politics that seeks to recover democratic rights against systemic pressures. The media, in this respect, is the main location where these largely symbolic struggles and circulations are organised and staged. Whereas previous democratic struggles have been organised in more material public spaces like the workplace and the city centre; the new politics of risk is mostly played through a mediated cultural dimension. The omnipresence of ecological danger that is translated into stories of toxic waste, depleted fish stocks, poisonous air and global warming have provided groups like Greenpeace with the possibility of repoliticising areas as wide ranging as science, advertising and consumption. In other words, despite Habermas's pessimism, it is quite plausible to point to the emergence of a new politics out of a global civil society *because of* the widespread impacts of instrumental reason. Sub-politics therefore introduces the possibility for a rebirth of more dialogic and communicative sensibilities.

Read somewhat differently there is another important sense within which the structures of everyday life contribute towards rather than detract from the meaningfulness of the life-world, that is that the technological development of the media has been accompanied by the proliferation of popular narratives. Whether these narratives are realist, internally referential in terms of other media production, concerned with the reporting of distant wars or play in post-modern fashion with intertextual references they provide an important resource in the construction of identity. Narrativity, in this respect, can be seen as an ontological feature of social life and should be viewed as a meeting place between structure and agency. Actors in the modern world are routinely surrounded and constituted by a multiplicity of narratives that vary across time, space and relational setting (Somers, 1994). The connection between narrative and identity has been most expertly investigated by Paul Ricoeur (1991a, 1991b) who argues that narrative provides the interconnection between an identity which is chosen out of a range of discourses, and identity that is neither fixed and final nor in a permanent flux. Identity in this understanding is like a story that is always in the process of being retold, reformulated and realised in differing social contexts. Narratives find an anchor point in human life in that they provide historical reference points by organising our memories, and by helping us realise that our life itself can be seen as being part of interconnected stories that link us to the world, other people and our sense of self. Building on Socrates's maxim that the unexamined life is not worth living, our lives are made meaningful the extent to which we are able to gain self-knowledge by attending to the ways in which we are woven into and outside of narrative structures. To have an identity, then, is also to have the capacity to tell a story about one's own self. To be able to plot the interrelation between the self and community means to be able to produce a story out of multiple incidents, events and seemingly disconnected happenings. These stories can be public or private, concerned with individual or collective identity, but they all provide a bridge between life as it is lived and stories that are told in the media. There remains, however, as Christopher Bollas (1992) reminds us, unconscious experiences that resist being categorised into narrative experience. To be a character, in Bollas's terms, depends not only upon our ability to turn raw experience into narratives, but on our capacity to gain a sense of our internal self that resists intelligibility. Maturity therefore comes not only through an ability to be able cognitively to map ourselves in self- styled narratives, but through an increasing perception of our own uncertainty as to who we are and our relationship with the community. This paradoxically leads to an enhanced awareness of both the importance of narrative to our sense of who we are, and life's unconscious dimensions that retain a degree of mystery.

If the self is constituted through narrative and the explosion of mass communication has witnessed the proliferation of popular narratives there must seemingly be connections between identity formation and the media. This particular dynamic is explored by Ken Plummer (1995) in that he argues that the development of the media of mass communication have witnessed the eruption of a variety of sexual scripts into the public realm. These stories concern a variety of previously taboo topics covering a range of sexual practices. The narrative construction of sexuality can either become orient- ated around modernist stories of redemption, survival and overcoming, or post-modern tales that emphasise an uncertain, fragmented and mediated world of pluralised difference. These stories form the backcloth to a new kind of intimate citizenship where the public sphere has become orientated less around questions of justice and emancipation, and more overtly concerned with issues connected to self-identity. Through talk shows, soap operas, true-life stories and radio phone-ins the fabric of everyday life has been transformed. The partial decline of the traditional family has witnessed the emergence of a space for experimentation with regard to sexuality. The con- temporary presence of a plurality of different narratives through the media constantly remind us that there are many different ways of living your life and constructing your identity. What Giddens (1991) calls life politics is orientated around the question of 'How shall I live?' which has an obvious connection to questions of sexual identity. Just as the media remains con- nected to emancipatory questions of justice, the proliferation of sexual, ethical and personal narratives means that it is also a constitutive feature of the very practices which give our most intimate of relations meaning. The media then both detract from the meaningfulness of everyday life by promoting a technocratic consciousness, while simultaneously suggesting new narrative identities which may be become increasingly accommodated as we struggle to find our barings in a post-traditional society.

Cultural politics

The interrelated dimensions of social justice, recognition and meaningfulness points towards a renewed concern with cultural citizenship and cultural practice within society. The emergent media order – if these comments are followed (and despite its changing form) remains caught between critical opportunities and the maintenance of hegemonic and powerful structures. The mediated struggles for justice, recognition and meaningfulness through the media of mass communication will become increasingly sharpened as we move towards the end of the century. The diversity of political groupings and identities that make up civil society will increasingly see the mass media as the place where collective fates are decided. The struggle to see one's own life or shared culture represented fairly through the dominant institutions of the mass media is likely to intensify the more the same said media becomes determined by the global economy rather than public directives. This process is also likely to be heightened by the fact that the media in general are more caught up with the social definition of society than ever before.

In the determination of these questions the position of the nation-state is paradoxical in that it is likely both to gain and lose power through media globalisation. First, and most obviously, they lose the capacity to control information flow within their own borders given the new opportunities available for symbolic exchange at the local and global levels. However, the commercialisation of media images and structures gives nations new opportunities to use their sovereignty to limit global corporations access to internal markets, and thereby influence the content of media stories. This situation is further complicated in that those nations that fall outside of the intensified zone of global capital are unlikely to be able to use any such influence leaving the travelling tribes of journalists largely free to represent conflicts as they so wish or to ignore them altogether. At the global level a truly 'civilised' world society in terms of cultural exchange is unlikely to be ushered in by systemic forces. What is required in respect of a reinvigorated global civil society is an active citizenry seeking mediated justice, recognition and meaningfulness. These demands seemingly go beyond those heard in connection with the struggle to bring about a media free of bias and partiality. The increasingly deregulated communications universe will come to mirror the growing gap globally between the Earth's prosperous and poorer regions. The so-called development of the information rich and poor is likely to mirror more material indications that predict growing global social polarisation. Yet just as economic productivity has no obvious relation to the communally felt quality of life, so the increased volume of communications heralded by the super information highway will not of necessity lead to media that meet our personal and collective needs, hopes and desires. How far a democratic politics allied with a humane global sensibility will serve to restructure global media cultures, it is still too soon to say. There can, however, be little doubt that the technical development and globalisation of the media will provide critical theory and citizenship studies with new opportunities to balance maturely reasons for hope against bleaker visions.

CHAPTER 4

Cultural citizenship

The words culture and citizenship are rarely closely connected within contemporary debates. The term 'culture' is usually associated with a mix of public and private institutions including museums, libraries, schools, cinemas and the media, while more specifically being concerned with the dialogic production of meaning through a variety of practices. Citizenship, on the other hand, is more properly thought to be about questions of membership, belonging, rights and obligations. In institutional terms the terrain of citizenship is usually marked out by abstract legal definitions as to who is to be included and excluded from the political community.

More recently however, there has been a growing interest in how 'culture' and 'citizenship' might be more closely interrelated. First, to concern oneself with questions of inclusion and exclusion from a legally defined community will inevitably raise questions of a cultural nature. Whose histories are to be taught in our schools, which languages are to be preserved, what film and documentary projects are deserving of public money? To be excluded from a political community involves civil, political, social and *cultural* questions. To talk of cultural citizenship therefore is to be concerned with the various ways in which membership is both determined and constructed. Are you an insider or an outsider, accepted or rejected, embraced or shunned by contemporary society? Secondly, it is notable that as the basis for social citizenship has been undermined by privatisation, the running down of the welfare state, under-employment and increasing material divisions, demands for wider forms of cultural inclusion have grown louder. Processes of globalisation and cultural fragmentation have given new impetus to previously excluded groups to make claims for equal recognition and respect within the cultural sphere. While it is misleading to suggest that the decline in social citizenship is inversely related to the rise in cultural citizenship, they are undoubtedly connected. For example, the de-traditionalisation and individuation of modernity has contributed towards the partial displacement of class politics. The emergence of new areas of social contestation such as disability, animal rights and sexuality amongst others have appeared in the cracks inadequately occupied by more traditional forms of politics. However, it is worth reminding ourselves that claims to social and cultural citizenship are not necessarily in opposition as both seek to widen the fabric of modern society. While there is a danger that 'cultural' questions could come to displace those of material entitlement, more often such concerns are likely to be linked within the responses of social movements. Further, many of the claims for a genuinely pluralist public culture have in themselves implications for social resources. Publicly funded libraries, museums, education systems and media all make claims for revenue raised primarily through taxation. Thirdly, as we shall see, the institutional organisation and reproduction of culture entails that 'culture' is the site of relatively durable social practices which can be viewed in terms of rights and duties. The demand that our shared ways of life and overlapping identities be 'fairly' represented by a host of cultural institutions remains a pressing concern for many social groups. That more 'inclusive' images, representations and cultural practices more generally should be underwritten by rights and obligations seems an obvious way forward. Finally, 'cultural' citizenship should not become overly identified with abstract legal definitions. The cultural aspect of citizenship signifies a connection with the politics of 'everyday life' that is continually being rewritten by the reflexive incorporation of new ideas, narratives and frameworks.

However, if we take certain strands of contemporary debate then it would seem anachronistic to talk of cultural citizenship at any level. To discuss cultural citizenship in a globalised placeless culture like our own is to exhibit a certain nostalgia for the real and to suggest the fragmented nature of contemporary post-modern culture can somehow be put back together again. For Baudrillard (1993) modern culture can be described as an *obscene* culture where the world has become immediate and transparent in that it is has both globalised and eliminated the distinctions between the public and the private. The close-up universe of the television screen, newspaper and magazine has abolished the prospects for critical reflection, as subjects become reduced to terminals of a bland, fast-moving culture. The global village replaces a hierarchical national culture with one that is depthless, kitsch and placeless. Whereas once cultural citizenship might have been seen as the gradual widening of access to an elite cultural sensibility, such distinctions have since imploded and been replaced by commercialism, irony and play. Old national hierarchies that sought to bind time and space through literature, history, heritage, ceremony and myth have been replaced by spatialised communication flows. Vertical national traditions have become floating signifiers in a mediated horizontal global culture.

Such descriptions, if we pause for a moment, certainly seem to have a degree of credibility. The emergence of global information flows through CNN news and Rupert Murdoch's rapidly evolving version of the global village link up the world through a seemingly homogeneous cultural space. Yet it is my dual strategy to argue that such projections are both vastly exaggerated and fail to connect with at least three ways in which we might talk about cultural citizenship. It will emerge that while the nation-state is currently being permeated by global economic, political and cultural transformations it remains an important domain, and still most likely to be the place where issues related to cultural citizenship are settled.

To illustrate these concerns in respect of cultural citizenship and media culture my point of reference will be contemporary Western society, with specific reference to Britain and Western Europe. I will talk about cultural citizenship in terms of the emergence of (1) a cosmopolitan culture and the continuation of national cultures; (2) the application of specific rights and duties which concern the operation of cultural institutions; and (3) more informal obligations that make up the sphere of civil society. I will argue that cultural citizenship is a multifaceted concept that resists a singular definition and that each of the three strands outlined above point to a variety of legitimate means of employing the term. It is not my aim here to proscribe the dimensions the debate around cultural citizenship should take, but instead to point towards an unfolding field of inquiry. To do just that I shall offer a short discussion of each of these overlapping concerns in the context of post-national societies and cultures, while remaining sceptical regarding certain claims made by post-modernism and those who suppose national cultures are disappearing. *Cultural citizenship can be said to have been met the extent to which society makes commonly available semiotic material cultures that are necessary in order to both make social life meaningful, critique practices of domination, and allow for the recognition of difference under conditions of tolerance and mutual respect.* In this regard, cultural citizenship builds upon the arguments presented within the two proceeding chapters. First, questions of cultural citizenship are both moral (what is right for the community) and ethical (what is right for the individual?) and provide public space for the circulation for critical questions within the media. Relatedly, unless the media allow questions of justice, recognition and more everyday notions to be the subject of chronic debate the 'cultural' dimension of citizenship would be unforefilled. Questions of justice, recognition and ethics all have implications for the ways in which the media are organised, controlled and regulated. However, taken together these concerns also introduce questions of inclusion and exclusion. Exclusions from cultural citizenship can appear along the following axes: (1) the attempt to erect rigid boundaries between insiders and outsiders; (2) the hegemonic operation of political, economic and cultural forces in society that seek to maintain a conservative agenda constructed on certitude and tradition; (3) the increasing tendency to subject the distribution, circulation and exchange of symbolic forms to practices that seek to reinforce relations of dominance and; (4) the capacity of social life to become drained of all meaning and purposefulness through the pervasion of cynical reason evident in much mainstream culture.

Previously it might have been argued that to be excluded from cultural citizenship was to be excluded from full membership of the national community. Such a cultural view of citizenship would emphasise that the symbolic inheritance of the nation and participation in its cultural institutions should be the subject of wide-ranging forms of participation. Cultural exclusion was synonymous with exclusion from the life of the nation. Despite many of the social transformations I shall discuss here, this aspect of cultural citizenship remains an ongoing concern, that is, a crucial aspect of cultural citizenship remains the 'inclusive' participation within and the reshaping of national life. This remains a crucial agenda given the continued importance of the national dimension, and the need to include peripherally defined cultures and perspectives. Such cultural strategies, for instance, would seek to make sure that the dominant imagery carried by the media and personnel who work in the cultural industries are fully 'inclusive' of previously marginalised social groups. Yet if this agenda is currently the dominant definition offered by modernity, then an emergent post-modern version of cultural citizenship is suggested by processes of globalisation and the increasingly heterogeneous nature of civil society. These dimensions, as we shall see, press the importance of cultural pluralism over attempts to reinscribe dominant homogeneous cultures. For instance, the 'inclusion' of sexualities other than heterosexuality could not simply be achieved through the extension of common rights (the right of lesbian and gay couples to marry one another) but would also have implications for the dominant heterosexual culture requiring the deconstruction of heterosexism (Richardson, 1996). The most important aspect, in terms of my discussion, of this emergent dimension concerns the maintenance of pluralistic public spheres at the level of the local, the national and the global. The cultivation of overlapping and interconnected public spheres that seek to balance the rights of the individual or group against their obligations to the wider community is increasingly the dimension where access to cultural citizenship is determined. Hence cultural citizenship is becoming not so much a product of national membership – although as we shall see this is still important – but the outcome of the critical linkage of reflexive and heterogeneous cultural practices related to self and society. However, despite many of those who think otherwise, this political and cultural agenda continues to remain subordinate to the dimensions of the nation-state, instrumental reason and commodification processes.

In the following discussions I want primarily, although not exclusively, to draw out the importance of these debates in the context of complex systems of mass communication. It is hoped that to view cultural citizenship in this context I will be able to avoid vague formulations and be able convincingly to express why I believe the concept should be applied to institutions and more everyday social practices alike.

Global cosmopolitan cultures

A number of theorists have pointed to the emergence of a global cosmopolitan culture as being significant in terms of questions related to citizenship. As Giddens (1994) argues, globalisation should not be simply conceptualised as capitalisation as such features include the technological ability of satellite communication to recontextualise imagery and information across time and space. Contemporary societies have witnessed the development of time–space distanciation that was not evident in pre-modern societies. By this he means that within the pre-modern period time and space were always strongly located in terms of physical place. The turning of night into day or the passing of the seasons served to act as localised markers of time and space. With the invention of clock time we could say that time has become separated from space, and that time and space have become empty phenomena. The pulling apart of time and space can be visualised in calendars, railway timetables and maps. These devices enable time and space to be coordinated without any reference to notions of place – they are abstract means of ordering social activity. These processes can also be connected to what Giddens calls the disembedding of social systems. Modernity, according to Giddens, is a post-traditional social order, where the 'emptying out' of time and space allows for the stretching of social relations. If we think for a moment about the globalisation of television networks this should serve as an illustration. While global does not mean universal, international media organisations are able to transport images and representations across time and space and onto the television sets of the globe's citizens. For Giddens, the relocation of information from localised contexts, evident within modern communication networks, is made possible via the uncoupling of time and space, and disembedding mechanisms such as technical media. These devices involve the separation of social relations 'from local contexts of interaction and their restructuring across indefinite spans of time–space' (Giddens, 1990: 21). For example, Giddens argues, expert systems exhibit many of these features as the knowledge they deploy has a validity independent of those agents who make use of them. Expert systems are part of the fabric of everyday life and have the capacity to extend social relations in time and space. Every time I read a popular feature on health care, expert frames of reference are being recontextualised in terms of certain lifestyle decisions that I might make. The decision to stop eating meat might be formed by an article I read in a women's magazine, a leaflet attacking MacDonald's, or my mistrust of the assurances offered by state-employed scientists – these are all examples of the way technical knowledge becomes routinely reconstituted in modernity.

Giddens (1991: 24–27) explicitly recognises the role played by technical media in his short discussion of the cultural make-up of newspapers. It was the invention of the telegraph that allowed the early newspapers to separate space from notions of place. Up until this point, the content of the press had been determined by whether or not news items were close at hand. The telegraph, through its capacity to disembed information from social location, meant that media content was less determined by proximity in space and time, while allowing newspapers to become much more event driven. These institutional transformations arguably make possible the increasingly global scope of much contemporary entertainment and news, and more crucially such processes produce cultural diasporas in that communities of taste, habit and belief become detached from national contexts. The self-definition of community was until recently thought to be the primary responsibility of the nation-state. However, the legislative force of the state and ideas of community have become progressively decoupled. These cultural transformations along with the implosion of expert cultures into everyday life have helped promote a world of culturally accomplished 'clever people' (Giddens, 1994: 94). By this he means that the populace of Western societies are used to eating foreign foods, challenging the professional power of their doctors and being informed about global events. Resisting the cultural pessimism of Baudrillard, Giddens cheerfully notes the world is better informed than it ever has been. Thus modern culture has both democratised expert cultures and made widely available a surface familiarity with other ways of life that are distant in time and space. As Urry (1995) notes, mass communications, along with other cultural processes, such as the internationalisation of tourism, have helped produce a certain openness to the rich patterns of geographical and historical cultures the globe has to offer. These changes, as Urry in particular seems aware, have certain implications for cultural citizenship. First, people are increasingly becoming citizens through their ability to be able to purchase goods in a global market, hence citizenship becomes less about formalised rights and duties – about which more later – and more about the consumption of exotic foods, Hollywood cinema, Madonna CDs and Australian wine. To be excluded from these commercial goods is to be excluded from citizenship (that is full membership) of modern Western societies. As Bauman (1992) notes, social control in societies where capital has been emancipated from labour is maintained through the dual poles of 'seduction' and 'repression'. That is, in its present phase, capitalism is legitimated more through the pleasures of the market (and the repression of those excluded from it) than it is through the normative acceptability of political ideologies. Secondly, other than participating in the consumption of goods, the other main plank of modern cosmopolitanism can be connected to notions of free mobility. That is, those nations that seek to prevent the free traffic of tourists, images and information across borders are seen as infringing human rights. Urry concludes global citizenship involves practices that enable us to consume other cultures and places distant from our own.

However, I would argue, the political implications of global cosmopolitanism are difficult to track and are probably ambivalent in terms of their overall effects. For example, read pessimistically the spread of a global market culture based upon pleasure and enjoyment might be held to bracket off certain obligations for others such as future generations. That is, modern cosmopolitan cultures are market cultures based upon practices of individualised consumption and destructive hedonism which are currently destroying fragile ecosystems, contributing towards global warming and adding to pollution levels. Viewed negatively cosmopolitan cultures can be linked to what Galbraith (1992) has described as the 'culture of contentment' which prevents radical political change at the level of individual nation-states. Here the good life is enjoyed through the marketplace by those in full-time employment (roughly two-thirds of the population) and ensures that those who seek to put up taxes are immediately politically punished, thereby adding to the misery of those excluded from the labour market. Further, and perhaps most critically of all, it is not currently evident the extent to which commercial cosmopolitanism actually opens out an engagement with the other, or merely reaffirms certain rights to pleasure. Here I think that both Giddens and Urry read the emergence of global cosmopolitanism in an overly optimistic way. The development of a marketised culture has indeed developed a far wider range of choice of consumer goods than those that have been made traditionally available. For instance, the magazine market currently carries lifestyle magazines for men, Asian newspapers, women's weeklies and monthlies, covering a range of topics from new technology to domestic pets. Yet could not a consequence of this be both the forming of new consumptive communities as well as the avoidance of more troubling topics that are deliberately excluded from 'cultural comfort zones'? It is probably the case, for example, that the recent arrival of men's fashion magazines has as much to do with the handling of masculine disappointment and the promotion of consumerism as it has with the development of critical forms of subjectivity. Our culture through the proliferation of different niche markets and the explosion of the number of cultural forms made available puts such avoidance within everyone's reach. Read in this way, cultural cosmopolitanism is less about helping us understand our specific identities and our obligations towards others than it is concerned with a placeless fragmented culture and the narcissistic pleasures of consumption.

Market cultures, in George Steiner's (1974: 174) terms, depend upon 'maximum impact and instant obsolescence'. That is, the very thing that makes market cultures so exciting and vibrant – the search for the new, the dramatic and the novel – makes substantive intellectual and cultural exchange difficult to achieve. In such an atmosphere, the nation can provide a site of obligation and connection (sometimes dangerously so) while notions of the public open up a critical domain that should be free from colonising (money and power) pressures. Indeed, referring back to Giddens's reflections, it is arguable that the nation continues to glue together space and time through the organisation of collective memory. Recently Britain's state institutions and media commemorated V.E. day (50 years since the end of the Second

World War); despite much evidence of the state creating national myths in order to foster its own legitimacy, the day also provided an opportunity for experiences to be communicated across generations in a meaningful way. Popular newspaper articles, television and radio programmes, it seemed, were concerned both to bring the nation together by interviewing 'ordinary people' who served in the war and to communicate a sense of the war's importance in shaping modernity. This provided a platform for an older generation to speak of their disappointments, hopes and dreams all of which have faded given Britain's economic decline. The nation then, despite the development of a global cosmopolitan culture, still provides a locale where the organisation of space (the legitimate use of force in a given zone) and time (collective memory) are hinged together. This is most definitely not to argue that national cultures should not be opened up to critique. But I would suggest that national cultures remain more permanent formations than either Giddens or Urry seem to allow. Instead I would argue that European nationalism is both a relatively enduring force and part of an ambivalent heritage.

First, nationalist claims have been made by both powerful social groups, and significantly by oppressed minorities, in an endeavour to extend citizenship rights. For instance, the idea of nationhood enabled the working-class movement to claim certain civil, political and social rights, while attempting to impose corresponding obligations on social elites. On the other hand, post-modernism has made us aware of the extent to which identity is based upon the unfolding of exclusive as well as inclusive social processes. However, it was probably Freud (1966) who first pointed out that the warm feelings of community are related to more troubling identifications being projected outside of the group. If nationalism has helped foster certain progressive ends it has also diverted our attention away from social relations that are external to the nation-state, while paradoxically providing an ideology that legitimated European dominance over the colonies. In a post-colonial context, nationalism remains an ambivalent force in that it contains a locus for communalism, while obscuring the complexities of residual and emergent global intersubjective dimensions. I shall now give some examples of these features.

While I have read the emergence of cultural cosmopolitanism less generously than others; as J. B. Thompson (1994: 94) notes, currently global media cultures subject the world's nation-states to a form of *global scrutiny*. By this he means that the exercise of political power increasingly takes place upon a visible world stage. The medium of mass communication makes the actions of despotic states, such as the suppression of the Chinese pro-democracy movement, ever visible to the globe's citizens. This process can also be coupled to the global re-mooring of images and perspectives that give individuals some idea of forms of life different from their own. This surface knowledge of other cultures, Thompson (1995) argues, gives individuals a social resource, enabling them to distance themselves from more official state-driven viewpoints. But, even here, nation-states are still granted a considerable degree of autonomy. While the Chinese state was unable to prevent critical observations being formulated by the Western media it was more successful in persuading the Murdoch controlled Star television corporation to abandon the practice of transmitting BBC news. Again, as with tourism, the restriction of global flows of information is widely perceived as a violation of citizenship. But the problem with J. B. Thompson's argument in this context is that it comes close to Murdoch's own verbose rhetoric regarding the democratising effect of global media corporations. What this analysis neglects is that when the chips were down Murdoch put his commercial interests before some of the loftier notions of democracy that he had previously claimed global media corporations could be associated with. Further, it has also been claimed, despite the global condemnation of the Bosnian Serbs, that their own state-controlled media regularly suggested that the UN and the Muslims are effectively fighting on the same side. These transmissions have undoubtedly had a marked impact on the internal population despite long-term economic and political pressures exerted by the international community. To claim the globalisation of the media places restrictions on the activities of nation-states is undoubtedly correct, but as the Chinese and the Bosnian examples bear out, such states, dependent on social context, still have considerable powers to isolate themselves from the internal impacts of global criticism, no matter how self-defeating this might prove over the longer term. Thus, in terms of cultural citizenship, cosmopolitan practices of consumption lead in ambiguous directions and are subject to the mediating effect of national cultures and states.

My argument is then that the 'globalisation thesis' is in danger of underestimating the relative permanence of national cultures and their ability to respond to such changes. Whether it is through national holidays, watching television, reading newspapers, listening to the radio, speaking a language or applying for a passport, the nation remains a primary form of 'cultural' address. The question that now has to be asked is what kinds of cultural citizenship are promoted in the national domain.

National citizenship

Most of the debate in respect of contemporary nationalism makes a clear distinction between ethnic and civic nationalism. Ethnic nationalism holds that citizenship is based upon a common cultural identity. This particular version of nationalism has been associated with the more destructive features of national cultures, that is, it is commonly held that ethnic nationalism's attempt to impose a 'pure' and homogeneous construction on the plurality of the 'people' is connected in late modernity to the cultural barbarism of ethnic cleansing. On the other hand, national cultures and identities are irrevocably Janus-faced, as ideas of nationhood have informed struggles to extend commonly held rights and obligations and have provided the backdrop for anti-colonial struggles. This attitude, offering a less pessimistic view of national cultures, brings us to civic nationalism. Here membership and basic citizenship entitlements are tied to a 'legal–political' definition of community. The rights and obligations of the national community are in this respect universal not culturally specific. For instance, critical-liberals, such as Habermas (1994), in the German context, have defended a conception of nationalism that he calls 'constitutional patriotism'. Habermas argues that while nationalism and democracy have 'grown up' together they are analytically separable. Feelings of loyalty and obligation should be constructed around universally agreed procedures rather than specific ethnic groups. Habermas, in this view, comes close to the liberal view that the state or national community should remain agnostic concerning members' particular views of the good life, within of course certain boundaries. There are however a number of objections to such formulations.

On the question of nationalism, Anthony D. Smith (1995) argues that all national identities contain a common ethnic content. Indeed, in this respect, Habermas does not so much propose a different national identity, as ignore it all together. Against the notion that the nation is purely a cultural construct of modernity, or in Anderson's (1983) term 'imagined community', Smith claims that nations actually developed out of pre-modern ethnic communities. These communities are obviously of different types and are held together by common symbols, rituals and customs. In the modern era there existed, in varying degrees, feelings of ethnic sentiment which have been the foundation stone of contemporary nationalism. Further, it is noticeable that many modern nation-states have built upon, not constructed, core ethnic identities. There is no doubting that these identities have been reinforced by nation-states, but what is being questioned here is that we can make any simplistic contrast between ethnic and civic nationalism. Even rights-based nationalisms are likely to be defined by a core ethnic content. What is compelling about this view is that it radically questions whether the modern state can be rationally reformulated in the way that Habermas suggests. As Berlin (1991) argues the major blind spot for rationalists, liberals and socialists of all shapes and sizes has been the success of nationalism. However, Smith undoubtedly goes too far in running together ideas of the nation based upon common political participation, and notions which are orientated around a shared ethnic identity. As Katherine Verdery (1993) has argued, it is plausible, given competing definitions of the nation, that it is open to a multitude of meanings that may become contested by different groups. Further, while Smith, correctly in my view, perceives a less than contingent tie between nationhood and community his more conservative reflections obscure the need to foster more fully inclusive national public spaces. What is not being problematised is the political question as to how national cohesiveness and a sense of belonging could be granted a more multicultural anchoring. Smith also fails to give adequate recognition to what might be described as the emergence of post-modern nationalism. This describes a new form of nationalism whereby a cultural community's demand for a state is rapidly invented as a matter of strategic political or economic advantage. The simulation of cultural communities who might become national communities is therefore as much a feature of the contemporary era as old style nationalism. As Enzensberger (1994) reports the recent upsurge of ethnic nationalism in Eastern Europe is more likely to be born out of psychic hatred, post-modern violence and the need to fill an inner void than the complex working through of deeply held convictions. Nationalism therefore is a mixture between traditionalism (the relative permance of pre-modern communities), modernity (regulated order imposed from above by legal legitimate authority) and post-modernity (break up of larger units and narratives along with the cultural simulation of new collective identities). Yet the partial deconstruction of ethnic and civic nationalism also critiques the attitude, prevalent in the social sciences, that nationalism is always someone else's problem. Michael Billig (1995), in a penetrative study, has revealed the ways in which the culture of nationhood is an ordinary, or in his terms a banal, phenomenon, which is reproduced through common sense discourses. Nationalism embraces patterns of thinking that make it almost second nature to think in terms of distinctions between 'us' and 'them'. Banal nationalism then is blind to the ways collective identities are commonly maintained, and presents the division of the world into nation-states as part of the natural environment. The national 'we' is the regular mode of address adopted by the media of mass communication. Hence, the problem with post-modern accounts of identity is that national affiliations can not be changed like yesterday's clothes, and that most citizens, although not all, take the reproduction of a common homeland for granted. There remains, then, a tie between citizenship and nationhood that can never be wholly deconstructed or ignored, depite its emergent post-modern elements. This perhaps inescapable fact poses cultural citizenship with problems as to how to reconcile increasingly multicultural communities with notions of national identity.

This leads to our second point. Charles Taylor (1992), in an important essay, seeks to link what he calls the 'struggle for recognition' with the politics of multiculturalism. Taylor starts from the view that both personal and collective identities are shaped by the intersubjective processes of recognition and misrecognition. That is, images of the self are mirrored back by intimate relations, social institutions and, most importantly in our view, the media of mass communication informing our individual and collective identities. The struggle for recognition is a dialogic process that is negotiated with intimate or distant others. These processes, for Taylor, encompass certain basic human needs that depend upon the recognition of the uniqueness of our identities and notions of equal respect. Many of the objections that have been raised against the dominant imagery of the communications media are that they have presented stereotypes of the poor, women, old people, the disabled and marginalised ethnic groups. The symbolic, as opposed to the material, struggles of these groups have attempted to 'interrupt' dominant hegemonic discourses in order that the media take a fuller account of their dignity and their difference. The problem comes however in reconciling the universal demand for equal dignity, while our differences are also respected. The politics of equal respect, which is most often associated with liberalism, requires that we treat others in a difference-neutral way. The difficulty with such a view, however, is that a blind universalism is of itself representative of a particular culture, and that if we are not receptive to difference, then this actually suppresses the uniqueness of our identity formations. To return to the culture of liberalism, it has wanted to secure equal respect, while remaining indifferent to the specific identity formations chosen by its citizens.

In other contexts, feminist theorists have sought to reconcile the dimensions of equality and difference. Phillips (1993) argues that the abstract individualism of liberalism imposes a unitary conception of human needs, which thereby marginalises groups who differ from the norm. Universalistic thinking has been increasingly abandoned by feminists as the suspicion is that appeals to equality, liberty and community have sought to encode a neutral subject. As much feminist research has now uncovered, the so-called ideologically neutral subject often took the male as its norm. The discursive shattering of the universal subject has led to the emergence of a politics of difference. The problem is, that difference feminism is unable to make pronouncements on common goods and principles. The solution to this thorny problem perhaps lies in an extended dialogue between abstract principles and concrete identities. According to Phillips (1991) this is exactly what members of the jury are typically asked to do. Jurors are, on the one hand, asked to lay aside their prejudices in order to reach a 'just' decision, and, on the other, to take account of the specific concrete circumstances of the defendant. The point is that, should politics simply become the assertion of specific identities, this would leave little space for processes of negotiation, compromise and even the reformation of our interests and identities. Phillips reasons that if women's identities were excluded from politics then it would be unlikely that previously defined 'private' social relations would ever have been politicised by their male counterparts. Yet the recognition of women's cultural 'difference' needs to be accompanied by their universal respect and recognition so that they might expand a notion of the common good.

Similarly Taylor, arguing in more overtly cultural terms, also maintains that liberalism is inhospitable to difference. Liberalism is unable to secure the collective conditions for the maintenance of minority cultures. Such cultures, in a framework of individual choice, are unlikely to flourish unless they are granted collective rights. However, Taylor is clear that the provision of such rights would not guarantee that equal forms of respect are granted towards minority cultures. To be clear, such rights, for ethnic minorities or any other such groups, could not ensure the recognition that they seek, however, they could help open the public space necessary for their survival. Minority cultural rights, to preserve a language, way of life, religion, etc., could, on this reading, help secure the public presence and visibility of previously marginalised traditions, symbols and practices. Elsewhere, Taylor (1995) argues that the liberal state can not actually afford to be neutral in respect of fostering a sense of patriotic identification amongst its peoples. A common sense of patriotic identification means that there is a commitment to a common sense of identity and the values of a political community. It is precisely this common focus which generates a shared sense of outrage among citizens within media debates. If we take the American reaction to Watergate, or the disgust of the British on discovery that Members of Parliament were taking cash for questions, these reactions were motivated by a sense of common identity being compromised. A sense of common identification then is likely to be fostered the extent to which national forms of identification allow themselves to become defined through their openness to plural ways of living.

Both the criticisms outlined above have important consequences for cultural citizenship. The first is that, despite post-modern arguments concerning the fluidity of modern identities, the national 'cultural' dimension is still a major point within modernity for the negotiation of identity. The other point is that national identities themselves need to be constantly re-negotiated to admit a diverse range of identity constructs.

The perceived fragility of most dominant constructions of national identity has provided the political space that has recently become occupied by those who wish to promote counter discursive hegemonic practices around notions of difference (Bhabha, 1988; Hall, 1987; Mercer, 1994). Much of this work, in a British context, has sought to both expose the cultural racism of the New Right, connect the construction of 'other' identity formations through a diasporic culture, and deconstruct discursive strategies employed by the state to construct homogeneous national identities. These moves are absolutely crucial if a more genuine cultural citizenship is to develop where difference is allowed to flourish and the dominant version of Englishness is decentred to become just another ethnic group. This would allow for notions of citizenship to become progressively detached from *overtly* cultural criteria and ethnic exclusiveness. The political impetus behind much of this work is to argue for a more genuinely multicultural national space than is likely to be delivered by globalisation processes alone. Yet, as most of these authors are well aware, in the British context at least, more multicultural forms of recognition are a long way off. Further, I would argue, there are also a number of problems that theories of difference have failed to address. First, while nation-states continue to have interests in symbolically defining a particular region they will impose a certain form of cultural uniformity upon it. Ernest Gellner (1983) argues that the universalisation of linguistic practices within nation-states is essential in highly mobile societies where citizens need to be able to communicate with one another. In order for bureaucracies to ensure social reproduction the state will need to ensure a shared minimal culture. That is, while Bhabha (1988) is perfectly justified in wanting to talk of cultural difference and incommensurability that resists accommodation within universalistic frameworks, it is likely that as long as nation-states survive plural cultures and dominant national cultures will have to enter into new social contracts. I think this is probably what Raymond Williams was hinting at when he wrote:

> We want to speak as ourselves, and so elements of the past of the language, that we received from our parents, are always alive. At the same time, in an extending community, we want to speak with each other, reserving our actual differences but reducing those we find irrelevant. (Williams, 1965: 252)

While Williams came close to defining citizenship in overtly cultural terms in his later writing, here, largely concerned with class difference, he recognises that if we are to communicate with one another in democratically reformulated public spaces then there has to be some minimal sense of a shared identity. This is also recognised by Parekh (1991) who argues for a citizenship that should be based around institutionally embedded multicultural practices rather than assimilation or mere tolerance. That is, new forms of national cohesion could be promoted by providing the social space for the recognition of difference, and also vitally, *commonality*. This process could be carried out through a mixture of formal and informally held rights and obligations that applied to both minorities and majorities. It remains the task of those who wish to foster a genuinely multicultural nation-state to consider how difference might be reconciled with a minimal universalism. Secondly, national cultures have been, and are likely to remain, important sources of legitimacy for nation-states, that is, the attempt by governments to foster a sense of a shared destiny and culture are crucial in binding together the population. As many recent commentators have noticed, along with the cultural fragmentation of Western democracies has come a growing decline in relations of trust between members of the political class and the people. In this respect, I would argue, there will be renewed attempts through the construction of a shared national culture to breathe new life into this relationship. National cultures and their constant resimulation will continue to play an important role in bridging the gap between the political class and the people. Finally, it is evident that all nation-states seek to represent themselves through organised ceremonies and rituals and, increasingly, through the construction of a shared national heritage. It is for this reason that nations are unlikely to become exponents of a pluralised postmodernism. The temptation here on the part of the Left has been, in many cases quite rightly, to point to certain exclusions in this process, and to argue that the nation can not be defined in terms of a homogeneous culture. Yet opponents of national exclusivity have yet to grapple with the problem as to how more multicultural symbols can be imagined, while fostering a shared minimal identity.[1]

What then are the implications of these reflections for a notion of cultural citizenship? I think they are threefold. First, globalisation processes have delivered increasingly cosmopolitan cultures which have fostered a number of common expectations (free mobility of peoples and information, access to the global market) among members of Western democracies. Significantly, to be excluded from these practices is to be excluded from citizenship. Secondly, I also pointed out that a more genuinely cosmopolitan culture could only be delivered through the reform of national cultures which remain more powerful constellations than many seem aware. For this to occur national cultures will need to enter into new partnerships with previously excluded ethnic and regional cultures. Despite the undoubted importance of diasporic cultural processes the decentring of national cultures is unlikely to be secured by global flows of people and images alone. Finally, national cultures are increasingly operating in new cultural contexts defined by the movement of peoples and images through the dimensions of time and space. Emergent cultural zones of identification are being shaped by processes occurring both above and below the contours of the originally defined national community. These factors are unlikely to mean the end of nationalism and national identity, in fact they give such questions a more pressing pertinence than was previously assumed. The question as to what constitutes collective as well as individual identities is considerably sharpened by the discordant traffic of globalising processes. This delivers risks in that national identity could become the focus of ethnic exclusionary moments and tendencies and opportunities, in that our identities are at least partially open for reconstruction.

I shall now connect these concerns with the reflections evident in the previous two chapters. What is being argued for here is for a public sphere that is just, allows for equal forms of recognition and is meaningful, but equally, we cannot afford to ignore the national domain. Further, we should be careful to avoid a false universalism that simply gestures towards the equality of the globe's cultures and avoid a form of cosmopolitan optimism that assumes that national cultures do not remain important centres of power and identity.

Cultural citizenship or cultural policy?

The next aspect of cultural citizenship I would like to investigate concerns the development of specific rights and duties that can be attached to cultural industries, or what might more loosely be defined as cultural policy. The idea of cultural policy is, at the time of writing, a growing one. The argument here is that cultural studies during the 1970s and 1980s retreated from wider political and economic concerns into the text and semiotic forms of analysis. Correspondingly cultural policy formulated by the state only applied to 'small corners' of cultural experience. Here the nation-state sought to preserve the culture of an elite (subsidising theatres, concert halls and galleries) leaving popular pleasure to be defined by the marketplace. Culture was about the redistribution of previously elite cultures. The hope was that such measures would civilise the masses away from immediate pleasures, into the deferred forms of gratification offered by high cultures. As a range of critics from Raymond Williams (1965) to Mulgan and Worpole (1986) have recognised, new sets of cultural policies need to be developed to cover electronic and print media, music culture, heritage parks, museums and public libraries, to name just a few. These developments can be linked to the increasingly widespread recognition that cultural pursuits are now a matter for public intervention.

The other developments in cultural policy are in two different directions; they concern the economic regeneration of urban areas and more specific interventions that can be linked to a Foucaultian conception of politics. Here I want to argue that these are both important and interesting developments, however, that both lack the normative and critical dimension of the version of cultural citizenship I am seeking to develop. My argument in this respect is for cultural citizenship rather than the more instrumentally defined cultural policy. Each will be considered briefly in turn.

The development of cultural strategies by regions and cities has been widely recognised as a means of generating employment in both tourist industries and in the service sector. In this respect, Lash and Urry (1994) argue, modern capitalism has been both reorientated around new flexible modes of production (where power is relocated through the dominance of certain distributors) while becoming more heavily reliant upon product design. Old style manufacturing, in the West at least, has been replaced by a culturally coded service sector. By the year 2000 the single largest item in terms of world trade will be international tourism. The production of tourism is of course heavily reliant upon the semiotic aspects of the social and physical locations of those places to be visited. Global tourism has not meant that the world is increasingly coming to look the same. In this context, we might consider my home city of Sheffield. Recently, due to the collapse of heavy industry (coal and steel) in the mid 1980s, the city has attempted to rework its image through a variety of cultural strategies including the provision of sports facilities, holding of the world student games, and the development of a cultural quarter (plans for a museum of popular music, the introduction of an arts cinema and the development of recording studios and a photographic gallery). These strategies are built around partnerships between local authorities and commercial concerns, and employ postmodern definitions of culture which undermine older distinctions between high and low. Viewed positively, such strategies aim to secure more culturally inclusive policies and counter trends towards privatisation by developing democratic forms of civic identity through the organisation of arts festivals and other activities. On the other hand, despite the democratic origins of such policies, doubts remain concerning their ability to be genuinely inclusive while the main emphasis in the 1980s was placed upon maximising the economic growth of cultural industries (Griffiths, 1993). Indeed, as we shall see later in my discussion of television and film, distinct dangers remain in viewing culture in purely economic terms. Further, the extent to which such policies have been pursued continues, for a large part, to depend upon their national context. In Britain, during the 1980s, city-based cultural policies were largely developed as national centres were either unwilling or unable to offer much in the way of alleviating long-term unemployment – it of course remains an open question concerning the effectiveness of cultural policies in this regard. But in other European countries, especially in areas with less-centralised decision-making structures, there is evidence of a deeper commitment to such policies. These important issues aside, my current concern is that the notion of cultural citizenship which is being offered here is: culture = economic growth. It is my argument that what needs to be found is a more substantive notion of what culture is for, if it is not to be pulverised by economic reason. My reflections, therefore, maintain a deep connection with certain branches of critical theory that sought to develop a critique of commodifying process which bracketed off more critical forms of engagement. By this I do not mean to imply that cultural strategies of attracting capital to urban centres should be abandoned, as such a view would fail to appreciate many of the positive impacts such strategies have had on improving the quality of city life. What I am suggesting however is that cultural dimensions retain a connection to public and aesthetic dimensions, which should not become subordinate to the movement of capital.

If cultural policies harbour the possibility of becoming overly economically driven, the other major development in cultural policy shows signs of becoming a technocratic enterprise.Tony Bennett (1992) argues that cultural policy studies should view culture as a particular area of government that requires specific forms of intervention in order to transform identifiable social practices. Bennett, utilising Foucault's work on govermentality, argues that culture may be defined as a:

> specific set of institutionally embedded relations of government in which the forms of thought and extended populations are targeted for transformation. (Bennett, 1992: 26)

Thus if cultural policy studies are ever to get off the ground, what is required is the production of concrete forms of knowledge that can be applied to specific fields of practice. The problem here, as with Foucault's work in general, is that culture is reduced to an effect of power, disallows intersubjective forms of recognition and is ethically neutral. Again, as with cultural policy that becomes subservient to economic forms of reason, notions of critique and meaningfulness are bracketed off to serve a technocratic enterprise.[2] The idea of culture becomes reduced to the specific sets of power relations that go into formulating museum policies, Hollywood movies or keep-fit videos. Such an argument, again similarly with economic forms of reason, could not demonstrate why all cultural relations should not be privatised and subordinated to the needs of capital. Further, as I indicated above, Bennett's remarks come close to advocating technical fixes to specifically cultural problems, the end result of which is nihilism and meaninglessness. Thus, while at first glance Bennett seems to be offering cultural studies an opportunity for critical intervention, on closer inspection his proposals come closer to an advocation of instrumental or technical reason.

Technology, as Lorenzo Simpson (1995) has pointed out, is both a response to our finitude as human beings and is end orientated. That is, technology seeks to deal with our anxiety regarding death by domesticating time and making the future predictable, while instrumentally aiming to achieve certain ends. Technology, in this reading, tends to be totalitarian in that it reduces 'worldly things' to means and 'de-realises' time by attempting to relieve us from the burden of having to wait. Ideologically, technology operates as if it were a disinterested objectivist practice, which it most definitely is not. This view seeks to both legitimise its domination over the life-world and translate a concern with meanings into an obsession with goals. For instance, the practice of intervening in a debate concerning the future of television can only, in Bennett's terms, be considered successful if it results in the achievement of certain ends. This brackets off a hermeneutic concern with what I might learn from the debate, the dialogic identities that become constructed through conversation, and perhaps the feelings of disappointment I might have if certain voices are systematically excluded from the conversation. There is therefore a connection between a technological project and the nihilistic loss of meaning which now pervades modernity.The political point here, as it is with Habermas (1989a), is to reform the relationship between instrumentalist and more communicative concerns. Thus by concentrating on the achievement of ends, Bennett fails to address the question as to what culture is for and why it is important.

Culture, if it is about anything, is intimately connected with meaningfulness. Arguably it is not so much about the preconceived ends of strategic intervention as it is concerned with the negotiation of identity and selfhood. Mature selfhood arguably can only emerge through coming to terms with nature, history and the perspectives of others – all of which resists the narcissistic projections of the playful post-modern subject and a technocratic obsession with ends. These reflections, I would argue, offer a more normative form of cultural citizenship and hold out the prospect of what Williams often referred to as an *educated* and participatory democracy. I shall now develop these concerns with respect to questions of citizenship and audio-visual communications.

The concept of citizenship is usually linked with the writing of the sociologist T. H. Marshall. Marshall (1992) divided citizenship into three dimensions that were originally meant to have a specifically national institutional location. The first of these was civil rights (property rights, rights to a fair trial) which largely developed in the eighteenth century. The next century saw the development of political rights in respect of the right to vote in democratically held elections and freedom of association. Finally, in the twentieth century, there emerged along with the welfare state social rights in the form of protection against poverty, unemployment and ill-health. These rights automatically implied certain obligations, and were meant to be definitive of a certain status of membership. In more recent years, while proving influential, this legacy has become controversial for a number of reasons. These include Marshall's evolutionary emphasis, the overly passive way in which citizenship claims have been isolated from the context of social struggle, his neglect of inequalities other than class, the restricted focus of social rights and his concentration upon the nation-state (Roche, 1992; Turner, 1993). To these diverse strands of criticism, I should like to add that Marshall failed to address questions of cultural citizenship. Along with civil, political and social dimensions we need to add cultural rights and obligations. Hence the concept of citizenship should be thought of as a four-tiered model, rather than the usual three-layered component. My approach, however, differs from that of other writers who have stressed cultural citizenship. The central locus for the application of citizenship in respect of culture remains the spheres of education and mass communication. Both Turner (1994a) and Wexler (1990) provide interesting discussions of cultural citizenship, and yet altogether ignore these dimensions. Here I will aim to readdress this balance with respect to the film and television industry. Yet, as we shall see, while the nation remains the primary forum within which these rights and obligations are to be claimed they can not be thought of as wholly separate from the intersection of globalising and regionalising processes.

The television media in the Western European context grew up in a specifically national system of regulation. Public systems of communication have developed in a sphere that has been offered some protection historically from commodifying processes, have a deep connection to national identity and are governed by the state. The first point to make is that public service broadcasting in Western Europe is directly tied into a specifically national form of citizenship. In modern Western democracies, television broadcasting has established an asymmetrical relation with the public. On the one hand, television institutions research the audience to uncover its viewing tastes and preferences. On the other, both public and private means of organising television feed back a sense of a global, national and regional identity, forms of drama and entertainment, and the political information necessary for the functioning of democracy. However, as is widely recognised, the notion of a specifically nationally defined public service is being undermined by more globally orientated commercial networks. The growing importance of transnational media has liberated the audience from certain socially imposed notions of the national community, accelerated processes of depoliticisation and 'privatised' previously publicly defined national sporting events. In the British context, national public service broadcasting was always tied to certain notions of democracy, Englishness and nationhood. Reith's original conception of public service broadcasting was based upon the principles of universality, equality of access, as well as the desire to educate the populace while binding them together in a nationally imagined community. Until the impact of commercial networks the BBC had a rather deferential disposition towards the establishment, and only a weak appreciation of questions related to pluralism. The problem with the BBC, therefore, was that the need to preserve a quality service became entangled with the dominance of the south-east of England over more regional and multicultural identities. This provided the space for commercial contributors to satisfy the needs of different publics. For instance, it is noticeable that independent commercial television has historically had a much stronger following with working-class as opposed to middle-class viewers. Further, the BBC, as the above makes particularly clear, has been traditionally associated with a hegemonic English regional culture that is predominantly white, middle class and male.

Why then, given the BBC's tie to an elitist version of the national culture, should we not simply privatise public service broadcasting? There are several reasons for wishing to maintain notions of a national public against more commercial definitions. Indeed, we might even argue that it is in the interests of pluralism that we do so. For example, a commercially driven culture is unlikely to experiment with innovative material that has no obvious target audience, is likely to play safe to secure income revenue from the advertisers and may become prey to the operation of vested interests. We might ask how serious are commercial stations likely to take so-called 'minority' broadcasting, what kind of broadcasting would flourish in a culture driven by a global market, and is a cultural diet of cheap imports really in the public interest?

More obviously it is the identities of citizen and consumer that are confused by such arguments. For instance, BSky TV's recent attempts to capture major national sporting events viewed from the point of view of a consumer makes a certain sense. The football cup final, Olympic games and the Wimbledon tennis tournament are seen as cultural goods which can be bought and sold on the market. Alternatively, read through a notion of citizenship, such a view would emphasise that certain sporting events are a shared communal good that belong to a national public. Such a cultural view of citizenship would seek to articulate the communal participation in the wider symbols of the nation. This does not necessarily mean that everyone has to be a tennis fan to be part of the nation, but that 'we' have the opportunity to 'take part' in the definition of major sporting occasions if we so wish. Again, I think this points to the link between citizenship and national culture, that is more than a form of unregulated pluralism.

There are a number of transformations currently taking place within Britain's internal and external television markets. Broadly speaking these involve processes of privatisation, globalisation, increasing production costs and the introduction of new technology. Britain is currently witnessing the shift away from national public service broadcasting in favour of a more deregulated and commercial climate. Originally, as we saw, public service broadcasting encompassed the institutionalisation of certain values (universal service, equal access, educated perspectives) and a hegemonic version of cultural Englishness. The charges levelled at the institution by the New Right is that such arrangements restrict the commercial development of television, prevent competition and, perhaps most plausibly of all, allow a cultural elite to dictate the tastes of the nation. The public service channels are currently being forced into commercial partnerships with large conglomerates to produce programmes for the world market, and are under pressure to connect more firmly with popular tastes. Further, in the future it is likely to face increased competition from cable and satellite companies which are slowly establishing inroads into the UK market. Given the current reshaping of the market this will undermine the BBC's legitimacy and replace broadcasting (publicly defined service) with television (commercial strategies geared towards profits).[3]

These changes have been accelerated by government policy which has sought to redefine notions of citizenship. Public broadcasting is no longer about the construction of an educated electorate, but the provision of services for consumers (HMSO, 1994). While public service broadcasting is still considered to have an overwhelmingly national role, the government are clearly seeking to make the institution more competitive gaining a broader entry into world markets. The problems here are further compounded as the cultural Left have either abandoned institutional analysis or have sought nostalgically to defend the golden days of the BBC. This is because, in the case of the former, post-modernism has abandoned institutional critique, whereas the Labourist Left has sought to defend public service broadcasting as it has provided a certain amount of protection against both state power and the dominance of the market. The obvious problem here is that the Right becomes the radical force for change, while the Left exhibits a misplaced uncritical pluralism or cultural conservatism.

There have, however, been a number of more critical interventions into the debate which address some of the traditional failings of public broadcasting and point towards a more substantial version of cultural citizenship. I shall now introduce three more elements into the equation. The first, picking up on some of the points I have already made, suggests that the BBC should be both pluralised and regionalised away from the metropolitan centre (Harvey and Robins, 1994). This view argues that the unitary national culture of the BBC could become reorientated around a greater recognition of difference if it were relocated into the regions. In this respect, Harvey and Robins (1994) argue that a reasonable target for regional broadcasting should be about 50 per cent of total radio and television output. This is an important argument, however, I think it is unlikely to make much impact. This is due for the most part to the BBC's pivotal role in the national culture, and its historic connection with the nation-state. Part of the way in which the BBC has maintained its legitimacy in current political rows over its importance has been to argue that it represents the national public interest over the more sectional interests of either the business community or politicians. Further, the role of public service broadcasting continues to reflect the importance of national politics over those at the local and European levels.[4]

Linked to a desire to regionalise public service broadcasting there is a growing conviction in certain quarters that citizenship is becoming increasingly defined more around the city rather than the nation. Holsten and Appadurai (1996), for instance, point to the appearance in Los Angeles and San Paulo of a walled city where local communities use private security guards and vigilantism to regulate the flow of outsiders. The world's major cities have recently been transformed through the emergence of genuinely multicultural spaces, and social movements fighting for immigrant rights in the city. The influx of migrant and immigrant labour into the city transforms the boundaries of citizenship in that loyalty is not so much held to the nation as diasporic identities. However, despite Holsten and Appadurai's focus upon the city, they also recognise that citizens require protection of their formal civil, political and economic rights. Further, they underestimate the extent to which, dependent upon a range of factors, new arrivals are likely to embody a form of overlapping national citizenship. This can be seen in the adoption of titles such as Asian-British or African-American. The city, then, is unlikely to be the centre of citizenship claims unless political power that is centralised at the national level is deconcentrated to allow for more local forms of participation and dialogic exchange. We might then arguably see more intensified political moves to develop electronic public spaces at different levels. Yet it is the case that more locally and transnationally defined public spaces are, while still subordinate, beginning to attract a mounting degree of attention. John Keane (1996) has defined a pluralist notion of the public-sphere as being comprised of:

> micropublic spheres in which there are dozens, hundreds or thousands of disputants interacting at the sub-nation-state level; mesopublic spheres which normally comprise millions of people interacting at the level of the nation-state framework; and the macropublic spheres which normally encompass hundreds of millions and even billions of people enmeshed in disputes at the supranational and global levels of power. (Keane, 1996: 169)

We can point to the micro-public spheres evident within locally defined media most often found within newspapers and radio, but might also include small-scale radical publications or even homemade videos made for personal, professional or political purposes. The national public sphere comprises the majority of the 'big' media, including national television networks, radio and the press. Here local and international issues are filtered through a national optic and are considered along with matters of national importance. Finally, a global public sphere informs individuals of events taking place in contexts far removed from their own. These might be news reports of war zones, documentaries concerning human rights abuse, or dramas based in global cities such as New York and Tokyo. The idea of an overlapping public-sphere, therefore, is to provide the symbolic and material cultures necessary for the operation of cultural citizenship. However, I shall argue that the national dimension retains a structural dominance over public-spheres formed at more macro and micro levels. Martin Shaw (1995) has recently argued that media interest in 'distant' wars and other events is usually defined by the national government's position from which they take their cue. The most striking case is the recent war in Angola. Despite evidence of hundreds of thousands of people being killed in a civil war it was largely ignored by the global media. This, it seems, was largely due to the fact that Western governments had no significant interests at stake in the region.

The next important intervention, and one that largely mirrors my own, has come from Graham Murdock (1994) who argues for the recognition of cultural rights. These rights are informed by a broad definition of citizenship which is based on the right to participate in 'existing patterns of social life' (Murdock, 1994: 158). These rights would include rights to what could be broadly defined as information, representation, knowledge and communication. The universal acceptance of these rights would recognise the broader cultural importance of television rather than a narrower commercial definition. The strength of Murdock's proposals is that these rights would be collectively held by citizens and could protect them both from statist ambitions to censure debate, and the exclusions on the basis of price a more commercialised system of communications would inevitably introduce. Yet I think, while I broadly welcome these proposals, Murdock does not consider corresponding communicative obligations. For instance, Murdock argues we have rights as citizens to contribute and participate within debates on matters of public importance. For Habermas (1989a) participation in discussion obliges us to attend to the claims of the other, and to respond rationally. Similarly, the writing of Zygmunt Bauman (1993) urges us to reimagine ourselves in terms of the other, and to recognise our accountability. It is only, Bauman reasons, the extent to which we are prepared to accept responsibility for the other that we can avoid perpetuating a culture without ethical content. The general point remains that free communication is unlikely to foster reciprocal relations of trust and respect unless participants are obliged to engage with views very different from their own. The alternative, it seems to me, is a system very similar to American talk radio, where everyone asserts their rights to speech without anyone being bothered to listen. A more substantive citizenship of communication in respect of television would do well to take account of citizens' rights and obligations. Let us take, for the moment, an example from the press. At present Britain has an almost exclusively white national press which tends, as numerous research studies have demonstrated, to represent black people as a social problem (Van Dijk, 1992). In distinction, there has recently emerged a number of weekly black newspapers (e.g. *The Voice*) aimed at a specifically metropolitan black middle class, which have displaced the campaign journalism that was previously connected with more radical publications (e.g. *Caribbean Times*). In terms of cultural citizenship, and I think these points build on those made by Parekh (1991), black people have a right to expect that a whole range of issues from housing to racism are properly treated by the national press. But unless, referring back to my argument, the national press recognises it has *obligations* towards the black community it is both unlikely to respect these rights, or do so only in a grudging manner. While post-modernists might point to the increased plurality of perspectives that the emergence of the black press has opened out, it has to be remembered that the predominately white national press maintains a structurally powerful position. That is, it is not enough to point to the emergence of an independent black press, while the mainstream dailies continue to misrepresent black people in their pages. However, we have to remember that communicative 'obligations' can not ensure that all sections of the community are open to argument and persuasion.

Finally, at the European level, there has recently been talk of creating a European public sphere. The idea here is that national public service broadcasting provided an integrative culture at the level of the nation-state and a trans-national governmental organ could contribute a similar function at the European level. As both Schlesinger (1993) and Robins (1993) recognise, European government is likely to become increasingly significant in the future regulation of media systems. Notwithstanding, such a technocratic enterprise is almost bound to fail. Cultural identities can not be proscribed by the policy remits of European bureaucrats, and public service broadcasting due to linguistic and cultural reasons is likely to remain tied to the nation-state. Indeed, I would argue, the best way to preserve a European identity and to ward off the threat of Americanisation is by European government acting to preserve national public service broadcasting systems. This is likely to prove important in the future given the growing dominance of media moguls like Rupert Murdoch, and the extreme difficulties experienced by those attempting to regulate at the national level. Television's immediate future lies at the national level, while its most pressing task is to articulate a more multicultural national culture than it has been able to achieve thus far. To this end, public service broadcasting should be protected by instituted rights and obligations seeking to serve a diverse national community. In achieving this end it should forge alliances with other European systems of public broadcasting. This would potentially open up the prospects for trans-national partnerships and operations that might lead to the exchange of information, joint projects and means of establishing an institutional dimension that is able to look beyond the most exclusivist ambitions of the nation-state.

Alternatively I would also argue a more informed European public sphere is beginning to be created less through the imposition of cultural cohesion, but more through talk about the EC government. While a European public sphere on the level of the nation-state is unlikely to emerge, what is evident is that European membership will increase the volume of information on European issues, develop European networks and lead to an increase in demand to be properly informed regarding EC matters (Weymouth and Lamizet, 1996). The emergence of European as opposed to national citizenship is likely to set new agendas for the home-based media. As Elizabeth Meehan (1993) argues the four main dimensions of European citizenship can be conceptualised as: (1) rights of free mobility; (2) community social policy; (3) common civil rights that can trump national policy; and (4) the emergence of the idea of common European standards. As these dimensions gather pace we are likely to see at least three elements emerging through the media. The first will be that the practices of the nations of Europe are increasingly likely to provide a point of comparison. How does Italy regulate the media in the light of Berlusconni? Do German fathers have more rights than those in Britain? However, as has been in evidence in the 'British beef ban', we will see these conflicts played through a specifically national dimension. Secondly, and more globally, the media are likely to carry stories that involve the linkage European nations and other parts of the world. This might involve a relationship between European nations and former colonies, nuclear weapons tests, and visits by European diplomats to world powers or world crisis points. Finally, with regard to the symbolic representation of Europe, it is likely that we will witness a continuing struggle between the need for common standards, and the demand that specific national cultures and perspectives are to be defended. The media then are increasingly likely to be caught in debates concerning national autonomy within a common European community.

Television aside, what of the film industry? Currently, Hollywood film productions dominate the world market in video, television and cinema film presentation. This has been achieved by the major film producers diversifying their products, capitalising on huge home markets and by keeping a keen eye over developments in new technology. Recent years has also witnessed the increasing importance of overseas markets in providing a 'safety net' in terms of product expansion. In particular Europe has become an ever-expanding market with nine of the top fifteen overseas markets being located on the continent (Wasko, 1994: 224). In 1992 US audio-visual exports to Europe were valued at 3.7 billion dollars, while equivalent EC exports to the USA only amounted to 288 million (Cockburn, 1995). The secret of Hollywood's global dominance lies in the diversification of risks. For instance, Paramount's commercial interests include motion pictures, video, television shows and the cable industry as well as book companies like Simon and Schuster and sports teams such as the New York Nicks and the New York Rangers. The introduction of more flexible forms of production (which involves the making of films such as *Batman* in London due to the excellence of certain special effects production staff) and co-production ventures have transformed film production. These moves, it seems, are as much to do with the avoidance of European attempts to regulate American film distribution as they are economic (Wasko, 1994; Lash and Urry, 1994). This is not to argue, as some have implied, that this is a simple one-way relationship with Britain's national cultural expression being asphyxiated by American cheapness. Aspects of British culture from the Beatles to Fawlty Towers have been successfully exported to the USA. Yet more disturbingly, it is undoubtedly the case that US conglomerates dominate this relationship, and there is much evidence to suggest that the images of Englishness, that have gained popularity in the USA, are of an island that is white, quaint and repressed (Murdock, 1989). Contemporary image cultures between the USA and the UK suggest a global intersubjective dimension that is based upon misrecognition and unequal forms of cultural exchange.

It is notable that 80 per cent of European film production, unlike that of Hollywood, never leaves the country of its origin (Wasko, 1994: 226). This is largely because of language barriers, Hollywood's dominance over distribution and the cultural specificity of European film products. These processes are particularly marked in Britain where a combination of government policy, American domination and decline in audiences has destroyed the British film industry. The removal of the Eady levy, the abolition of the requirement of distributors to handle a percentage of British films and the drying up of state and commercial resources has deregulated home market production (Hill, 1993). As I indicated above, Britain has shifted from being a producer of films to a supplier of specialised skills and scenic locations. This has brought a closer relationship with Channel 4 (which has a public service dimension) playing an increasingly significant role in the organisation of film production. The collapse of British film companies such as EMI, Goldcrest and Virgin in the 1980s has meant that Channel 4 by 1989 had a role in funding almost half of the films produced in the UK. This situation is further exaggerated when you consider that the Hollywood majors also control distribution networks and that the deregulation of television is likely to put further financial pressure on Channel 4.

Do these developments matter? Surely, it could be objected, that films, like television are only entertainment, although of course it is a great shame that the British film industry has collapsed given the contribution it could be making to our economy. To view the interconnection between institutions, culture and values in this way is to disregard the way in which we form our identities and commitments, and to view culture too instrumentally. My argument is not that Britain should seal its borders and return to the good old nationalist cinema characteristic of the war years. The circulation of American films provides an important critical function often opening up questions our own national cultures find embarrassing, while contributing to our understanding of one of the most powerful and vibrant cultures on the planet. Further, it is likely that black British audiences have gained pleasure and a sense of self from Spike Lee films such as *Malcolm X* and

Do the Right Thing. To maintain the importance of a British and European public culture in respect of cinema and video production is to recognise that this could also be an important domain where cultural differences can be revealed and dialogically negotiated. Culture then is an intersubjectively produced, publicly held phenomenon. It helps provide a source of identity, means of social exchange and a sense of community. My claim is that a multicultural British film culture could open out more multiple versions of Britishness than we are likely to see in a global market dominated by Hollywood. Recent films funded by Channel 4 have included *Barji on the Beech* (first British film produced by an Asian woman), *My Beautiful Laundrette* (critical exposition of ethnicity and gay sexuality) and *Raining Stones* (which concerns regionality and class). That these films seek to exhibit a critical view of the national dimension made primarily for a national audience makes important contributions to what I have termed cultural citizenship. Television and film cultures are currently both instrumentally and economically defined by governments, intellectuals and the lay population, but this belies the critical potential of these important mediums. Again it is likely that any simple minded or merely well-intentioned attempt to revive the British film industry (given my earlier comments) could play into the hands of nationalist currents. But against such fears, I would argue that the complexities and hybridities of the British are unlikely to be opened out by the Hollywood film industry.

Civil society, values and obligations

One of the central paradoxes currently facing modernity is that the more interdependent global systems become, the fewer agreed-upon rules there seem to be regarding our obligations towards each other. The growing 'connexity' of social systems seemingly has the effect of loosening more traditional codes of conduct given that we are made aware of alternatives (Mulgan, 1997). Further, as Alan Wolfe (1989) has pointed out, the problem with national governments trying to institutionalise obligations is that the more abstract and impersonal they are the more people will try and resist them. The state's attempt to legislate moral rules hands them over into the domain of experts which fails to recognise that obligations are not just a matter of public policy prescriptions but are an essential part of civil society. Civil society might, in this understanding, be described as the self-organised domain of social life that depends upon taken-for-granted rules and expectations (Keane, 1989). A thriving civil society therefore could only be secured if areas of spontaneity and independence were protected and reinforced by the state. Civil society, in this understanding, should be thought of as a cluster of institutions such as trade unions, religious associations, media, literary formations and households. It is civil society's ability to act as a pluralistic realm of overlapping identities with a degree of ideological distance from the state that has made it such an important category for social and political theory. Yet this is the sector of social life that the communitarians have recently argued is in need of renewal. Etzioni (1993) maintains that our general moral sense has been eroded by an individualistic rights-based culture. In brief, he maintains that the consensual and morally restrained society of the 1950s has been replaced by hedonism, selfishness and rampant individualism. This has eroded older values such as civil responsibility and mutual recognition to the detriment of all citizens. Etzioni calls for the communal rebirth of an American culture that has mistakenly looked to the state or the market to resolve societal problems. In particular Etzoni is concerned with child-rearing practices and our obligations to future generations. He points out that women's entry into the labour market, large numbers of one-parent families and high divorce rates has created what he calls the parenting deficit. What is required in Etzioni's vision is a shift from the values of consumerism and careerism into values which reaffirm bonds with other adults and children. Etzioni is adamant that by this he does not mean an attempt to turn the clock back to the 1950s by forcing women to re-enter the home. Instead there needs to be a new partnership between the sexes, and moral and institutional reform to help *both* parents become actively involved in the upbringing of children.

One of the problems with Etzioni's attempt to rework civil society is that he presupposes a moral consensus that is significantly lacking in all modern democracies. Modern societies through diasporic social processes have become increasingly multicultural societies which hold a number of competing traditions and elements at any one time. Indeed, the problem is that the appearance of a 'moral consensus' is more often the result of repression and power, than the recognition of difference and open forms of communication. This is not to argue that communitarianism does not offer certain possibilities regarding the re-moralisation of public dialogue away from the atomised individual of the 1980s. As I have already indicated such possibilities would more resolutely involve a reconstruction of both the national culture (through difference) and more international dimensions. Ezioni in current conditions inadequately appreciates the plurality of modern societies (despite many of the qualifications I made in this respect) and foregoes the logics and the processes through which common moralities are made. The appeal, as we saw earlier, to intensify communal bonds and beliefs is nearly always accompanied with the displacement of more ambivalent feelings and projections. In other words, Etzioni's call for national moral renewal would undoubtedly, if carried through politically, have a number of negative consequences. For instance, Etzioni offers a brief description of the moral unity that united fellow Americans during the Gulf War. However, he singularly fails to mention that the public sphere offered only the narrowest interpretation of events due to the operation of hegemonic groups and formations (Kellner, 1992). Further, as Said (1993) points out, ideologically the conflict was seen as an internal matter for the Americans to decide.

Etzioni's programme for moral unity reproduces a certain blindness concerning America's global dominance both past and present. That is, questions of obligations and morality are viewed as being mainly internal to the nation-state and not about other parts of the world. As a consequence, Etzioni's tribalism does not adequately locate the United States in terms of a geo-political understanding of international power relations. A 're-moralised' America could either turn inwards obscuring its relations with the rest of the world, or give new life to imperialist projections which would seek to re-order the globe in its own image. That these concerns never occupy the foreground of Etzioni's projections is of itself grounds for unease.

Zygmunt Bauman (1993), whose own concerns with moral responsibility are similar to those of Wolfe, also warns against the forms of communitarianism represented by those like Etzioni. He argues that rather than renewing moral resources communitarianism has more in common with the desire to convert communal relations into a new form of social discipline. Such measures, like the older legislative ambitions of the nation, are likely to be avoided or be submitted to instead of actively cultivating individual moral selves. Bauman argues that rather than merely seeking to uphold the moral convictions of the community or tradition of which we happen to be part, or searching fruitlessly for universal norms, we should embrace the irredeemably ambivalent nature of the moral self. Moral consciousness and responsibility is more the matter of everyday practice than seeking law-like guarantees from an intellectual class who have served to hand down moral orders to the masses. The basis for all moral sentiment are feelings of responsibility and a commitment towards other people. Again, returning to the paradox with which I opened this section, modernity's attempt to discipline individual selves into feelings of obligation has resulted in the privatised retreat from such public concerns. The new communitarians, on this reading, are to be found in middle-class suburbs where strangers are distrusted, private security guards employed and burglar alarms are on constant standby. Attempts to legislate morality and the retreat from the public, evident in individualised escape attempts (the privatisation of public morality), forego attempts to build upon the moral resources of the self. However, for Bauman at least, new sources of hope are to be found in the partial collapse of national identities and cultures. The splintering of the hinge that bound state and society has led paradoxically to both nationalism's increasing appeal (it seems to offer firm foundations where there are none) and its withering away in a society whose dominant motif is the vagabond. Bauman writes:

> The vagabond does not know how long he will stay where he is now, and more often than not it will not be for him to decide when the stay will come to an end. Once on the move again, he sets his destinations as he goes and as he reads the road-signs, but even then he cannot be sure whether he will stop, and for how

long, at the next station. What he does know is that more likely than not the stopover will be but temporary. What keeps him on the move is disillusionment with the last place of sojourn and the forever smouldering hope that the next place which he has not visited yet, perhaps the place after next, may be free from the faults which repulsed him in the places he has already tasted. Pulled forward by hope untested, pushed forward by hope frustrated. The vagabond is a pilgrim without a destination; a nomad without an itinerary. (Bauman, 1993: 240)

This metaphor of contemporary post-modern culture is meant to apply as much to the hyperactive lifestyles of the globalised business class as the refugees fleeing war-torn cities in search of a new home. This condition it seems, while spelling considerable dangers, offers new possibilities for the development of moral sentiments free from the legislative ambitions of state and society. Again, such an account, I would argue, has both considerable merit as well as corresponding limitations. Whereas Etzioni's remarks seem to be built on a form of moral repression, Bauman, I think, often forgoes attempts to view the interconnection between a moral dimension and institutional forms of analysis. Bauman is so occupied with a primal form of moral ambivalence that he arguably neglects attempts to link institutions and moral sentiment. This is also linked, as we shall see, to my second point that Bauman's metaphoric adoption of the vagrant neglects more permanent cultural contours like the maintenance of national cultures. On the first of these points it is undoubtedly the case that sociology from Durkheim to Althusser has reduced feelings of obligation to the determination of social structures. Hannah Arendt's (1958) warning that this robs human-beings of their uniqueness and responsibility for one another is well taken in this context. On the other hand, as Bauman well understands, shouting from the roof tops, telling people to be better behaved, neglects wider questions of social context and structure. But I am still left feeling uneasy that the wider connections between institutions, values and cultures are left out of his analysis. For instance, Bauman argues that moral responsibility prompts us to care for others, but the problem is that those others are often close at hand. Morality, he reasons, particularly in globalised contexts, needs to grow much longer arms. Bauman would probably point to the various war zones that are scattered around the globe, and argue that we all share a sense of responsibility for those who are currently suffering. The post-modern aspect of this recognition is that an acceptance of responsibility does not always deliver any notion of what the *right* action to take might be. This has been amply demonstrated through recent debates which have wanted to appear to be doing something in the face of ethnic cleansing in Bosnia, genocide in Rwanda and community violence in Northern Ireland. Media reporting seems to be underlined with a sense that we should do something, but it was not clear what that should be. Why, asks Shaw (1995), is it that media and other political and social movements of civil society have persistently failed to respond adequately to global civil conflicts? He answers that the dimensions of civil society are less likely to take their character from individual responses to global crisis than institutional organisations that are either pro or anti the particular position adopted by the host nation-state. Thus despite Bauman's description of the vagabond, the nation will remain for most of its citizens most of the time the main feature that organises a sense of obligation and focus around which to campaign. Again, my sense of what is being neglected is the relation between self and society, or individual and community. In his classic study of nationalism, Benedict Anderson (1983) argued that, as a cultural force, imagined national cultures are more often bound with the idea of self-sacrificing love than the projection of hatred. This is probably why both Etzioni and the British moral lobby appeal to particular national dimensions. It seems, to me at least, that hegemonic movements will continue to trade upon nationalist sentiments. The question is less about moral ambivalence and more about how counter-hegemonic strategies in the areas of class, sexuality and ethnicity mobilise a pluralised ethical discourse that reveals difference and what we share through open, equal and respectful dialogue. What we need to search for is how this might be achieved in solidarity with those outside of the porous walls of the nation-state.

What, if any, are the implications of these reflections for questions of cultural citizenship and mass communication? First, attempts to rework civil society within the world's culturally dominant regions (the media are still mostly American) are likely to have global effects. These effects are, of course, unpredictable and unstable but they are unlikely to remain confined within a national arena. Next, given the ambivalent nature of modernity, media-led campaigns to discipline and punish the population are unlikely to have clear-cut results. This is not to argue that they may not have significant effects and even become culturally hegemonic for a while. The claim that is being made however is that within civil society such strategies are likely to be coloured by mixed feelings and associations. Finally, in a European context, national and local communicative spaces are likely to remain important despite the increasing globalisation of the media. For instance, many of the new environmental campaigns employ handheld video equipment both to promote their cause and provide evidence of the police's disregard of civil liberties. Such information is then fed into national networks and perhaps even into worldwide networks. Yet given the 'national' character of those they are seeking to mobilise, it is likely they will attempt to lock into national rather than more overtly global structures. Further, where I think Bauman's analysis leads us astray, is to view nationalism as something which is mainly imposed from above onto the masses. Contrary to this view, I would prefer to see national concerns and sentiments as a hegemonic domain of popular practices which are intersected by state and civil society. In this respect, the institutions of media and culture have a crucial responsibility to decentre national traditions, and make their citizens aware of other perspectives from a diversity of the world's peoples. My joint concerns of cultural citizenship and mass communication would be combined when the local–national option is revealed as being one among the many on offer.

The promotion of a trans-national civil society which shares perspectives on the fate of the globe's citizens is, as I have indicated, only slowly beginning to emerge. If I take a casual glance at my morning newspaper, located on the front page is a photograph of a Bosnian Catholic church holding its first mass in three years, made possible by the peace agreement (*The Guardian*, 5.2.96). However, each of the other four front page features (the Scott Report on the arms to Iraq scandal, the privatisation of the rail service, the death of a woman fire-fighter from Bristol, and the return of a thirteen year old girl who had caused a national outrage by marrying a Turkish waiter) concerns issues with an overtly British focus. While both Iraq and Turkey are mentioned both only receive attention because they are considered of interest to a British readership. While the modern period has witnessed the partial de-coupling of national sentiment from the borders of nation-states and, in certain respects, a decline in the idea of obligations towards the nation, such tendencies remain. Again, it has probably been nationalism's capacity to speak a warm moral language, against the cold rationalism of the market and bureaucracy, that continues to account for its popularity. Here, Tom Nairn (1997) offers a hilarious and persuasive critique of some of the pretensions of englightenment internationalism. The idea that progress and reason would eventually witness the end of all national distinctions has surely run its course. This ambition, as the historical record shows, has been consistently frustrated to the despair of liberal and socialist intellectuals alike. Nairn's point that nationalism is here to stay concurs with my own. I want to hold this view while pressing that one of the greatest problems facing our public media is the cosmopolitan decentring of overly chauvanistic dimensions, but that this is likely to meet with little success unless we recognise the relative permanence of national sentiments and connections. That is, before we understand the needs, projections and complexities of others, we must first understand ourselves.

The third tier of what I have referred to as cultural citizenship concerns the sense of duty and obligation we have for others that can not be legislated into existence. As the communitarians rightly claim we can institute free speech and certain laws protecting others, but this will not ensure I attend to the claims of the others or consider their opinions worth listening to. The building of relations of solidarity, particularly with those who are distant from the places in which we live, calls for what Habermas (1990a) has called an 'ethic of compassion' or what Cornel West (1994) has called an 'ethic of love'. What both of these thinkers maintain is how the sustenance of such a civil society is intercut by wider relations of culture and society. That the kinds of nihilism and economic reason that I described earlier continually threaten to disrupt relations of solidarity and *meaningfulness* is warning enough against intellectual complacency. Again, it seems that while

Bauman has been critical of many post-modern formulations for neglecting moral questions, he has inherited a tendency to overstate the excessive indeterminacy of the modern subject, and a neglect of some of modernity's more stable features.

Cultural citizenship: a future?

To reiterate then, the development of global cosmopolitan cultures and the cultural industries have opened new questions that link culture and citizenship. Viewed in terms of the two previous chapters these developments open out a number of normative considerations. Moral and ethical questions are being transformed by the development of media cultures. First, despite many of the permanent dimensions and features that continue to inform contemporary culture, previously repressed questions of morality and ethics are coming to the fore. For instance, while felt obligations still remain, local and national new complexities are being opened out by more global flows. Pertinent moral and ethical qustions here are how should a global media be regulated, and in terms of what principles? How might we learn to live, learn and engage with one another in increasingly pluralised public spaces? What obligations do we have to those outside the traditional frameworks of family and nation? These questions are hardly new, however, they are given added force under conditions of a radically mediated society. Secondly, we might also seek to understand what kinds of ideological understanding and intersubjective recognition are promoted within and between different world regions? What is the connection between these symbolic dimensions and more mutual relations? How do different intersubjective cultural forms help promote democracy, trust and feelings of attachment in civil society? Thirdly, and finally, how has the transformation of the media restructured the rhythms of everyday life? This might be through the fostering of new ethical dimensions, the opening of new narratives of self or of promoting familarity with other forms of life. My anwers to these questions has been that for now (and most certainly in the near future) domains of nation and state remain central if no longer determining.

CHAPTER 5

Global media cultures: contours in village life or cultural imperialist dominance?

Unlike other strands within the social sciences much of the writing that can be connected with the study of communications systems has maintained an analysis of space as well as time. This is rare given the established patterns in social theory that tended until recently to equate society with the nation-state. Spatial thinking, as is well known, has also assumed a prominent place within post-modern attempts to understand the disorganised flux of modernity. Through the separation of the signifier and signified, the uncoupling of the 'experience' of place from physical location, and the shrinking of the world evident in global travel and global media events the 'social' now seems a more unstable construction than was previously assumed. Notably in such formulations the television set is often presented as a prominent metaphor. Dick Hebdige (1990) has described the experience of watching television in the 1990s as a form of time and spatial travel fostering in the Western world an everyday form of cosmopolitanism.

However, to become engaged in such talk is often to encounter a lapse of memory as to how previous generations have sought to think about global relations. In this respect, I think we can point to two main traditions evident within media studies that are focused around questions of media imperialism and the technical capacities of media technology as information storage and shifting devices. These two approaches gained intellectual prominence in the 1960s when technological optimists like Marshall McLuhan talked of a global village, and more pessimistic, politically radical voices warned that the expansion of media systems actually lead to the cultural dominance of the 'Third World' by Western consumerism. Seemingly the backdrop to these debates was the global prominence of Western forms of culture, and technology becoming apparent in trans-national media events such as the Vietnam War, the space race and large-scale music festivals such as Woodstock. Since the 1960s, global concerns have made a dramatic return and in part reinvention. What is interesting is that while McLuhan's zany predictions concerning a global media village were quickly dismissed three decades ago, today they seem to be back in favour. On the other hand, questions associated with the cultural dominance of Western societies that can be connected with a political economy of mass communications systems are currently granted a more peripheral significance. If anything today there seems to be a bias against thinking about the ways that media cultures might reinforce hegemonic structures and patterns of dominance. This is in part attributable to some of the more obvious failings of the older models of media imperialism and a retreat from class analysis more generally. Here I want to look for ways of rejoining media theory with an understanding of the material structures of late capitalism and the symbolic spaces and geographies that can be associated with them. To start with, as I have indicated, this will lead me in two separate directions looking at earlier models of media imperialism and what McLuhan termed media implosion. This will connect into current debates by post-modern and post-colonial concerns in respect of the impacts of media cultures. These ideas will then be reflected back upon those earlier formulations before opening up some final critical remarks. From what I have said, it will be argued that to represent global communications systems adequately, it is insufficient to remain at the level of their continued capacity to structurate global communicative relations or of their ability to introduce cultural forms of disorder. Moreover my task remains the careful unfolding of the dialectical relations between the two perspectives.

Media and cultural imperialism reconsidered

Media imperialism is usually discussed with reference to the broader theory of cultural imperialism. This has proved to be a notoriously difficult concept to define. John Tomlinson (1991) has identified at least four (possibly five) ways of talking about cultural imperialism with media imperialism only one aspect. These include definitions of cultural imperialism: (1) as a form of domination associated with empire; (2) as the media saturation of local products through America's domination of mediums of communication; (3) as the external repression of autonomous forms of local and national culture; (4) as a critique of the political and economic dominance of global capitalism; and (5) as a critique of global modernity (including mass communication, nation-states, consumerism and instrumental forms of reason). All of these aspects, claims Tomlinson, maintain the ways in which we have attempted to think about cultural imperialism. But, whereas Tomlinson, on the whole, wants to talk of cultural imperialism in the fifth sense, I think each of the dimensions he opens out has something of value to contribute. Or to put the point in more Wittgensteinian terms, I am less interested in a precise definition of how we may talk of cultural imperialism, than I am in looking at how it has been talked about and in asking whether or not it maintains a critical purchase. This emphasis will displace a concern to deliver the correct definition enabling the analysis to concentrate upon a field of related social practices that we might call cultural and media imperialism. Thus, while Tomlinson offers some suggestive remarks in regard to cultural imperialism, I want to turn elsewhere for a looser, more workable definition.

The most obvious place to start is with the two words imperialism and culture. The study of imperialism, according to Said (1993: 8) involves 'the practice, the theory, and the attitudes of the dominating metropolitan centre ruling a distant territory'. He quickly goes on to argue that imperialism is nearly always linked to that of empire whereby one state utilises force and consent to control that of another. Yet, he points out that, in our own time, direct forms of control have largely been ended, but that imperialism can be said to persist when it *lingers* in the cultural sphere. By this Said means that nostalgia for empire, ideologies of cultural superiority and dominance, and racist projections of hostility and violence against cultural 'others' could all in certain contexts be said to be imperialist. Said clearly argues that these sentiments are realised within a global intersubjective dimension, but that they are often disguised as simple-minded patriotism. According to Said our collective task is to give up claims to ethnic superiority and exclusiveness mask and learn to think *contrapuntally* about the relationship between others and ourselves. What national systems do in their insistence of our uniqueness and our superiority is effectively to silence the various ways in which our histories and identities are 'mixed in with one another' (Said, 1993: 401). To think contrapuntally then is to offer a form of ideology critique against reified imperialist and nationalist attempts to make us forget our global interdependencies past, present and future. One such strategy that Said adopts is the interrogation of the ways in which imperialist assumptions have impinged upon the national literatures of old colonial powers such as Britain and France, and the way that modern media cultures are interrupted by the pretensions of American foreign policy. While it is true that Said's 'literary' distance from any precise analysis of the formal structures which uphold and reinforce these practices leaves much to be desired his case studies beautifully demonstrate how imperialistic assumptions can be as much part of CNN news as they are of the novels of Conrad and Camus. However, if Said manages to offer some good examples as to how imperialist frames embed themselves within literary texts, he is less precise on the matter of media cultures. Most of his book, with the exception of the final chapter, is concerned with 'great works' of literature rather than the mediated electric culture of television screens, cinema and video, etc. Obviously any wider definition of cultural and symbolic processes must take a fuller account of the operation of the media of mass communication.

If 'imperialism' has historically been utilised to signify a range of practices the same can also be said for 'culture'. Raymond Williams (1976) argues that Western societies have talked about culture in connection with the normative development of humanity, the particular 'life-worlds' of specific nations and social groups, and, finally, the distinctive activity of intellectuals and artists. These meanings, as one might suspect, continue to overlap and inform one another, while providing the intellectual context within which we will continue to think about cultural patterns. Further, as I think Williams (1974) also reminds us, the study of culture should be rejoined with an understanding of the dominant social relations and institutions which help shape and determine their distribution and social exchange. I will argue in accordance with Williams that cultural studies should both respect the specificity of economic, political and cultural levels of analysis while seeking to unravel the relations of determination that exist between them. This would redefine notions of cultural imperialism in that the analysis would seek to unravel the multiple ways in which metropolitan dominance is maintained through a cultural dimension and the ways this has been sustained by economic and political practices. As we shall see, this is exactly what the media imperialism thesis initially tried to achieve.

According to neo-Marxist theories of dependency the breakdown of older forms of direct control instigated by imperialism was replaced by new forms of manipulation of which media imperialism was just a small part. Until the impacts of European colonialism pre-colonial Africa, Latin America and Asia were largely oral cultures. Thus when modern media such as the press was introduced into the 'Third World' it was in the language of the colonist. This provided a source of cultural power in that it legitimated the languages and cultural practices of the coloniser rather than the colonised. The languages and styles of the old empires became the languages of the national governing classes while informing governmental and media organisations. Media forms, it was also argued, were tied into the maintenance of an unjust global system. Since the breakdown of direct rule the media had been targeted by a number of political interventions in order to foster the correct 'social attitudes' to promote capitalist orientations and practices. Mass communications, it was assumed, would play a key role in the integration of 'Third World' nations into the global economy. Media cultures would reverse traditional practices and beliefs that lead to current levels of underdevelopment. Yet the major break offered by dependency theorists was to move the analysis beyond the *attitudes* of the world's poor into an investigation of the structural relations that promote unequal relations between rich and poor nations.

Theorists like Walerstein (1974) argued that the capitalist world system was divided into three tiers of states, those of the core, the semi-periphery and the periphery. This enabled the core states through the unequal distribution of economic, political and cultural power to manipulate the workings of the global system in its own interests. Media and cultural imperialism, it was assumed, provided the ideological mechanisms through which relations of dependence were fostered and practised. In short, the shift from developmentalist perspectives to dependency theory challenged the assumption that peripheral nation-states were ever going to achieve global equity with their more powerful counterparts. The appeal of dependency theory, in this and other respects, was that it was able to challenge the Eurocentric leanings of developmentalism. Samir Amin (1989) argues that the cornerstones of Euro-centric thinking are the twin assumptions that *internal* factors determine the development of national societies, and that Western models of capitalism were generalisable to the inclusion of the whole planet. Dependency theory made a crucial intervention in that it attempted to represent the way that global economic, political and cultural interconnections reinforced relations of dominance. The best working definition of media imperialism I have come across is supplied by Fejes:

> media imperialism shall be used in a broad and general manner to describe the process by which modern communication media have operated to create, maintain and expand systems of domination and dependence on a world scale. (Fejes, 1981: 281)

As should be obvious from the preceding discussion, the terms domination and dependency are directly drawn from the theoretical interventions of neo-Marxists who sought to think globally and critically. The aim was to extend what was originally an explanation of economic forms of power and exploitation to cultural and ideological modes of domination. It followed that if the nations of the core were dominating those at the periphery economically then this relation was also being reinforced through the superstructure (politics and culture). In the equation being drawn here there is a direct correspondence between economic and cultural levels of domination. The arguments concerning media imperialism for Boyd-Barrett (1977) have three different levels that can be stated as follows:

1 The development of the technologies of communication by Western capital meant that they were able to shape the vehicles of communication (radio, press, television, video, cinema). The technologies were first exported by colonialism and then sustained through relations of *dependency* fostered by late capitalism. New technology is mostly brought from the capitalist West rather than developed by the 'Third World' due the prohibitive cost of more local production. This, in effect, served to marginalise more 'authentic' local forms of communication based upon the native traditions of host cultures.
2 The purchasing of media technology automatically involves dependent nations in the financial and organisational structures of late capitalism. The growth of transnational media corporations has meant that Western capital and knowhow has been used in the setting up of communication systems in economically subordinate nation-states. This has led to a replication of capitalist forms of organisational structure and control.
3 Western professional norms (objectivity, balance) are also evident within media organisations. The moulding of the professional norms of journalists by imperial Western values again displaces the impact that more

local cultures might have made. However the most pertinent form of media imperialism is carried in the ideological messages and assumptions that are evident within Western produced films, television programmes, radio broadcasts, and press and magazine culture. These cultural forms both promote certain Western values (read consumerism), while stifling more critical perspectives.

Politically such views have proved to be important in mobilising resistance against Western control of media production and symbolic exchange. The challenge offered by a 1974 UNESCO report was that the structural and cultural dominance of the West meant that the rest of the globe (75 per cent) were economically deprived and culturally saturated by Western images, news and perspectives. These concerns then led to the 1978 report produced by the McBride Commission (*Many Voices, One World*) that strengthened these arguments. As Anthony Smith (1980) put it at the time, the imperative of the market and the free flow of information had replaced Christianity as the West's 'cultural gift' to the South. The report called for a new information order which would allow 'Third World' nations' cultural autonomy and the possibility of reversing the one-way flow of mediated cultures. The West's response to such demands was to point out that the free flow of opinion was essential to the development of democracy and an unacceptable intrusion into the operation of market principles. Thus whereas the South complained that their own national and cultural identities were being asphyxiated by the West, the West perceived an attempt to restrict free trade and democratic expression. Viewed from the perspective of 'Third World' nations the political importance of the media imperialism thesis and the dependency model was that it revealed relations of force in place of those of development and progress. The media imperialism thesis therefore provided a political point of identification for *dependent* nations to criticise the West both materially and symbolically.

If this argument is followed the cultural values and forms of Western capitalism have been imposed upon subordinate states through economic means. Primarily it is the West's dominance of economic relations that leads inexorably to cultural forms of dominance. However it is arguable that the character of global capitalism and culture has changed considerably since the 1960s and the 1970s. Slightly different and more sophisticated versions of this thesis are offered by Herb Schiller (1992, 1996) and the Mattlelarts (Mattlelart *et al.*, 1984; Mattlelart and Mattlelart, 1992). Of these two distinct approaches it is Schiller who most forcefully ties the production of culture into the defence of empire. Schiller argues that the 1960s represented the apex of American economic and cultural power. Since this period, the globe has become increasingly complex with competing centres of economic power and activity. The US response to these challenges has been to move its efforts more forcefully into the cultural industries through the development of new communication technologies. These developments have aided the increasingly global spread of American multinationals, the deregulation of public networks and the spreading commercialisation of the mass media.

In Schiller's (1996) most recent defence of this argument he focuses upon the capitalist driven nature and commodification of American popular culture before transferring this model to the rest of the world. The globe, it seems, is being remade in America's own image. American capitalist culture, according to Schiller, is being developed by the expansion of credit, rampant consumerism, advertising and the systematic displacement of traditional forms of constraint. Capitalism American style has largely arisen in a national context that lacks any recognisable tradition of social democracy and where working-class labour organisations have only the weakest public presence. Such an environment has fostered the integration of information and culture into the dominant structures of the finance economy. Popular culture in America is driven by capitalist accumulation strategies. Economic forces are the main structures behind technological developments such as the super information highway and the internet, and they also help determine the superficiality of much of mainstream mass culture. The dominance of the economic system over other social spheres helps foster a culture of conformity rather than critique, of sensation rather than substance and technique rather than reflection. Cultural concerns, other than for a small intellectual elite, are run, managed and determined by the parameters of economics. For this reason, American culture carries ideological messages of consumerism and promotes acquisitive behaviour in the host and the world population in general. Mass forms of entertainment, therefore, act as a form of compensation for a disintegrating communal life while encouraging the displacement of critical questions connected to a divided society. Schiller argues that the expansion in entertainment services not only provides new markets for advertisers, but masks important social issues such as the growing underclass, widening social divisions and a spiralling prison population. Mass culture thereby insulates the well-off from the poor, and is utilised increasingly by private as opposed to public interests.

Schiller maintains that while America has declined in its overall position within the world economy, it has maintained its hegemony over the globe's culture. Since the 1980s, culture everywhere has become increasingly Americanised and penetrated by economic reason. The increasing integration of media products into the global market, and the rapid deregulation of public cultures has promoted worldwide processes of Americanisation. This has been achieved thorough the direct promotion of American products, and the local copying of American television styles and formats. Just as American capitalism was able to marginalise oppositional structures at home, so with the running down of public cultures abroad it has been able to penetrate into new markets. Commercially driven media, which are the main carriers of American products, are currently overrunning a passive world. Significantly it is the global economy rather than the nation-state which is the new mechanism of governance. In the face of networks of global capital the nation is struggling to maintain its cultural autonomy and preserve the distinctiveness of internally constructed social identities. Indeed the development of global communications has been driven less by individual states than by the world's rich and powerful seeking to cordon themselves off from the poor. In this reading, again mirroring developments within American society, the globe's wealthy consumers will become the targets of accumulation strategies, thereby repressing questions concerning deepening global inequalities, that will inevitably be avoided by overtly capitalist controlled media structures. A world dominated less by the governance of the nation, and more by the commercial imperatives of global capitalism will foster a social environment where a few prosper and many are marginalised.

The Mattlearts (Mattlelart *et al.*, 1984; Mattlelart and Mattlelart, 1992), on the other hand, have broken more decisively with the argument that the main role of media cultures is the legitimation of a declining American empire. This however is not to doubt the universal and global presence of American media products. They report that between 1970 and 1981 only France and Japan succeeded in securing a majority share of their domestic market in film (Mattelart *et al.*, 1984: 20). Further, in 1982 American advertising firms held 30 of the top 50 places in the global market. Yet the most marked change since America's overwhelming cultural dominance of the 1960s has been the arrival of a multi-polar world. In particular the 1980s has witnessed the development of new cultural exporters in both the 'Third World' and the so-called developed world which has changed the shape of international image markets. For instance, in Brazil the formation of the audio-visual conglomerate TV Globo was set up through a series of local initiatives and without the involvement of substantial amounts of foreign capital (Mader, 1993). While it depends upon revenue from transnational advertisers, the company grew in the 1980s experiencing financial turnovers equivalent to those of the combined efforts of French television channels.

Other more detailed analyses of global media flow have revealed a more complex picture than the one offered by advocates of media imperialism. For instance, just as economic analysis has questioned the supposed unity behind concepts like the 'Third World', media analysis has also become more attuned to its complexity. According to Reeves (1993) it makes little analytic sense to put Brazil and India into the same categories as some of the poorer African nations. In 1985 India produced 912 feature length films and Brazil 86; this not only overwhelms Africa (where the numbers are so low they are often not recorded) but also European nations like France (151) and Italy (73) with strong traditions of independent cinema. These figures also disrupt simple assumptions that economic development has any direct and unmediated impact upon the production of cultural goods. Hence the argument that cultural development can be assumed to 'mirror' economic development can no longer be seen to apply. The shift in perspectives hinted at by these structural changes has lead the Mattlearts (Mattlelart *et al.*, 1984; Mattlelart and Mattlelart, 1992) to argue for the abandonment of the media imperialism thesis. They argue that, while the dimensions of political economy remain important in the production of culture, it should be tied to a more specific appreciation of the intersection between different global regions and local conditions. They now argue that, while the media imperialism thesis has been historically important in raising the consciousness of those nations outside of the rich capitalist club, the theory no longer adequately maps (if indeed it ever did) global communicative relations. Further, the Mattlelarts hold that media imperialism always had its weaknesses as it consistently failed to account for the cultural relations within 'Third World' states and the uneven distribution of capitalist technology. In order to account for global relations the 'media imperialist' thesis needs to be replaced by a different theoretical paradigm. More recently the Mattlearts (Mattlelart and Mattlelart 1992) have pointed to the increasing commercialisation and economic penetration of shared public spaces as the most promising contender for the new paradigm. Such arguments have the added advantage of ditching ethnocentric notions of Westernisation and talk instead of a multi-polar commercial culture. The problem for those interested in global political economy is no longer the imposition of cultural homogeneity through Americanisation, but concerns the transformation and privatisation of social spaces in a world economy. These transformations, especially within Europe, have undermined national public service models of media production through the processes of deregulation and the need to compete within international markets.

Whatever the adequacy of these reflections, I think the main stumbling block for the media imperialist thesis lay in its economic essentialism. As I have indicated those who advocate forms of media imperialism largely derived their studies from dependency theory. The flaw in this argument is that cultural identities and processes are thought to reflect material social structures. That is, for Schiller, if America was the dominant cultural power in the 1960s this was a direct reflection of America's economic standing. Further, if we can demonstrate the global nature of American culture then it is quite proper to assume that the world's peoples are being ideologically indoctrinated by its influence. The impact of audience and more ethnographic approaches to cultural studies have also added new levels of complexity to such arguments. In addition, Schiller's hermeneutic both misrepresents global economic trends and marginalises other more cultural patterns. For example, Robertson (1992) has pointed towards a growing political and cultural realisation that critical questions related to AIDS, nuclear disasters and ecological degradation are truly global questions. The rich and powerful are of course in a much better position to be able to shield themselves from the negative impacts of such developments, but there remains a sense in which they are *everyone's* responsibility. These dimensions arguably offer a more nuanced understanding of the new identities being fostered by processes such as the technological development of the media that can not be captured by patterns of consumerism alone. Indeed, we might go further, and suggest that the intensification of the capitalist economy has produced both cultural homogeneity as well as cultural difference. For example, in the media and mass communication we can point to the development of niche marketing where consumers are explicitly targeted depending upon lifestyle criteria, income bracket and other information. Yet we can also read this argument in reverse and suggest that the expansion of commodity capitalism into the cultural arena has developed globally recognised products from Coca-Cola to Disneyworld. The point here is that we need not make a choice between homogeneity and difference but learn to understand how they inform one another.

The impact of audience studies and more ethnographic approaches to cultural studies – as I have indicated – have also added new levels of complexity to such arguments. In particular, Ien Ang's (1985) study of *Dallas* has pointed to the inadequacy of these arguments. While Ang was compiling her study, *Dallas* was being shown in 90 countries and had become part of a global culture. Indeed, according to Ang, in her own country the Netherlands, during the spring of 1982, *Dallas* was being watched by just over half the population. The programme itself, for those who have never seen it, concerns the personal relations of a family made rich by Texan oil. Ang's book is an attempt to account for the popularity of the series through an interpretative understanding of the pleasures of the audience and her own evident enjoyment of the programme. At the time, the main reason that was being offered for the success of *Dallas* within the Dutch media was the media imperialism thesis. By this Ang means an account that represents a synthetic global American culture that is repressing more authentic national cultures. For Ang the implications of this argument would be to restrict free trade in commercial culture to enable national forms of cultural production. Such a perspective, on her account, is flawed in that it would probably lead to cheap attempts by nation-states to imitate *Dallas*'s glossy production, but, more importantly, such a view fails to account for the reasons why the audience tune in each week. The related argument that the arrival of *Dallas* is explained through media hype and the dominance of the culture industry is similarly dismissed as by implication it reduces the audience to cultural dopes. Instead, insists Ang, *Dallas* was enjoyed through a structure of feeling of tragedy. That is, the very reasons why it was enjoyed can be related to the emotional feel of tragedy and melodrama with which viewers tended to identify. Ang's own study, and those that have been developed since, have argued that the meanings generated through the practice of viewing are inherently unstable and depend on a number of structural and cultural factors.

These studies have discredited simplistic assumptions that the meanings of popular culture can be understood independently of the audience that

makes sense of them. In global contexts this argument speaks less of cultural imperialism and more of difference, polysemic meanings and diverse patterns of identification. Yet it would seem that if these reflections are carried to their logical conclusion they would cancel any concern with structural levels of power and authority. In short, while Ang focuses attention upon the fluid practices of the audience she displaces any concern for the effects the media might have on the sustenance of collective identity and the impact that a political economy of culture might also have on these levels. If our level of attention is focused upon the different interpretations offered of popular programmes our analysis is likely to reveal how different ethnicities, nationalities, genders, age groups and social classes interpret a diversity of media products. As important as these perspectives undoubtedly are, what is absent is the way that wider structural and institutional changes continue to inform the 'life-world' contexts of the users of mass communication. It is certainly the case that the older forms of media and cultural imperialism need to be radically redrawn if they are to represent the present adequately; however, I am not convinced that connections can not still be made between the levels of media production, content and reception. This points to an understanding of media that rethinks the predominant arguments of neo-Marxists, that the economy has causal effects on the levels of cultural identity, and the so-called 'new revisionists', who assume a more radical disjuncture between these different levels.[1] Instead what is being insisted upon here is that the media should be seen in terms of a wider cultural political economy that it is connected with both structural as well as democratic normative dimensions. Before going on specifically to address these questions, I want once more to return to the 1960s, before considering more recent post-modern and post-colonial perspectives on media cultures.

Post-modernism, post-colonialism and the global flow of the information society

Many of the current arguments that detail the way in which the global media reorganise space and time can be traced back to Marshall McLuhan. McLuhan famously argued that the modern world had moved through three modes of information exchange which include oral, print and electric mediums of communication. He claimed that what was more important than the content of the messages society decided to send were the mediums through which this communication took place. The transition to the medium of electronic communication can be connected with a change in the experiential nature of modernity. This is best represented through the gradual displacement of hot mediums with cool mediums. For McLuhan a hot medium disallows participation and is high in informational content. Conversely, cooler media leave more spaces for the audience to participate, and exhibit lower levels of information intensity. McLuhan explains:

> speech is a cool medium of low definition, because so little is given and so much has to be filled in by the listener. On the other hand, hot media do not leave so much to be filled in or completed by the audience. Hot media are, therefore, low in participation, and cool media are high in participation or completion by the audience. (McLuhan, 1994: 23)

The most obvious example of a cool medium is perhaps the internet. The internet is a dialogic medium that converts subjects into both senders and receivers of information. Conversely, print culture remains a hot medium as the activity of reading makes fewer demands upon the subject in shaping the flow of information. In McLuhan's terms the telephone, like the internet, 'demands complete participation, unlike the written and printed page' (McLuhan, 1994: 267). In addition, McLuhan is also aware that the telephone, by making its users constantly available, also has the effect of changing relations of power, and those of the public and the private. For instance, book culture was dependent upon reading practices that took place in private as opposed to public spaces, and knowledge production was undertaken by a small cast of authors. Cooler mediums, like the telephone and the internet, decentralise the production of knowledge as they involve a wider range of participants and thereby democratise the formation of opinion. Interestingly, McLuhan argues, that it is a characteristic of *bookish* intellectuals to wish to extend so-called enlightened perspectives into society's more backward regions. This, if the argument is followed, is the effect of an increasingly outmoded form of communication that depends upon centralised forms of knowledge production. McLuhan predicted that the new media would end relations of dominance within communicative relations and would produce a system which no central authority could govern.

The reconstitution of media into electric forms of communication, as I have indicated, also has implications for the reworking of space and time. Previously McLuhan had largely followed Innis (1951) by arguing that whereas oral societies were time biased, literate cultures were space biased. By this Innis meant that media such as stone and clay were time biased as they were difficult to transport through space. On the other hand, media such as printed paper is spatially biased as it is able to shift information through space. But for McLuhan the displacement of print by electronic circuitry had rendered Innis's earlier reflections redundant. Space and time have been annihilated through the impact of electronic media. Under modern conditions, according to McLuhan, cultural forms pour 'upon us instantly and continuously' (McLuhan and Fiore, 1967: 16). The interaction between modern subjects and communication networks is no longer confined to a few lonely hours before bedtime. Today the lives of the globe's citizens are wrapped around a seemingly endless encounter with material and symbolic modes of communication. Here communication systems put us in constant and immediate touch with different perspectives. The coordinates of time and space have vanished to herald a world where the sense of individualised detachment fostered by a book culture has given way to one where everyone is 'profoundly involved with everyone else' (McLuhan and Fiore, 1967: 61). The explosion of the new media has disrupted the visual bias of written forms of communication returning the globe's citizens to a shared culture that has much in common with that of oral societies. The global village has swept aside the hierarchical, uniform and individualising culture of print production and replaced it with a more tactile culture of simultaneous happenings. A culture driven along by electricity does not flow from any one place or location, but is quite literally organised into networks that have no connecting centre. The technology of communication, therefore, extends our central nervous system into a sensuous global embrace with the rest of humanity. This, as should by now be clear, renders redundant temporal (past and present) and spatial (near and far) distinctions. If we take a look at our morning newspaper we can immediately see that it inhabits a radically different form from the traditional novel. In place of the linear progression of a narrative we are confronted by what McLuhan calls a 'communal mosaic' (McLuhan, 1994: 204). That is, a newspaper has a multiplicity of authors and a variety of features and sections (sports page, fashion section, foreign news, editorial) that resists the single point of view evident within the book. The collage-like layout of the modern newspaper will also contain a number of items that have been transmitted from contexts far removed from those who either read or produce the newspaper. The speeding up and globalisation of news gathering practices will mean that temporality and distance will become progressively unimportant in governing newspaper content. Further, McLuhan explicitly argues that it is the consumers rather than those that own and control the relations of production who determine the content (McLuhan, 1994: 216). Hence as space and time, as well as patterns of ownership, become irrelevant to the content of the newspaper it is the audience's need for participation that shapes this process. This is nurtured by the fact that modern forms of communication enable audiences to travel through time and space. Before the mass production of photographs travel was practised 'to encounter the strange and unfamiliar' (McLuhan, 1994: 198). Now, returning to our morning paper, we can familiarise ourselves with the Grand Canyon or the Eiffel Tower by glancing at the travel pages. But just as space has been abolished so have linear conceptions of time. Under electric forms of communication the globe has become both historically and spatially visible. When we scan the newspaper we may be moving our eyes across stories from different parts of the world and events from human history. A single newspaper might contain articles regarding a new film on the Russian revolution, photographs of what our city looked like in the 1920s, or a feature on youth culture's attempt to revive the 1970s. The globe has imploded vertically, temporally and horizontally. Electric cultures have therefore introduced a new global sensibility pulverising the boundaries of nation-states and have undermined the linear and elitist modes of thought that can be associated with print cultures.

These arguments, while deeply problematic, remain provocative and maintain a deep connection with many of the post-modern currents which are presently in vogue. The main difference is that whereas McLuhan argues that technical landscapes directly impact on human senses, post-modern accounts prefer to take a more interpretative turn by investigating the way that global cultures impact upon modern identity formations. However, like McLuhan, the main emphasis is placed upon the media's capacity to transform relations of time and space. The argument here is that the era of imperialism has been replaced by that of globalisation: where imperialism was driven by the attempts of nation-states to impose a uniform culture on inferior populations, globalisation lacks a single centre and is marked by cultural difference. New forms of cultural pluralism are available through the uncoupling of peoples and symbolic goods from particular times and spaces. This can be achieved, as McLuhan thought through technical means, and as the post-modernists prefer by the reassembly of a global bricolage.

Bhabha (1994) argues that the post-colonial and the post-modern both attempt to reverse a series of binary oppositions between the 'Third' and the 'First World'. Both perspectives do this by rejecting 'holistic' explanations by more explicitly focusing upon complex cultural and political spheres. The political aim is neither to reduce the 'Third World' to the homogeneous other of the West (as was evident in the media imperialism thesis) nor vacuously to celebrate cultural plurality. Thus the movement of peoples and information has jumbled up established boundaries with the 'Third' World appearing in the 'First' World and the other way round. The aim here is critically to disrupt the imposition of sameness that is the product of 'First' and 'Third' World nationalism. The nation, in this respect, attempts to order time as a linear narrative and discipline space into definite boundaries. The post-colonial and post-modern moment seeks to deconstruct specifically national-led attempts to displace the anxiety of plural onto reordered spaces. Against what Bhabha (1994: 160) describes as the nation's obligation to forget the post-colonial view articulates an ambivalent 'experience' that talks of the in-betweenness of cultural identities. Cultural identities, therefore, are neither fixed nor linear but are the shifting mediations of specific discourses, histories and spaces. Bhabha most graphically illustrates these ideas through what he refers to as the 'Third Space'. The 'Third Space' is an ambiguous public space that has no primordial fixity and appears at the moment of articulation between the I and the You. Cultural meaning then is a dialogic construction borne out by the uncertain backwards and forwards of conversation. Yet this is also the space of cultural struggle, difference, translation and hybridity which resists ethnic nationalists' talk of 'purity' and the banal liberalism of 'diversity'. For Bhabha, and many others in the post-colonial tradition, the maps of meaning that characterise modernity should continue to resist hegemonic attempts to stabilise and order uncertain cultural flow.

There would seem at first glance to be a world of difference between post-structuralist intellectuals like Bhabha and the technological obsessions of McLuhan. But on closer inspection both provide a description of a decentred communications universe that has destroyed the temporal and spatial fixity of the nation-state and the printed word. Whereas McLuhan is mostly concerned with the media and Bhabha with literary texts, both offer a disordered cultural universe that grants new opportunities for cultural connection and articulation beyond the ambitions of the nation-state. They differ in that McLuhan presents the communications universe as providing new forms of unification, whereas Bhabha is more concerned with the estrangement of cultural difference. In this sense, as we shall see later, I think it is possible to reconsider both of these contributions as articulating partial truths. It may be possible, as many cultural critics seem to be aware, to reconcile the production of homogeneity and difference through an analysis of new forms of communication technology. However both McLuhan's and Bhabha's concerns are evident in post-modern attempts to reconsider the communications universe of the late twentieth century. The unhinging of stable locations of time and space has changed our shared cultural landscapes forever. Finally, it is also worth mentioning that they differ substantially in that for McLuhan media technologies have a direct impact on the sensory impressions of modern subjects, whereas for Bhabha, taking the linguistic turn in philosophy, cultural meanings are a product of the discourses through which we view the world. In other words, if McLuhan predates post-modernism in certain respects, in others he remains the product of an earlier epoch.

Both patterns of unification and difference are particularly apparent in more recent papers by Appadurai (1990), Luke (1995) and Goonatilake (1995), to name but a few. These contributions are marked within the literature by a need to rethink global systems of communications in the light of post-modern social theory and the redundancy of the media imperialism paradigm. Appadurai (1990) insists that despite the global reach of media technology it has not produced homogeneous spaces and cultures. More to the point are the diverse concerns of the Sri Lankans about Indianisation, the Baltics and Armenians of Russianisation, and the Koreans of Japanisation. These concerns mark the end of centre and periphery models in connection with cultural imperialism and speak instead of post-modern disorder and disjunction. The analysis of global culture points to at least five transnational phenomena that may be differentially combined with one another, in different contexts and with different effects. Appadurai outlines a disjunctive global cultural economy as being made up of: (1) *ethnoscapes* as the movement of peoples evident within disporas, tourism and migrations; (2) *technoscapes* as the uneven distribution of global technology; (3) *finanscapes* as the operation of global commodity speculation; (4) *mediascapes* as the transportation of semiotic cultures that open up imagined worlds across the boundaries of time and space and (5) *ideoscapes* which point to the transnational mobilisation of hegemonic and counter-hegemonic ideologies which are then recombined in different contexts to different effects. These levels are described by Appadurai as disjunctive as they have no necessary belonging and connection with each other.

Let us take the 'fictitious' example of a small community of Bosnian refugees who happened to have settled in a large northern city in Britain to outline these features. Displacement from the former Yugoslavia has had a paradoxical impact in that their relocation in a declining part of Britain has made it difficult for these peoples to find work despite their previously held professional status. Further our 'fictitious' community have all discovered despite their different ethnic origins that they have a great deal in common and now espouse principles of multiculturalism rather than ethnic nationalism. Yet Serbian, Crotian and Muslim refugees are able to continue a sense of connection with their particular ethnic groups as well as their host culture through media reports concerning the breakup of the former Yugoslavia. This can be achieved through the unofficial transportation of film and video, correspondence from family and friends, as well as viewing British national television. As this example demonstrates the particular combination of each of these elements does not so much produce sameness as much as heterogeneity. The flow of ideologies, images, money, technology and people is continually recombined to different effect in different global regions.

Similarly Luke (1995) and Goonatilake (1995) also register the discordant and chaotic flux of global media cultures. Luke (1995) argues that the transnational movement of a simulated culture has produced a global technosphere that is having a creolising effect upon local cultures, making the nation-states' desire to impose fundamental identities impossible to enforce. The global nature of new media technologies means that time and space have become increasingly compressed providing new linkages between different spatial and temporal dimensions. As Goonatilake (1995) observes, the new forms of global interconnection that are made possible by modern information technology increasingly make fundamentalist ambitions impossible to achieve over any longer term. The new levels of global interdependency that have become increasingly apparent since the 1960s has meant that different virtual communities have been able to communicate with one another across the borders of nation-states. In a world of overlapping cultures, the attempt on the part of nations to achieve ethnic purity is turned increasingly into a pyrrhic victory. The purified zone is likely to remain dependent upon global technology, expert systems and other cultural processes if it is to thrive economically, politically and culturally. Thus even a concerted policy of cultural imperialism that was consciously implemented would be unlikely to succeed in modern communications environments.

Considerations of cultural fragmentation and unification have much to offer theoretical perspectives within mass communication. It seems from McLuhan to more recently framed post-colonial and post-modern perspectives that the connections sought by notions of cultural imperialism between levels of political economy, media content and cultural identity should be quietly abandoned. Noticeably, critical concerns are now less impressed by the capacity of large-scale multinationals to enforce cultural homogeneity and more by corresponding processes of hybridisation and time and spatial travel. Yet, it seems to me, that while these are considerable correctives to some of the more obvious failings of the media imperialism thesis, it is clear that notions of political economy and ideological domination are being discontinued altogether. For instance, post-colonial attempts to describe the new cultural landscape have been attacked by both Arif Dirlik (1994) and Aijaz Ahmad (1995) who have both argued that a concern for plural identities has replaced that of global capitalism as the main theoretical touchstone. This, they argue, is a mistake. As Dirlik (1994) in particular points out, without the economic power of capitalism, 'Eurocentrism' would not have been a global ideological force but merely a local ethnocentrism. The cultural concerns of more 'post-modern' perspectives to map a global hybridity ideologically masks the emergence of a new phase of capitalism. Increasingly fluid forms of capital require cultural fragmentation (the packaging of distinctive markets), weak nation-states (so that financial flows can be directed by money markets rather than sources of social power) and the transportability of relatively standardised products (more global than local). As both Pieterse and Parekh (1995) similarly remark, the blind spot of post-modernism and post-colonialism is the renewed importance of notions of global political economy in an increasingly commercially driven world.

What then are the implications of these perspectives to global media cultures? I think they are at least threefold. The first is to argue that it remains important to map the changing contours of the cultural industries while remembering that these will have unintended as well as mediated effects upon cultural identities. However, I also think that the analysis should remain open to the diversity of ways that economies and cultures remain more than contingently related. This is the main problem with Appadurai's influential remarks. It remains the case that the structurating impacts of both money and power globally have done much to prevent the emergence of more democratic cultures. The systematic commercialisation and commodification of global media cultures of course has different effects within different contexts and this is missed by those who simply stress the 'economic colonisation of the life-world' (Habermas, 1989a). Beyond this, however, the pulverisation of cultural practices by the economy has hardly fostered the material social conditions necessary for enlightened conversation and democracy. Secondly, I think that critical mass communications theory is giving up a great deal if it fails to map the contours of the global village. This need not lead us to return to simplistic frameworks where the economic is held completely to determine the cultural. Instead, any sensible considera-tion of this theme would seek to trace through the relations between eco-nomic, political and cultural levels. Further, as Frederick Jameson (1991: 411) has pointed out, an appreciation of the ways in which global capitalism has transformed space can not be generated through immediate lived experience. The audience researchers may be able to point to the diverse quality of con-temporary subject positions but are unable to offer much on the structural coordinates that are systematically re-ordering contemporary media. Further, as perceptive as many of the post-colonial concerns are about the increasing hybridisation of identity formations, they are seemingly unable to account for the more durable elements of collective identity formation, such as nationalism. In terms of media and communications this might be because by seeing all social relations as equally contingent they are rendering them-selves incapable of identifying some of the more stable features of the modern era. Finally, post-modern perspectives have consistently failed to offer con-sideration of more normative levels of theorising. A more pejorative theory which placed communicative rather than identity concerns at the centre of the debate would ask different questions, and thereby lead to a more overtly political set of concerns. For instance, is it really the case that the globe's citizens are as informed as they should be about one another's hopes and concerns? If indeed they are, why has modernity presided over an increas-ingly widening gap between the material advantages of the rich western nations and some of the poorer nations on the planet? If viewers are really zipping backwards and forwards in time and space and national cultures are losing their permanence, then why are they not appalled by ever-widening global divisions? These are some of the questions I aim to address.

Global media in the age of informational capitalism: speed cultures and spatial dimensions of power

In this final section, I want to drive a critical wedge between the old style economism of the media imperialism thesis and the more divergent cul-turalism of post-modernism and certain post-colonial perspectives. I shall do this by investigating the following items: (1) the changing nature of global political economy with respect to the arrival of trans-national media; (2) the general speeding up of temporal dimensions; (3) the emergence of what I shall call spatial zones of power in respect of media cultures; (4) the need for a worldwide and genuinely global communicative democracy.

1 Media and cultural studies are currently marked by a lack of analysis of the economic determinants of mass communications systems. This is particularly striking given the current debates on questions of globalisation

and the arrival of new technologies such as satellite, cable and digital television. The problem with most media analysis at present is that through the attempt to represent media cultures as disorganised symbolic systems the more material questions concerning its functioning seem to have been sidelined. Here I aim to show how the changing structures of global capitalism have helped shape the emergent processes of what could be called a *new media order*. That is, the 1980s have witnessed the slow breakup of national media systems and their displacement and partial erosion by more global concerns. Of all the current works on global culture it is probably Frederick Jameson (1991) whose theory of post-modern culture is most dependent upon economic forms of analysis. Post-modernism, according to Jameson (1991), is the emergent culture of global society. The problem is that despite the welcome need to link cultural and economic practices Jameson paradoxically has a good deal to say about the former and very little about the latter. Jameson (1991: 36), taking his lead from Mandel, indicates that global capitalism through technical developments in media and advertising has moved into a Third Machine Age. The capitalism of our own time is becoming progressively purer in that it has penetrated hitherto uncommodified areas like nature, the unconscious and the 'Third World'. I want to argue that Jameson's descriptions on the ultimate triumph of consumer capitalism are as insightful as they are vague and lacking in precision. Perhaps the most important point I want to take from Jameson is the idea that if we want to understand the changing political economy of culture we should start with an analysis of the current changes taking place within global capital.

A more reliable guide to the changes impacting upon global economies is Manuel Castells (1993). Castells argues that the development of capitalism and world trade throughout the 1980s has become increasingly dependent upon the application of science and technology. In this new stage of capitalism, which Castells calls the informational economy, it is the application of knowledge and technology in customised production that best ensures economic success. The technological level of the enterprise is a much better guide to competitiveness than older indexes such as labour costs. For Castells (1989) the 1980s witnessed the rapid development of information technology which enabled capitalism to restructure itself internationally after the breakdown of national Keynesianism. The application of new technology has enabled capital to become increasingly placeless by rapidly providing investors with information regarding new market opportunities, opening up markets that were previously spatially distant, and also massively increasing the rate of capital turnover on global markets. The impact of new technology has enabled large-scale organisations to reconstruct the internal organisation of their institutional structures. This has been achieved through increasing flexibility (division of workers into core and periphery), the growing concentration of internal knowledge generation and the shift from centralised to decentralised organisational networks. The creation of horizontal and less-vertical structures, however, has not meant that small businesses now have the upper hand over large-scale multinationals. In fact, the opposite is true, as new technology has enabled large structures to coordinate their activities world wide, while building in reflexive inputs so that they can quickly respond to the current state of the market and benefit from economies of scale (Castells and Hall, 1994). According to Castells then, the fundamental source of wealth generation lies in the ability of capitalist concerns to be able to cash in on the information revolution. This is not to argue that economic success is not also dependent upon access to large integrated markets (especially the US, the EEC and Japan), the cooperation of compliant nation-states and distinctions between production costs and market prices. Instead Castells is revitalising an older Marxist argument that global capitalism remains dependent upon the tie between productive forces (the application of technology and knowledge) and the social relations of production. These economic forces, argues Castells, are the main economic motors that are restructuring global capital flows.

More recently Castells (1996) has argued that information technology is irrevocably tied into such processes in ways that are poorly appreciated by more traditional political economy perspectives. According to Castells the new informational economy has replaced old-style capitalism in that its source of productivity is knowledge and information. The development of information technologies in Silicon Valley, USA, during the 1970s has paved the way for the revitalisation of capitalism during the 1980s. That is to say, whereas industrialism was orientated towards economic growth, informationalism is more concerned with the development of knowledge and the creation of networks. The digitalisation of knowledge bases allows information to be processed and stored across huge distances. Capitalism is therefore becoming less dependent upon the state and more upon the ability of a common informational system to transmit knowledge across distanciated networks. Yet Castells is clear that this situation is not creating a global capitalist class or even the universalisation of capitalism. The global economy however explicitly does not include all the regions of the planetary economy but involves the intensification of sectors within Europe, North America and the Asian Pacific Region. The more dormant zones of the world economy, on this reading, are being increasingly reduced to a position of structural irrelevance. In information technology, then, it is notable that the most information over-loaded media cultures are likely to develop within areas where the global economy is at its most intensive.

The growth of information technology has both globalised capital and become a significant source of wealth in its own right. For example, Netscape (the current most popular browser for the internet) had in 1996 been installed in an estimated 30 million computers. Notably it is currently worth $5billion, although this was achieved by the company giving away its product. The internet is one of the fastest-growing activities in the world today. In 1995 there was an estimated 1 million people using the web, whereas today it is closer to 40 million (Keegan, 1997). However, the information revolution has not empowered the world's impoverished zones, but has significantly contributed to the creation of a global super rich where 358 people own as much as the poorest half of the world. The development of new information technologies has both intensified the division between the winners and losers of the global economy, and shifted its operation onto a 'real-time' basis. The vast fortunes accrued by the likes of Bill Gates, Li Ka-Shing, Paul Allen and Kenneth Tomson (all of whom are currently among the globe's richest people) are strongly connected with their role in the buying and selling of new media and information technology (Keegan, 1996). Such a 'material' analysis of the media and information revolution could also point towards the increasing significance of global media magnates like Rupert Murdoch. The digitalisation of information (the conversion of all information forms into binary codes) will enable the information distributors to improve the quality of television pictures and dramatically expand the number of channels that can commonly be made available. The digital revolution is therefore likely to increase the financial and political power of those like Murdoch who will control the hardware that delivers the new information culture (Porter, 1996).

These concerns help us understand a great deal about the increasing economic and cultural power of large-scale multi-media organisations. As Morley and Robins (1995) argue, the development of new technology and the willingness of capital to invest in media industries has meant that a small number of global players are manoeuvring for dominance over new information markets. The participants include Time Warner, Murdoch's News International, Ted Turner's CNN and Sony who are all heavily investing in communications technologies and delivery systems. What is noticeable is that, while America remains the main national force, it is becoming increasingly challenged by Japanese and European concerns. The amount of investment taking place in these enterprises is perhaps not surprising given Castells's arguments concerning the importance of technology in determining economic success or failure. Media organisations like Murdoch's News International and Sony are directly involved in the selling of technological hardware as well as the distribution of the products which will inevitably benefit from more sophisticated means of transmission. In other words, many of the larger transnational concerns are in a position to benefit doubly from technologising capitalism. Media multinationals are able to strike global deals while offering the latest and most up-to-date technological means and informational goods to its customers. Further, it is notable that all of the major players have been able to keep ahead of their competitors by securing access to the most lucrative markets as well as utilising new forms of technology in the production and distribution of media forms. From News International's switch to the Wapping print plant in Britain to Disney's successful attempts at product diversification, the major players have kept well ahead of technological developments.

We have also witnessed so-called 'merger mania' in the main media multi-nationals. In the Spring of 1995, Murdoch announced a multi-million dollar deal with MCI communications (the world's second largest telecommunications company) which was followed in August by Walt Disney's takeover of Capital Cities/ABC television network (*Economist*, 1995a) Time Warner, seemingly not to be outdone by their major rivals, subsequently merged with Ted Turner's company TBS to form the *current* world's largest entertainment and communications business (*Economist*, 1995b). These transformations have a number of consequences that any attempt to reformulate the significance of political economy and mass communications should consider. First, consistently with Castell's arguments, these media companies are global rather than universal concerns. If we take Murdoch's News International it is significant that his media business stretches across the world's most developed or rapidly developing economic regions, notably ignoring most of the world's poorer nation-states. The critical point about the new global economy, and for that matter the *new media order*, is that it is becoming increasingly international and integrated at the same time. If economic performance is currently dependent upon high levels of technological development and access to the wealthiest world markets then most of Africa, parts of Latin America and the non-oil producers in the Middle East are being increasingly relegated to the sidelines.

These concerns could prove highly significant to the development of the so-called information revolution. It is undoubtedly the case that the strategies of product diversification, internationalisation and ownership concentration currently being followed by the new media conglomerates are attempts to place themselves in a dominant position so that they might benefit from the possible emergence of so-called new super information highways. The idea here is that the McLuhanite implosion of media technology (primarily the telephone, the computer and the television) will produce a new interactive medium. In Britain, an alliance between the Murdoch-owned B Sky B, British Telecom, Midland Bank and Matsushita Electric have joined forces to launch digital satellite services (Culf, 1997). Subscribers will eventually receive over 400 channels, the internet and a range of other facilities including home banking, shopping, computer games and other forms of public information. This will both increase the number of people who have access to a range of informational resources, while producing new axes of exclusion. Murdoch's nodal enterprise is no longer nationally based but is a global phenomena which allows him to avoid paying taxes, have undue influence on state-driven political structures, and promote an information culture based upon private consumption rather than more inclusive notions of public citizenship. In the British context however it is important to remember that the power of media barons like Murdoch have been fostered by state policies that have progressively provided opportunities for the commodification and globalisation of media structures. Indeed, at present, it is still not clear, despite the election of a centre Left government, what new forms of regulation, if any, are likely to be placed on Murdoch's looming power base (Toynbee, 1998). The responses of the 'new' Labour government to the increasing global nature of the big media has been at best contradictory. While it has been careful to distance itself from specific attempts to outlaw predatory pricing by Murdoch (who currently owns 41 per cent of the national newspaper readership) the culture secretary Chris Smith has argued that access to digital television needs to be as universal as possible (Ahmed, 1998). Yet in the absense of any clear strategy of definite policy pronouncements it is currently difficult to predict how far the government will go in challenging the power of News International. News International, then, is a good example of the new global economy as it is concentrated in the world's fastest accelerating regions and is a beneficiary of technological change and development. The development of global media corporations is more properly thought of as the extension of modernity through the emancipation of capital from the governance of the state, than some of the cultural complexities that have been associated with post-modern frames.

More explicitly, George Gilder (1992) and Mark Poster (1995) have argued that the digital revolution will disrupt the centralised one-way flow of television networks which depend upon passive viewers and mass audiences. The new media, both authors confidently predict, will allow audiences both to transmit and receive messages, will be less about passive consumerism than about active involvement. These developments will foster a deeper and more participatory democracy by opening up and making accessible a plethora of information. While I do not share the mostly undiluted enthusiasms of Gilder (1992) and Poster (1995), it is certainly the case that it is a similar vision to that which is offered by the global talk of the media moguls who front the communications conglomerates. Ted Turner echoes many of these sentiments:

> I think we need to test the phrase 'the Third World'. First, because two-thirds of the [world's] people live in the Third World, it's really the first world. And second, the word 'foreign' to describe other countries and other people on the planet is an outdated term. Five hundred, four hundred, even one hundred years ago, the world was foreign. It was far from one place to another. But now it's not. We're all neighbours in the world today. (Turner, 1994: 42)

The corporate speak of Turner seemingly ideologically masks as much as it reveals. New forms of unification are primarily being achieved through the application of technology which is largely owned and controlled by the economically core centres of global power. Despite Turner's view of global brotherhood, which is questionable from a number of positions, it is unlikely that more peripheral information zones are likely to foster cool interactive media cultures. It is then not so much the case, as the media imperialism thesis implied, that the indigenous peoples of these nations are being progressively swamped by an American culture. What will become more apparent is an information and technology gap that will progressively divide the

114

culturally saturated nations of the core markets and the less technologically sophisticated zones represented by poorer regions. Global visions like those of Turner mystify the structural dominance of core information centres which inevitably means that cultural goods will become progressively targeted to capture these markets, displaying only a limited concern for those regions external to the main centres of media activity. Further, it is also apparent that many of the nations that have become hooked into the global television age have placed restrictions on the material that can be transmitted into the country. This again questions the pretensions of the talk that has become associated with the global media. For instance, the Malayan prime minister, whose country receives transmissions from Murdoch's Hong Kong based Star TV, described the service as both 'friendly and useful'. This and other deals achieved by Murdoch with authoritarian heads of state makes a mockery of the suggestion that global television flows necessarily rests uneasily with political dictatorships. Murdoch's willingness to allow repressive nation-states to regulate communication flow seemingly undermines the earlier statements he made regarding global media's essentially democratic impact (Shawcross, 1995).

These features map onto a further aspect of the *new media order*, that is that it is better characterised through a concern to provide immediate up-to-the-minute information than it is to carry through a specific ideological project. Thus we may now speak of an emerging spatial and temporal bias in world communications flows rather than, say, Murdoch's desire to impose a particular political ideology. Of course this is not to say that the new global media will not carry material that is class biased, sexist, racist and Eurocentric. Indeed, despite the impact of post-Marxism, which has wanted to de-stabilise the assumed correspondence between patterns of ownership and media content, it remains the case that media moguls are unlikely to resource material that is highly experimental in form, unable to reach a sizeable proportion of the market and politically radical in content. However, what is most striking about the global media is the need to be as up to date technologically as in the information conveyed, and that the media are becoming increasingly spatially focused around the globe's most economically developed regions. These factors do not mark an end of ideology, but instead point to a new information and media age that is not adequately captured by either concerns around blanket media imperialism or post-modernism. My argument here is that the spatial and temporal dimensions of the media are becoming as important as the capacity of capital and sources of social power in the structuration of media flows and content. However, as I will go on to argue, I think it is a mistake to argue that one set of coordinates is replacing the other. More radically my suggestion is that the spatial power of the economically dominant world regions and the ever-quickening turnover of media imagery have now to be considered along with more traditional frameworks that are associated with the state and capital when considering the media of mass communication.

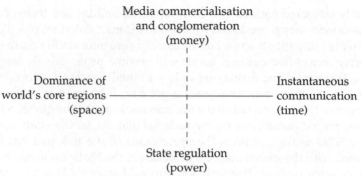

Media commercialisation
and conglomeration
(money)

Dominance of
world's core regions ———————————— communication
(space)

Instantaneous
communication
(time)

State regulation
(power)

Figure 1

Let us consider these features. There is much evidence that the new media order has considerably reordered the flows of other media. In the European context there is widespread concern that the expansion of commercial media, which is usually linked to the emerging conglomerates, has had a negative effect upon public channels. Petley and Romano (1993) report that Burlussconni's domination of Italian television has led to the growth of American news genres such as *infotainment*. The increasing competition between public and private broadcast networks has meant that news is increasingly organised into bit-sized chunks that depend upon the dramatic and the sensational while helping foster a 'star system' of highly paid presenters.

In Britain a recent report by the 'Campaign for Quality Television' has argued that the increasing commercialisation of television and the scramble for ratings among television companies has led to a serious decline in the number of documentary programmes being shown on terrestrial television (Mullholland, 1998). Martin-Barbero (1993) and Hallin (1994) in Latin America and North America respectively both argue that 'the people' in their plurality and difference have been progressively excluded from televised debates the extent to which the medium has been turned over to instrumental forms of reason. Both writers articulate this dimension in complimentary if divergent ways. Martin-Barbero argues that Latin America's particular route into modernity meant that the early media (film, press, etc.) connected the birth of nationalism and the appearance of the 'people' in public life. In particular popular genres like melodrama, whose overriding concern is with the everyday conflicts of 'ordinary life', allowed the public to experience themselves as a particular nation for the first time. The increasing capitalisation and transnationalisation of the media has largely readjusted information flows in terms of capitalist defined progress. This has meant that whereas radio and the press continue to form a close affinity with the nation it has been television which has become the main outlet for American popular culture. For instance, despite the independent productive base of TV Globo in Brazil, 99 per cent of the films that are shown are American. Further,

116

although TV Globo produces nearly 80 per cent of its own programmes, these are overwhelmingly orientated towards mass entertainment (Mader, 1993). For Martin-Barbero, while the media imperialism thesis has been considerably overstated, it retains an analytical value the extent to which national forms of imagining are asphyxiated by global cultural power. Duncan Hallin (1994), on the other hand, argues that the intensive search by the American media for new markets has led to processes of de-politicisation and a scientific obsession with 'facts' and 'objectivity'. The 'scientisation' of the media has meant that media news has been progressively turned into a product that requires very little by the way of participation by the audience. In other words, the commercialisation of the media of mass communication coupled with the dominance of technical reason has substituted a technocratic agenda for one that might have been associated with more communicative practices. This indeed connects with a strand of thinking available within the Mattlelarts' as well as Schiller's attempts to think global media cultures. That is, it is the multipolar triumph of commercialism and capitalism that is shaping global futures rather than homogeneous Americanisation. This said, as both the Mattlelarts and Schiller concur, American culture retains a global reach like no other currently available on the world stage.

Arguments concerning the standardisation and homogenisation of global media continue to have much to contribute. Indeed we might even argue that the media imperialism thesis could be reworked along Habermasian (1989a) lines. This would point to both the colonisation of the 'life-world' through the reification of communicative relations and the cultural forms of impoverishment that can be associated with passive forms of mass culture. This could then lead to a concern with a global communicative citizenship that stressed the dialogic rights and responsibilities of the globe's citizens. Yet it is not clear to me whether the globalisation of media cultures are not more unpredictable and torrid than such theses allow. The event driven nature of commercial media can mean that it acts against the interests of local elites who are attempting to rationalise and regulate image production through the media. The media in this respect regularly produces global information spirals where mediated events gather a momentum of their own. This opens up the possibility of unintended consequences and unpredictable outcomes. Whether it is through global pictures of famine, genocide, war or of ecological disaster they often embarrass powerful governments who are then presented with problems of presentation management. The globalisation of information also poses questions of responsibility for we can no longer claim that we did not know. In the contemporary version of McLuhan's global village we hear news of distant wars, political executions and miserable injustice all competing for and seemingly equally deserving of our attention.

The shifting uncertain world of radicalised modernity, which Beck (1992) has aptly entitled the risk society, has seemingly broken with the ordered progression of the rationalisation thesis. The media can produce globalised boomerang effects where seemingly large parts of the globe are all talking about the same issue all at once. These effects temporarily obliterate distinctions between the information rich and poor by providing vertical fields of communication and a global experience of unification. In this respect the new media order is pulling in two different directions simultaneously: towards the increasing rationaliation of information systems as well as the spiralling of uncontrollable flows of information. These seemingly contradictory movements, it seems to me, will become increasingly evident in the future. Again, the advantage of this model is that one is not forced to choose between the media offering new instances of control or disorder. This has largely been the error that has been made by those who have sought to jutapose modernity and post-modernity, and which was also evident in the rampant pessimism of the media imperialism thesis and the excessive optimism embodied in McLuhan's idea of the global village. A more differentiated account then enables us more consistently to think through the undoubted opportunities and dangers inherent in globalised media production.[2]

Ulrich Beck (1997) has more recently argued that cultural analysis that only points towards new instances of social control is insufficiently appreciative of what he calls 'reflexive modernisation'. Where modernity was the age of certainty and truth the coming of a second modernity is predicated on notions of radical doubt and uncertainty. From media stories concerning the horrors of ocean pollution to others speculating on the reasons for the fall in male fertility rates, social life is rendered and experienced as fragile. This does not mean that the world is 'objectively' a riskier place. What Beck is arguing is that individualisation, the decline of tradition and the rapid circulation of knowledge all contribute towards making risk assessment a key feature of contemporary life. Evidence of greater reflexivity has helped release repressed questions associated with modernity (particularly those connected with gender and ecology) but has also fostered more reactive attempts to construct certainty. Constructed certitude is an attempt to defend the self and community from questioning and doubt. It is the other side of modernity. For every television programme concerning the growing ecological crisis there is the hired spokesperson offering calm assurance and an unproblematic belief in the nature of experts. The development of new media has meant that, as never before, the world is full of questions that deny simple answers. What is the future of our planet? What are the long-term consequences of women taking the contraceptive pill? Can we trust politicians? While the organisational structures of the media impinge on the degree of reflexivity that is allowed to make itself publicly present in such disputes, similarly they can not ignore scare stories about mad cows, redundant males and rising sea levels. Indeed the climate of sensation, panic and instantaneous opinion formation can be as much about the colonisation of public discourse and dialogue as it can be about its disorder and problematisation. The pulversiation of the cultural sphere by the economy can both lend itself to tabloidisation and the more unstable logics of media

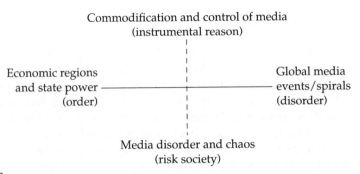

Commodification and control of media
(instrumental reason)

Economic regions   Global media
and state power ————————————— events/spirals
(order)   (disorder)

Media disorder and chaos
(risk society)

Figure 2

sensation. The arrival of new technologies such as personal computers and hand-held video-recorders has provided the possibility of alternative sources of information exchange underneath the structures of big media. We might represent these logics as in Figure 2.

2   The temporal dimensions of media cultures have strong connections to processes of globalisation. For instance, in the mid eighteenth century it used to take letters approximately 40 days to cross from Europe to the United States. Today, through the intervention of telephones, the World Wide Web and live broadcasts, as McLuhan predicted, we have entered the age of instantaneous and immediate communication. The emergence of new media conglomerates has seemingly accelerated this process bringing the most dramatic happenings into our homes on a daily basis. The experience of what Giddens (1990) has called 'time–space' compression has meant that the increasingly 'event' driven nature of media reporting has become exaggerated in correspondence with its global spread. Newspaper stories, television news items and radio programmes it seems are no longer determined by their immediate proximity to the location of their production. The linear and sequential nature of time that according to Benedict Anderson (1983) allowed the nation to imagine itself collectively progressing through history is being displaced by a global time of immediate and instantaneous transmission. The idea of historical progress through time by a hermetically sealed nation-state has been undermined by simultaneous global happenings and the blurring of strict boundaries between past, present and future. This new structure of feeling is propelled by a media culture of nostalgic revivals and pastiche where firmly distinct historical periods and sensations are difficult to maintain in an increasingly mongrel world. The displacement of temporal frames associated with the linear and sequential time frames of modernity by the speeded up disorganised dimensions of post-modernity has important consequences for the way we understand global media cultures. Hence the speeding up and disorganisation of the temporal flow of the media can lead to a situation where the rational forms of reflection necessary for democracy are undermined by the formation of

immediate opinions, collective forms of forgetting and a wider culture of uncertainty.

Let us take each of these cases in turn. The quickening of the time allowed for opinion formation can often lead to the production of superficial perspectives in place of those which should have taken a deeper and more substantial view of the subject. We might then be in a position to receive more information more quickly than ever before but denied the interpretative opportunities to make the world more meaningful. For example, the speeding up of events interferes with our capacity to feel empathy and disappointment. The media, it seems, are always moving on restlessly searching for fresh news and different viewpoints. This then makes the achievement of responsible and meaningful forms of reflection increasingly difficult in the modern age. In this respect, following a range of theorists after McLuhan who have stressed the importance of the medium rather than the message, the collapsing of time frames in mediated discourse makes it difficult to construct a narrative of the past and continous empathetic relations with distant others. Yet it is a mistake to proceed as if the media only colonise society's shared capacity to construct meaningful relations with others. For instance, the culture of immediacy and speed can also feed the idea that we the nation or international alliance, in a time of crisis, ought to do something. This can be invaluable if, say, we are considering offering immediate humanitarian aid to the victims of a disaster, but can also have other perhaps more negative consequences when the questions are connected with military intervention into a war zone. The rapidity at which these decisions are made might mean that a wide-ranging public discussion has not yet taken place and that not enough 'quality' information has been made available to make an informal judgement. Again I am struck by a basic ambivalence here between the need to receive information quickly and the consequences this might have for human reasoning. The wider point is that the temporal bias introduced by media cultures disrupts our capacity for critical reflection as well as providing a necessary service and influence on contemporary political culture. The issue here is to hold an intellectual concern regarding the lack of slowness in our culture against an appreciation of the political necessity of speeding up information exchange.

The recent 'Louise Woodward' case (Oct./Nov. 97) highlights many of these ambivalences. The televising of the trial of the British nanny who was accused of the murder of a small child simultaneously subjected the American legal system to critical scrutiny (particularly in Britain), while fostering the 'false' impression that distant publics were in a position to judge her guilt or innocence. The television reporting of the trial in 'real time' actually fostered the belief among much of the audience that they were 'closer' to the events than they were. It is difficult to avoid asking the question as to how many of the British audience were actually motivated by ordinary nationalistic sentiment, and how many of them were 'really' in a position to make an 'informed' judgement?

Secondly, I think that the daily overturning of opinion in the modern era has led to a tendency for collective memories to be shortened. This can also have unpredictable effects and consequences. In political terms it might lead to similar mistakes being made and an increasing inability to make sense of larger historical patterns and trends. This might lead to forgetting the historical struggles which have granted us with certain citizenship entitlements and leading us into a culture of complacency and neglect. It can also give the impression, as we become caught up in the immediacy of the present, that events that only happened a number of years ago are distant temporally. Yet again I think it important to stress the dialectical nature of such processes. The unintended consequence here might be an opening of human horizons free from the dead weight of the past that can offer new hope and energy to emancipatory groups of various kinds. This paradox can be illustrated if we take ecological movements. As Barbara Adam (1995) has expertly argued, ecological concerns have focused collective attention on time lags and latency periods caught between cause and effect. By this Adam means that modernity has increasingly made us aware of the risks that our present actions are shoring up if not for ourselves but for future generations. This again points us towards a different conception of temporal dimensions than existed with sequential and linear causality. However, the main problem for the green movement is that they have to persuade people to think over a longer period of time than is customary in a world fostered by speed capitalism and mass communication. The need to consider the material conditions of future generations, however, rests uneasily with the current desire to satisfy the immediate and the short term. But to complicate the situation further the concerns of the ecological movement, I would argue, have undoubtedly been shaped by new levels of global interconnection that global media regularly make available. The compression of space and time has both revealed global interconnections that were previously obscured and opened out a concern for wider collective futures. In short, the global media makes the world thinkable.

Finally, the changing temporal dimensions of our culture has helped foster a shared sense of the future which is deeply uncertain. The breakdown of narratives of progress and security that can be connected with linear time frames has developed culturally a good deal of anxiety about the future. Baudrillard (1994) has argued that fear of the future can be discovered in the arguments that have abounded about the 'end of history' as the twentieth century draws to a close. This can be detected in what he calls an 'event strike' where the aura of historical events has declined through the repetition and simulation of the twentieth century in the media. By this Baudrillard means that the history of our time is currently being re-run through a culture of ecological recycling, nostalgia for the French revolution evident in the 200 years celebration, and re-birth of liberalism after the fall of the Berlin wall. The desire to impose an 'end to history' and the current cultural re-running of the century exhibits a generalised global fear as to what the future might hold. However, while I think that Baudrillard's reflections are interesting, they displace what I take to be the key issue. That is, the break with linear time evident in the globalisation of the media and related processes itself reveals a sense of the future which is likely to be chaotic, disorganised and increasingly unpredictable. Again the event-driven nature of the global media helps foster an impression of a violent world that is running out of control. This sense could perhaps be linked to fundamentalist desires to re-order the world, a greater moral concern with the sufferings of others, passive forms of voyeurism or indeed even increasing indifference. Obviously then the handling of these different responses to globalised uncertainty will depend upon a variety of social and psychic responses of which the media form only a small part.

What then is the link between these hermeneutic questions and the arrival of the new media age? First, and most obviously, they are connected with an intensification of the global reach of modern media. The fact that we are able to witness at increasing speed global events is largely the product of research and investment into new technologies by the new media conglomerates. This was particularly evident in the live transmissions that were being broadcast by CNN during the Gulf War. These pictures were transmitted around the world and provided the basis of a global reference point available to many of the globe's peoples. Secondly, again as Adam (1995) points out, capitalism has long been associated with a culture of speed. Capitalism has a tendency to place value on that which can be performed and achieved in the shortest possible time. Traditionally this has meant that capital invests as little as possible in labour time, produces goods quickly and makes profits fast. As we saw earlier in the global age the movement of capital around the globe has increased as it has become emancipated from place. Increasing the value of time, in the commercial media time has become equated with money. As Dallas Smythe (1977) pointed out, media cultures are largely commercial cultures whereby audiences (calculated through time frames) are sold to advertisers. This shapes the content and production of media cultures in the interests of consumer capitalism. Interestingly, what this points to is that media cultures are still dependent upon time frames that are both disorganised and rationally calculable. This opens up a further contradiction that the disorganised temporal flows of the global media and the rationalised calculable form of time demanded by capital are simultaneously produced through commodification processes. This speaks of a temporal dimension that is neither modern nor for that matter post-modern. Indeed I think that post-modern aspects of time (disorganised frames) continue to co-exist with clock time (enabling the coordination necessary for satellite broadcasting) and national time (the extent to which the nation continues to be an important unit for the organisation of memory and sentiment). These concerns point towards a future not one where one homogeneous conception of time replaces another (e.g. global replaces national) but one where such dimensions co-exist.

3   The dimensions of space evident within the media imperialist argument was one where the so-called 'Third World' were denied cultural forms of autonomy through the imposition of specifically conceived Western hegemony. These arguments, as we saw, have been challenged by postmodern and post-colonial concerns that have resisted the reduction of 'Third World' nations to the Other of the West. This theoretical strategy centres upon theoretical complexity where Western cultures and local cultures are hybridised through a form of global bricolage. In other words, the postmodernists deconstruct the opposition between the West and the 'Third World' to reveal an unstable dimension of reinterpreted images, identities and perspectives.

Again I think this tends to ignore the spatial dominance and power of certain centres of communication flow. As Lash and Urry (1994) point out the new informational core zones globally are likely to be located within the USA, Europe and Japan. It is in these societies that the new super information highway is most likely to be developed. The concentration of advanced technology, sizeable markets and rapid transformation makes them media cultures unlike any other. In more peripheral zones like, say, Latin America the cultural production of the core is also likely to make itself felt despite the fact they are likely to lack the most up-to-date information technology, the regulatory capacity of core nations and the most developed markets. The important point about these developments in more peripheral zones is that it has increased the cultural reach of the core areas (the most dominant of which is America) in the absence of the mechanisms of state or civil society that help regulate such processes. To stay with Latin America, as Martin-Barbero (1993) pointed out earlier, the deregulation of the national domain has allowed cultural space to become increasingly colonised by the imperatives of capital, technology and American culture. However, while these transformations are significant other American nations outside the North are as of yet poorly served by cable networks and are likely to remain so unless they are able to offer concentrated markets in the future.

Yet it might be better, when discussing economic and cultural processes, to talk of regionalisation rather than globalisation. I would want to reserve the notion of globalisation to discuss the electronic transmission of image, sound and perspective across time and space that promotes more intensive cultural connectiveness. Regionalisation, on the other hand, more specifically represents the economic, political and cultural development of the media within world regions. Regionalisation then describes the development of multinational markets which are linked by geography, language and culture (Strabhuar, 1997). For instance, there have emerged markets in cultural goods linking Latin, Chinese, South East Asian and most obviously English languages. While American cultural products retain an international purchase unlike any other, the international dominance of the English language does provide opportunities for smaller cultural producers. In this context, Australia makes an interesting example in that it has become a significant exporter of light entertainment to Europe (who has not heard of the soap opera *Neighbours?*). According to Sinclair, Jacka and Cunningham (1997), between 1980 and 1991 Australia produced a total of 334 feature films, 172 mini series and 148 telemovies. Yet despite the opportunities for regionalisation offered by the dominance of 'English' this has not prevented the flows of media culture being dominated by the United States.

Kwane Karikari (1993) notes the most pressing problem in the African context can not really be construed as media imperialism. The lack of advertising revenue available has granted nation-states with considerable power in shaping the dominant communication flows within the continent. These markets have great difficulty in supporting television or print mediums (especially due to rising levels of illiteracy) which leaves the media in the control of transnationals already in operation in Africa or with the state. The other problem in Africa is that nation-states more often contain a plurality of languages which makes the production of television and film for home markets economically a very difficult achievement. In many African nations radio is more widespread than television, a factor which is particularly important in sustaining a local music industry (Reeves, 1993: 218). More to the point, a weak economic base and state forms of control mean that notions of civil society are culturally underdeveloped.

Again, we have to be careful not to homogenise different national experiences and contexts. The next chapter will reveal in detail how the communicative conditions in Rwanda could be linked to the practice of genocide, whereas in South Africa they would need to be connected to the development of a post-Apartheid state (Maingard, 1996). South Africa has witnessed progressive campaigns to wrest control of the national television and radio broadcasters away from the state. The redefinition of broadcasting in South Africa has sought to grant recognition to 11 different languages, provide space for independent film makers and reflect the plurality of South African society more generally. These examples make the point that despite the development of global media corporations the nation-state by and large remains the dominant force in the regulation of communicative relations. Indeed it is worth reminding ourselves in this context that as late as the 1970s only three regions in the world had any significant private media (North America, Latin America and Australia), the rest were either state dominated or heavily regulated by the state (Sinclair, Jacka and Cunningham, 1997).

While we are undoubtedly moving into a more market and technologically driven era the state retains a considerable capacity to structurate internal social relations in respect of mass communication. John Downing (1997) points out in his detailed study of the transformation of media in Eastern Europe that the state rather than the agents of media imperialism remains the most important mechanism in securing or disabling a pluralistic civil society. Before the liberal revolutions of 1989 the state in these societies had to manage a plurality of opinion while seeking to censor dissenting voices. The paradox remains however that if the state was the main force that repressed the plurality of civil society before 1989, after this date it has remained the dominant force. State support for the media remains one of the key ambiguities in post-socialist societies without which much private media would collapse. For example, in July 1995 approximately 85 per cent of Russian publications received aid from the state. Downing concludes that the main problem in the former Eastern bloc is not so much the colonisation by Western media mogels, but continued state patronage and control. Hence the withdrawal of state funding would lead to the collapse of the media while its continuation allows the state a substantial amount of influence within post-Communist societies. As these examples demonstrate it is overly simplistic to suggest blandly that a national public media has now been replaced by a more commercially driven global media. The current communications picture needs to attend to the context-specific interrelations between the continuing capacity of states to order communicative flow, and the cultural and economic relations between different world regions.

Does this then mean that media imperialism is a Eurocentric myth? The short answer to this question is not necessarily. There have indeed been historical instances, such as the Gulf War, where the defence of the economic interests of one of the global world powers was enhanced through the control of the global flow of electronic media. As Said (1993) argues the war was culturally governed by a form of global misrecognition that reinforced relations of *contrapunctal* dominance. In other words, the reinforcement of older imperialist ideologies of dominance will continue to play an important role in the future, however, they can not be assumed always to be already in place by pointing to the dominant structures of communication. Meaning does not depend upon how things are but more on how they are signified and interpreted. Of course the material relations that are structurating global information flow continue to impact upon these levels, however media forms of imperialism are more contingent phenomena than earlier schools of theorising seemed aware. In fact I would argue that the most significant bias within world communication is spatial and state based rather than imperialistic. By this I mean that new centres of regional cultural power and the nation-state are the current most important agents of governance in respect of systems of mass communication.

4   The image being presented here is of world communications caught somewhere between the ordered structuration of modernity, and the disordered flux of post-modernity. The need for a world-wide communicative democracy where public spaces are made available for plural identities, cross-cultural communication and a deeper understanding of the most pressing issues facing humanity, is unlikely to be delivered by commercial or exclusively national processes and passions. Yet the emergence of new communities of identification, the development of communication technology, the restructuring of national spaces, and the speeded up nature of communication

have all paradoxically helped force such considerations onto the agenda. This argument seems particularly pressing if viewed from the position of some of the Earth's poorer nations and regions.

In a study of media cultures in a small multicultural village in Podapadu, South India, 'information' about the outside world had three main sources. They were visitors, migrant workers and the media of mass communication (Hartmann *et al.*, 1989). The media were being developed in a context that had previously been dominated by traditional cultural practices that could be associated with drama (natakam) and the mixing of prose and poetry (katha). During the period of study these dimensions were being transformed, as it seemed that the young in particular displayed a growing desire for the medium of film. The impact of the newspaper industry was in turn restricted due to poor literacy levels, however most households had access to a radio. Despite the capacity of radio to reach most of the people within the village it was the local power holders who were most able to transform their structurally powerful position into political knowledge concerning development issues. To participate in the debates that affect us locally, nationally and more globally, world citizens need access to a range of material and symbolic resources.

This I think points to a dual strategy with regard to global media cultures. First, it remains important that plural media cultures are able to reach the world's citizens where they eat and sleep, where they work and love, and where they care for others and spend their leisure time. This presupposes specifically media strategies concerning the development of a rich mix of media cultures globally in such a way that respects the cultural autonomy and diversity evident within the world's regions. Complex plural debates should be encouraged in place of fundamentalist ambitions that silence and discipline open discussion. Such an aim would seek to deconstruct the dichotomy between market conceptions of the free flow of intellectual opinion held by the West, and the struggle for national autonomy most often represented by the 'Third World'. In its place a global form of citizenship would seek to ensure communicative rights and obligations that were held irrespective of ethnic identity. Secondly, such a desire also suggests an extra-media strategy that not only grants opportunities for participation but empowers people through literacy campaigns, the provision of rights of access and the local resources that enable the least powerful to have their voices heard. Such a dual strategy would reimagine a form of cultural citizenship where the diversity of world cultures might be simultaneously maintained, eroded and transformed by opening our horizons to the voices and perspectives of others. This would help us all to turn inwards to examine our collectively held identities, while simultaneously looking outwards protesting against the very limits of our experience. If such conditions began to be satisfied we might then be able to talk of a global cosmopolitanism that was not restricted to a conspicuous minority.

126

Such transformations could only be carried through by what might be termed a global ethic. Such an ethic would responsibly seek to open out communicative relations with others in a spirit which respects both rights and responsibilities. This would neither seek to impose a unified culture nor blandly celebrate the diversity of cultures. A global ethic would question national egoism, the pretensions of capital and the capacity of technology to deliver global forms of understanding and reciprocity. This ethic would not solve the world's mounting communication problems, but would at least try to ensure that human beings have access to the material and symbolic resources which would help provide the forms of interpretative understanding that are so desperately sought by those most in need of truthful representation, human rights and consideration. These concerns, as we have seen, are better orientated through the questions of cultural democratisation than they are through concerns of media imperialism and some of the more recent projections of post-modernism.

The ambivalences of media globalisation

Here I want to close by looking at some of the ambivalences of globalisation that are not really evident in talk that has become associated with concerns around blanket commercialisation and/or cultural fragmentation. More contradictory frames become strikingly evident if we consider two recent documents that concern the British context. The first is the parliamentary report on the BBC published in 1994 called *The Future of the BBC; Serving the Nation, Competing World-wide* (HMSO, 1994). The document commits the BBC to reflecting the national identity of the United Kingdom, to quality programming and to the promotion of diverse tastes among the audience, all of which have a long history in the provision of public service broadcasting. However a different tone is struck in other parts of the document where concern is expressed that the BBC is 'not exploiting its assets sufficiently'. The concern here is that the BBC should draw up a strategic proposal in order to reboot its commercial activities. Commercial pressures mean that, of course, the BBC like other public institutions can not afford to ignore market opportunities opened out by the information revolution. This is particularly evident if we consider that there is likely to be renewed pressure on the BBC's source of finance as its market share dips and as cable and satellite services are developed. Attempts by public broadcasters to juggle the very real contradictions that exist between the principles of a common citizenry ('serving the nation') and that of commercial enterprise ('competing world-wide') will become more pronounced in the future. That public service broadcasters need creatively to manage a commitment to certain values while taking risks in a global market is likely to be one of the key issues which determines the fate of communicative democracy. This is likely to prove increasingly difficult in that they will face competition from multinational media conglomerates, pressures by the state concerning revenue and an increasingly fragmented audience. However, in a world that is increasingly characterised, as we have seen, through the perception of risk and social division the provision of high-quality forms of information in the public interest remains paramount. The fact that the public broadcasters are regulated in ways that more commercial services are not means that they will remain important to the public in their ability to deliver knowledge that is both truthful, informative and high in quality.

A different set of dimensions is opened out by a another kind of report. The Third World and Environmental Broadcasting project's report *What in the World is going On? British Television and Global Affairs* in 1995 seeks to point to what they call the 'trend towards insularity' (Cleasby, 1995). They present a powerful case that increased economic competition within the British television market has led to a reduction in the amount of foreign news programmes and documentaries between 1989 and 1994. The paradox here then is that in an age of global interconnectedness British broadcasters are increasingly concerned with more local than global events in their coverage. The report documents what they claim to be a shift from international affairs to a more domestic focus. We might argue that there is an interesting contradiction emerging whereby the increased ability of journalists to send back high-quality forms of information due to the development of new technology (hand-held video-recorders) has been coupled with a more 'restricted' agenda set by broadcasters. In other words, while global media technology opens certain horizons, these are partially closed by the operation of market economics.

Both of these examples neatly point out that the connection between globalisation and the media can not be assumed to be in one direction. On the whole this is the problem with constructing the debate in terms of either full-scale economic colonisation or the promotion of difference and fragmentation. My argument here has been to try and tease out some of the uncertainties contained within a field that will undoubtedly remain in tension.

CHAPTER 6

Post-colonialism and mediated violence: Rwanda, genocide and global media cultures

It was always a question for many of us, me included, whether cultural studies wasn't in some way deeply embedded, even in an unconscious way we couldn't understand, in the problematic of western modernity, that it was untranslatable to other cultures: that there couldn't be an African or an Asian cultural studies. Of course this situation has changed. Globalisation itself, the historical process of globalisation, means that those boundaries are not where they were, even when cultural studies started. It's not the 1960s any more. There are practically no serious, well established forms of culture in the world that are self sufficient and autonomous, out of touch or out of communication with what is going on elsewhere.

[Stuart Hall, interviewed by Kuan-Hsing Chen, 1996: 399]

The intermixing and hybridisation of mobile cultures has become the defining motif of post-modernity. Time–space compression brought about by new media technologies, international travel, diasporic population movements and global economics has meant that whereas modernity became defined through time, post-modernity's dominant metaphor is space. This shift points to an awareness of new levels of global interconnection among the peoples of the Earth who were previously obscured through overtly national perspectives. The work of spatially oriented post-modernists continues to remind us that our experience of place has been radically transformed by the impact of a variety of new social experiences, including electronic media. The geographies in which we now live are not just of physical place, and notions of community may be defined more readily by those with whom we rarely enter into face-to-face relations. Yet while such descriptions have an obvious resonance what is not so clear is the precise relations of interconnection that are being articulated? Have these new forms of connectedness transformed the fate of the poor of the planet? Have images of global need, hardship and distress mobilised vigorous campaigns within dominant Western civil society on their behalf? What are the dominant impressions of 'other' non-Western cultures currently being fostered by global mechanisms of communication? Despite the capacity of the media to bring spatially distant cultures together, are they actually driven further apart by the maintainance of distinction, hierarchy and cultural superiority that has its roots in the colonial rather than the post-colonial world? Here I want to explore these and other questions, with particular reference to the relationship between the so-called First and Third Worlds. Relations here are changing through new migration patterns and economic development. The binary categories of First and Third Worlds no longer adequately map patterns of economic relation or cultural identity. For instance the USA by the year 2000 will no longer have a majority population categorised by a white European heritage (Morley, 1996). The centre of world culture therefore is not only losing its economic dominance but is being centrally transformed by the 'invasion' of peripheral cultures. These new dimensions of cultural complexity also have implications for British identity formation. The decolonisation of the British Empire has meant that 6.3 per cent of the population can be defined as ethnic minorities, while fostering a dominant national culture that has had great difficulty in accepting the multi-ethnic make-up of the nation along with the legitimacy of other interconnected cultures (Hall, 1996). As Stuart Hall (1996) has remarked, just as the myth of the self-sufficient economy has been debunked by the operation of global markets, so in terms of identity, through the play of similarity and difference, have our conceptions of self and other been reformulated. These insights are fostered by the notion that the clear demarcation between the First and Third Worlds, home and abroad, and familiar and foreign have been disrupted by cross-cultural interrelations. The 'Third World' it seems is not where we thought it was.

Despite these important theoretical developments, what is not clear is the significance of this new cultural intermixing. For instance, J. B. Thompson (1995) has recently claimed that through the development of global media individuals are able to gain a surface impression of lives and cultures which differ significantly from their own. This will obviously have different implications in different contexts. For instance, it might mean that the Earth's poor are familiar with the lifestyle of the globe's rich in that they are all acutely aware of what they do not have. However, what is not clear, is that the globe's rich and powerful are similarly acquainted with the material condition of the poor on their own doorstep and further afield. These are all examples of the new dimensions that have been opened up by global media, and yet if we are witnessing the renegotiation of what is central and what is marginal, there are features which remain under-theorised by the approach outlined so far. These can be characterised as: (1) the absence of social justice; (2) the maintenance of ethnocentrism; (3) the mediation of violence and its relation to civil society; (4) that most 'Third World' states suffer from an absence of modernity rather than post-modernism; and (5) the hybridised culture of post-modernism was prefigured by modernity. Let us take each of these points in turn.

1 The global traffic in peoples and symbolic goods has presided over an ever-increasing gulf between the poorest nations of the South and the richest nations of the North. According to the World Bank's development

report (in terms of GDP) the ratio of resources between the 20 per cent most developed nations and the 20 per cent least developed nations was 30 : 1 in 1960, 32 : 1 in 1970, 45 : 1 in 1980 and 60 : 1 in 1990 (Therborn, 1995). It is also notable that global environmental degradation is not primarily caused by the newly industrialised nations but by the richest 26 per cent who are responsible for three-quarters of the world's energy consumption, and yet it is likely that it will be the poorer nations of the South who are most affected by processes such as global warming. Indeed, it is a chilling statistic that 30 000 of the world's children die each day from preventable diseases, and that the basic nutritional and family planning needs of the planet could be met by 5 per cent of global military expenditure. Finally, if we add to this pessimistic equation that most of the world's global institutions (with the United Nations as a possible exception) including the World Bank, NATO and the IMF are directly controlled by the Earth's rich and powerful then this might lead to some tough questions being asked of the relation between cultural and more overtly *material* transformations. That is, the rapid flow of images and information across the borders of nations has had, it would seem, little impact upon more stable social relations that have been ushered in by modernity. The explosion of contemporary information cultures, it is true, can be linked to more transnational elements of civil society, however, this has yet to be forcibly reflected back upon the political organisation of the main centres of power and privilege that continue to exist within the world (*Real World Coalition*, 1996).

2   Another way of approaching post-colonial arguments in respect of hybrid cultures is to ask what kinds of images, perspectives and representations inform our citizens as to the life-world contexts of spatially connected others? In certain respects, modern media cultures routinely transmit the symbolic material of 'distant' cultures into more local contexts. The post-colonial thesis is that this process has made it much more difficult to differentiate between the 'First' and 'Third Worlds' with the production of films by black people settled in the old colonial countries, the global spread of news reports, the development of world cinema and large-scale media events such as Live Aid in 1985. Yet, as Julien and Mercer (1996) argue, the partial deconstruction of the centre and the margin has not meant that we have entered into a post-ethnocentric age. Any study of modern ethnocentrism, therefore, would have to examine the material and symbolic interconnections both internal and external to the nation. By this I mean that the study of ethnocentrism is a complex phenomena as it involves the discursive and intersubjective relations within and between nations.

3   Zygmunt Bauman (1994) argues that the global development of media technology has brought a new everyday barbarism into the fabric of our lives. The delivery of global news stories involving war, hatred, killing

and maiming has increasingly meant that 'ordinary' interactions take place against a backdrop of cruelty. Bauman reasons that the sheer monotony of such images has a wearing and desensitising effect on the viewer. An over-familiarity with atrocity creates a distancing effect between the viewer and the images represented on the screen. This mass indifference to an everyday 'carnival of cruelty' offsets feelings of obligation, connectedness and concern. The electronic mediation of real suffering has, for Bauman, begun to eradicate distinctions between information and entertainment, image and reality, and pleasure and moral obligation. For instance, in the televising of the Gulf War the spectacle of shooting and bombing could easily be confused with plot lines taken from Hollywood movies or the simulated effects of computer games. The culture fostered by the conversion of cruelty into a televisual experience is one of distance, indifference and finally boredom.

John Keane (1996) more precisely locates, like Bauman, the relatively secure democratic zones of peace which cover only a seventh of the world's population. The rest of the world, arguably, might consume such images in a less voyeuristic mode, in that they are living in zones of warlordism, civil and international wars and random acts of violence. A different disposition towards violence is potentially fostered by cultures which are relatively (although this ignores problems of criminal and domestic violence) peaceful. A diet of horror and slasher movies, video games, gruesome crime stories and tabloid murders is freely available to anyone within wealthy metropolitan cultures who wish to be shocked, thrilled or merely frightened silly by such material. This points to yet another stark contrast in that there is all the difference in the world between viewers whose main experience of violence is mediated and those who are living within the orbit of the constant threat of its eruption. This point is particularly evident in Schlesinger's (1993) study of women viewers of violent films. One of the many interesting aspects highlighted by the discussions was the 'distinctiveness' of the women who had been the victims of domestic and sexual violence. Even the most sympathetic portrayal of women who were subject to violence was viewed by women who had had similar experiences with extreme forms of ambivalence. The concern was, particularly in the case of sexual violence, that such acts, even if negatively portrayed, could be interpreted in a pleasurable way. This might then in turn lead to the legitimation of violent acts against women. There is then a distinction to be drawn between those who are able to enjoy relatively peaceful co-relations with one another where social struggles are mostly symbolic and dialogic, and places where the possibilities for democratic dialogue are negligible, given the continued threat of force. This inevitably leads to the notion that a diverse and pluralistic civil society, which allows for the negotiation of identity and critical rational exchange, also needs to be relatively peaceful. The public and private reduction of violence within civil society, which for democratic reasons needs to be made 'visible' by the media, is an essential component of any democratic society that does not want to run the risk of descending into law and order type solutions.

4   The relative decline of the nation-state has become one of the central topics of recent political and social theory. The argument, now well known, that the state is permeated by the flow of post-modern culture and economic capital has led to arguments in respect of a post-national or a post-colonial cultural condition. Michael Mann (1993) has argued that this view can only be accepted as long as we acknowledge that while state powers are diminishing in some areas they are intensifying in others. The states of developed Western nations have become increasingly involved in the regulation of 'private life' during the twentieth century. State authority has been progressively widened to include the regulation of smoking in public places, domestic violence, education and the care of children. The notion that nations are being universally post-modernised can also be challenged if we consider that many of the states in poorer countries are suffering from inadequate modernity, rather than post-modernity. That is, in the European context, nations progressively constructed centralised communications systems, national education systems and other national cultural institutions along with certain citizenship entitlements and obligations. However, in the less-developed world most states have been born through decolonisation processes set in train after the Second World War, and have poorly based state and civil society mechanisms. As Hannerz (1992) argues the states at the periphery often lack the material underpinning of European states and corresponding regulatory capacities to control the cultural traffic flowing from the metropolitan centre. This does not mean that 'softer' states are necessarily swamped with unwanted material (as the market may be negligible) but that there will occur a certain amount of 'cultural dumping' of cheap metropolitan goods past their sell-by date. These social conditions obviously make it difficult to foster the conditions necessary for the kind of pluralistic civil society necessary for democratic relations. The culture of democracy itself presupposes the maintenance of pluralistic communication systems, certain levels of education, relatively peaceful internal and external relations, diverse forms of political representation and the satisfaction of basic economic and material needs. Notably these preconditions are strikingly absent in the Earth's less-developed regions.

5   The final point to make, in this brief section, is that the newness of cultural mixing is a specifically Western experience given that previously colonised states have been living with diversity since the advent of modernity. We might translate the problematic of living with diversity as a problem of modernity rather than post-modernity if viewed from a Southern rather than a Western perspective. This would allow for the fact that Western modernity can be characterised through capitalist work practices and a rational bureaucracy developed at the level of the nation-state

obscuring their exploitative relation with the colonies. In this respect, many 'Third World' cities prefigure the development of more culturally fragmented and diverse identities evident in Western metropolitan conurbations (King, 1995).

In tandem, Cornel West (1993) has argued that the new cultural politics of difference should actually be understood in terms of the decline of Europe's dominance over the world during the twentieth century. In 1914 European colonial domination was such that the continent dominated half of the globe's land and a third of its people. The intellectual challenges to Euro-centrism and the political questions orientated around questions of difference have to be seen in the context of these changing historical and spatial relationships in world society.

What then do these items show? Taken together I think that they complicate some of the more overt post-modern rhetoric in respect of the series of transformations that have been ushered in by spatial flows of image and information. While it is understandable that those seeking to articulate the post-modern will search for what is new about these relations, there is a discernible tendency to displace other features which influence the mediated relations between so-called 'First' and 'Third Worlds'. Indeed a more normative focus might have been maintained if cultural questions were more forcibly tied to what I have termed cultural citizenship. Such dimensions then have implications for the wider structuration of cultural and political relations. For instance, the dominant construction of poorer nations is as a 'social problem' through the reporting of famine, refugee crisis, war and terrorism. Arguably the maintenance of these dominant frameworks can be connected to the continuation of both dependent and subordinate economic relations. This is most definitely not to argue (as in Marxist accounts of the base/superstructure) that economic relations of inequality functionally require ideological images and representations to support Western superiority. But there is surely more than a contingent relation between the fact that global news agencies like CNN, the BBC and NBC, etc. are predominantly owned and controlled by Western news corporations, and the ethnocentric bias that persists against the world's poorer regions and nations. These dimensions, however, can perhaps best be explored through a more detailed overview of the specific relations between different world regions in terms of the flow of images, opinion and critical commentary. However, if we are to take the point about spatial variability seriously then we would have to investigate the ways in which local, national and transnational public spheres interact with one another in order to help shape economic, political and cultural social relations. Therefore, before moving on to my main case study, I want to provide a brief discussion of the internal mediated relations between the white majority and black minorities in British society. This will enable the analysis to look at cultural relations internal to Rwanda and Britain in respect of ethnicity, and the dominant flow of images that took place between them during the genocide.

The black in the Union Jack

Much of the subsequent argument is focused upon the development of television and film industries in respect of the changing frontier in media cultures between a hegemonically defined white, southern, Englishness and more marginally defined black cultures in contemporary British society. The historical mutability of this relation has, as we shall see, helped bring questions of multiculturalism, ethnicity and national identity onto the agenda both academically and in terms of the practical focus of media policy. Karen Ross (1996) argues that the history of black people closely follows that of other marginalised groups in that in the 1950s and 1960s there was a very minimal black presence on television screens and when they did appear it was as negative myths and stereotypes. However, due to increasing demands for black people to have rights to *representation* and the more widely accepted need for blacks to have a more inclusive presence in British society, television began to take the context of a multicultural society more seriously. The determining political moment for this seems to have been the Brixton riots of 1981 and the subsequent Scarman Report that emphasised the import-ance of British institutions becoming more widely accessible to minority groups. This led to both the BBC and Channel 4 developing documentary style programming that sought to voice black people's problems with white racism. However, television of this type was soon replaced with magazine and discussion features (*Black on Black* and *Eastern Eye*) that displaced an overriding concern with racism with that of the exploration of multicultural difference. These programmes help deconstruct the previously assumed unitary category of an essential black subject, and emphasise the fact that there is no universal black perspective (Hall, 1996b). However, for Ross, this transition should also be viewed ambivalently, in that by displacing a concern around racism it opened the space for the more sensational tabloid style journalism of the 1990s that focused on black sexuality, crime and lifestyle more generally.

Despite these transitions the main problems that face black people and television are similar to those in other areas such as film. These would include ghettoisation (the appearance of one black sitcom, or one black news programme is considered enough), lack of access to the media in gen-eral and what might be termed the 'burden of representation'. This process, connected to questions of broader ethnocentrism, ghettoisation and access means that when black programmes are actually made they are expected to represent the whole community. This issue has been explored in British black film cultures by Kobena Mercer (1994) who argues that the devel-opment of a black British film aesthetics has been particularly important in challenging the representation of a homogeneous black British identity. Notably the history of black cinema in the British context has followed a similar path to that of television in that invisibility and racism in mostly white films is followed by the articulation of an essentialist black response and eventually a more deconstructive stance in the fluid representation of identity. Further, there is also, as I indicated, a recognised problem in the sense that there is so little space currently available for independent black culture that there is enormous pressure for black film makers and producers to be seen 'to get it right'. This promotes expectations (interestingly rarely experienced by whites) that they are speaking for all black people everywhere. These issues, we should remind ourselves, occur in a context where, despite some of the very real advances that have been made, more independent black voices are rarely heard among minority communities, but are especially absent among the white majority. The black in the Union Jack, as Paul Gilroy (1987) might say, is still largely defined in terms of the hegemonically defined majority culture that disallows uncomfortable expressions of difference and the re-negotiation of shared national symbols.

Quite apart from the current articulation of 'blackness' as a shared national identity it is not clear what the future of media cultures holds for minority communities in the British context. On one level, it is likely that minority groups will be attracted (if they are able to afford it) to cable and satellite productions orientated around niche marketing. There is already evidence of this process within British society with the development of IDTV (subsidiary of US company Black Entertainment Television) that includes entertainment from the USA, Africa and Asia. This network is Britain's first black entertainment channel, and was launched in June 1993 (Ross, 1996) The problem here, however, is that cable, given its overwhelmingly commercial orientation, is unlikely to become the focus of new and original programming relating to black British experience, will exclude those unable to afford the service, and will inevitably fail to engage white viewers on critical questions such as racism. The public channels, with their more overtly national focus and commitment to the inclusion of minority groups and development of multicultural broadcasting are more likely to be the successful target of interventionist struggles for the equal recognition of all non-white peoples in the national community. Yet, as we shall see, if black struggles have made some headway internally to the nation-state, the picture looks less optimistic when we consider the representation of non-white peoples through the global news media. Inevitably given the national orientation of black media struggles this has meant that the culture of reporting events at a distance has escaped the critical scrutiny of the host national culture. The aim of the following sections is to explore these issues in reporting the Rwandan genocide in the context of global media representations.

Media, representation and Africa

Recently many of the debates connected with post-colonialism have pointed to the ideological necessity of 'decolonising' the global or at least Western imagination (Pieterse and Parekh, 1995). This means critically reworking the West's cultural conception of itself in respect of its historical relation with colonialism and empire, and the continued relations of force between North and South. Such a project, as we have seen, entails deconstructing lingering forms of colonial nostalgia, breaking with Eurocentrism and rethinking existing relations through more culturally complex frameworks. The legacy of colonialism continues to inform contemporary images of 'non-Western' cultures as well as the West's own collective self-identity.

In traditional colonial imagery, Africa was seen as a world of nature rather than of culture. The most popular image of the African male was of a primitive savage or warrior who needed to be civilised and cultured by the West. The African's lack of technical know-how and ignoble customs represented a homogeneous people incapable of self-government or civilised behaviour. These cultural images and representations evident within Western literature and the newspapers of the colonial administration served to justify the continued dominance of European nations and maintain a sharp distinction between civilised and uncivilised cultures. It was an imperative of imperialist ideologies to repress any hint of similarity between the peoples of the North and South and thereby conceal the political and economic links that exist between them. Much of the research in this area has been built upon the directions opened out by Said (1978) who demonstrated how discourses, values and patterns of knowledge served to construct the facts about 'other' cultures. Said uncovers the ways in which Western forms of power and knowledge combine in order to divide the globe between the Occident and the Orient. The former is the site of human values and rationality, while the latter is seen as irrational, dangerous and exotic. Similar to what was described above, Orientalism reduced the complex interrelations between East and West to simple binary oppositions. The power of the West in relations with the East and the South was to be able to name the sites of cultural difference, while maintaining colonial inequalities. The discursive construction of difference served to mask ideological relations and repress more ambivalent cultural connections. Despite many of the criticisms that have been levelled at Said, he has sparked a number of works all pertaining to be more sensitive to the cultural construction of 'other' cultures (Turner, 1994b). However, according to Pieterse (1992), what is currently lacking in the literature is a detailed examination of the ways such assumptions are being rearticulated in contemporary image cultures.

These dimensions have been explored by all too few contemporary perspectives. Notably if we explore the cultural flow of imagery between the North and South it is overwhelmingly one way. That is, while representations of the 'Third World' remain important in terms of global intersubjective relations this should not obscure the fact that the vast amount of cultural representations and perspectives are moving in the opposite direction. Hence while the West use the South as a dumping group for out-of-date cultural products, the West receives images of the South that are discursively shaped by well-worn stereotypes. For instance, recent studies of the ideological construction of Africa in the British press and global media generally by Brooks (1995) and Sorenson (1991) point towards a remarkable consistency in this area. Although concerned with different aspects and time frames in the reporting of Africa, both Brookes and Sorenson argue that the media tend to naturalise African conflicts by inadequately contextualising the reported events in the appropriate political and historical context. Ideologically this reproduces a tendency to neglect the historical location of Africa within colonial and neo-colonial social relations. Africa, in this reading, is represented as intrinsically violent and anti-democratic while constituted through tribal rule and excessive use of force. Further, the continent's economic underdevelopment is often explained through anti-modern forms of superstition and cultural backwardness. Overall this promotes a view of the 'Third World' as a passive recipient of Western generosity as well as being intrinsically dangerous and insecure. Sorensen and Brookes speculate that these ideologies serve a dual purpose in that ethnocentric discourses promote satisfying feelings of Western superiority and that the otherwise troubling fact of 'Third World' poverty can be explained with reference to their own cultural lack. The perpetuation of Western superiority, in this reading, provides a forceful means of legitimating existing geo-political relations of dominance. This differs somewhat from the picture offered by those who simply want to talk about increasing cultural instability and displacement. Rather, these considerations point to a picture that is articulated through the mechanisms of modernity (relative stability, rigid forms of cultural dominance and difference, etc.) and post-modernity (more uncertain social relations and less predictable spatial flows of culture) than is evident in much of the literature.

Racism and the psyche

The complexity of contemporary racist ideology has brought about a number of new and original critical engagements at the border between sociological thinking and psychoanalysis. Racism has been explored through a number of theoretical traditions, the most prominent being Klienian and Lacanian tropes. Both approaches, I would argue, have much to offer a contemporary understanding of racist discourse in the context of modern popular culture. Psychoanalytic frames can contribute to our understanding of the functioning of racist ideologies through the introduction of concepts of psychic splitting, lack and projection, all of which help to explain the irrational fears and anxieties that inevitably accompany racist *thinking*. Racism, in this respect, is explained both through the ways in which *whiteness* and its other came to be defined through an encounter with dark-skinned people, and the accompanying cultural and unconscious dimensions that are played through. Both psychoanalytic and sociological dimensions are crucial if we are to understand the interlocking of modern institutions, and the often passionate responses of the self in the reproduction of racism. Both Klien (Mitchell, 1986) and Lacan (1977) offer what I would describe as different definitions of human nature that are not necessarily mutually exclusive requiring that we make a choice between them. There is not, however, the space here to enter into an extended debate with these two perspectives mainly because this has already been done elsewhere, and my own interest lies in the interpretative dimensions that they potentially reveal in modern racism (Elliott, 1992; Flax, 1990). This will inevitably mean that my expositions of the rich bodies of critical analysis that can be associated with Klien and Lacan can only be referred to briefly in this context.

The work of psychoanalyst Melanie Klien is built upon the idea that our unconscious desires and needs are structured by human relationships. Her research explores the emotional ambivalences that emerge in the inter-subjective space between infant and the primary caretaker in the earliest phases of human life. Klien famously opens out an understanding of the self through what she calls the 'paranoid–schizoid position' and the 'depressive position'. According to Klien, the dependent young infant fears that the carer (usually the mother) will withdraw emotional sustenance, which deflects early aggressive feelings outside of the self onto the adult's body. The emptying out of aggressive feelings onto the body of the carer however means that the body of the other comes to be experienced as bad. The return of the infant's destructive feelings leads to psychic splitting in an attempt to preserve good parts of the carer, against the projected bad parts. In this pre-Oedipal stage of development, the infant splits the carer into sustaining and persecuting objects. The forms of paranoid splitting characteristic of this phase acts as a defence against the fear that the young infant will be overwhelmed by the death drive and thereby annihilate the good object. The importance of loving and hating the same object is that it generates an anxiety that can only be partially resolved by projecting the bad feelings that emerge within the self into the body of the other. Good parts of the self are therefore protected at this and later stages through processes of denial, feelings of omnipotence and psychic splitting. Yet, and this is important, Klien emphasises that paranoid splitting paves the way for a more integrative emotional state. The infant realises that the good and bad objects are actually related to the same person, that is, the body of the primary carer. The depressive position, which emerges within this period, allows the infant to experience feelings of guilt and remorse as there is a growing unconscious sense that the object of love and hate are focused on the same object. Depressive feelings are the beginning of the recognition that connected others are also persons, not simply the receptacles for the projection of one's anxiety. As Thomas Ogden (1989) has argued, the depressive mode (feelings of resolution and containment) and the paranoid–schizoid mode (feelings of chaos and persecution) embody separate but related feelings. They both involve a relation to the other which is experienced as either a source of concern (depressive) or more instrumentally through what the other can either do to me or for me (paranoid–schizoid). How then might this admittedly condensed account of early psychic processes help us understand racist ideology?

Michael Rustin (1991) argues that racism often trades upon mechanisms of idealisation and denigration similar to those mapped by Klien. This does not of course mean that racism is a product of human nature, but that ideologically it may become embedded in psychic mechanisms that are extremely resistant to rational questioning. The splitting between positive and negative poles of identification can be linked to states of mind inherent in racist constructions. The denigration of an other could involve the satisfaction of an unconscious desire to expel something uncomfortable from the self or social group and thereby promote feelings of inner purity. For instance, Kovel (1995) claims that animality was projected onto black male bodies by colonists due to the deep unease that puritan capitalism experienced in respect of the sensuous nature of sexuality. Race then was an empty category into which the colonisers could empty anxieties concerning their own bodies and sexualities. The displacement of animality onto the 'other' therefore enabled the white colonisers to maintain an image of themselves as pure and unsullied by associations with nature. Notions of inner superiority are maintained by splitting away parts which would seemingly threaten this self-identity. What is being denied here is the onset of more ambivalent and, dare we say, depressive identifications that would view the other as being more similar to ourselves than racist ideologies care to admit.

Lacanian perspectives, on the other hand, build upon a view of the subject that is both constituted through language and the *imaginary* order. In Lacan's (1977) famous essay on the mirror stage, he describes how the infant, who is still unable to control basic bodily functions, recognises his or her self in a mirror thereby generating a sense of unified selfhood. The infant sees a reflection in the mirror and receives a gratifying image of an integrated self. This constitutes a process of ideological misrecognition in that the mirror provides an image of wholeness thereby alienating the infant from its actual condition of fragmentation and chaos. For Lacan the notion of a unified ego is born through a process of narcissistic illusion. Yet if the mirror phase speaks of an alienated subjectivity this is also true of the infant's entry into language. What happens here is that the infant's unity with the mother is torn apart by being inserted into the symbolic order. The small infant is forced to break with the body of the mother to encounter the domain of language under the law of the father. This constitutes a fundamental (read ontological) 'lack' in the human subject in that once separated from the mother's body it must represent its desires through language (the discourse of the 'other'). The individual is therefore excluded from the domain of the imaginary to be embedded within the significatory structure of patriarchal culture. The imaginary order of fullness and plenitude, the product of the mother–child relation and the mirror phase, is permanently displaced by the operation of language and culture. The problem is that, despite the impossibility of recovering from the narcissistic wound, the human subject will inevitably try to recover images and representations, like that of the phallus, that encourage fantasies of oneness. However, Lacan is clear, such strategies are doomed to failure as subjects are de-centred through the operation of language (we are all, if you like, fashioned by linguistic distinctions we do not author) and can never fully realise the demands we make for love. This introduces a fundamental and irreducible 'lack' into the drama of the human condition.

Homi Bhabha (1994) has utilised Lacanian theory in order to investigate the nature of colonialist discourse. The aim of such discursive practices, he claims, is to fix the 'other' unambiguously ideologically. For Bhabha the cultural strategies of racial superiority 'connotes rigidity and an unchanging order as well as disorder, degeneracy and demonic repetition' (Bhabha, 1994: 66). The most important trope here is that of the stereotype which must be endlessly repeated in order to ward off the anxiety that it could never be proven. The stereotype is 'excessive' and must be fetishistically repeated to mask more ambivalent forms of difference. Hence the racial stereotype, for Bhabha, does not so much mean the setting up of a false image but the projection of unconscious fantasy. For instance, the fixing of the black 'other' through discourse gives the white subject a narcissistic sense of wholeness and internal purity. The repetitive quality of the stereotypes could therefore be explained through an inevitably flawed attempt culturally to reify a sense of white omnipotence that is always threatened in Lacanian terms by lack. Just as the infant in the mirror stage is able to escape his or her own disintegration through a projected image of wholeness so colonialist discourse is able through its 'fullness' to project a sense of its own authority. Furthermore, the repetitive nature of the stereotype is underlined by the notion that, just as the child makes futile attempts to cling to the illusory nature of the ego, colonialist ideology is constantly being threatened by the irruption of heterogeneity from other positions. Bhabha's understanding of colonial discourse reveals a far more impermanent state of affairs than might otherwise be imagined through conventional uses of the term stereotype. Colonial discourse, like the relation between ego identity and more unconscious manifestations, is constantly shadowed and threatened by a fear of its own disintegration. Its continuous recycling through media images and the discourses of popular culture is both evidence of its power and its inscribing in 'lack'. As Castoriadis (1997) remarks the psyche takes refuge in racism as a means of refusing reality and the contagion of difference. Yet on the other side of racism there is an insistent voice which repeats 'our walls are made of plastic, our acropolis of papier-mâché' (Castoriadis, 1997: 29).

Whereas Rustin accounts for the paranoid nature of racist frames, Bhabha, as we saw above, gives a reading of its repetitive and rather obvious quality.

Yet while both of these approaches could contribute to an understanding of some of the more enduring features of racism, they are not intended as an explanation in and of themselves. As Kovel (1995) reminds us, racism is grounded in institutions and material social circumstances that underlie and help reproduce racism. In this view, racism depends not so much on the constant features of ontological lack or psychic splitting, as important as these undoubtedly are, but on the degradation of one group to the advantage of another. The racist representation of blacks in the West and images of 'cultural backwardness' of those in the South reinforces continued structural inequalities within and between these domains. My contention, as we shall see, is that such features continue to be present in contemporary image cultures.

Genocide and social theory

Social theorists have long been aware of the connection between the state and violence. Max Weber defined the state through this intellectual hinge when he argued that the state was a human community that claimed the 'monopoly of the legitimate use of physical force' within a given territory (Kasler, 1998). Indeed, Anthony Giddens (1994) argues that the pre-modern state may be distinguished from the modern state in that the political centre was unable to secure control over the mechanisms of violence. The modern state, by contrast, has through improved communications structures, the intensification of internal surveillance, the bureaucratisation of administration procedures and the creation of a professional military been largely internally pacified. Yet these features are perhaps more prevalent in the developed world (as we shall see) and do not distinguish between different kinds and categories of state violence. State violence can be connected to force used externally or internally, a police baton charge during a strike or industrial dispute, the daily punishment of prisoners or the systematic use of torture against political opponents. Perhaps because of the assumed unitary conception of violence it has meant that sociologists have rarely explored features such as genocide. Genocide arguably remains connected to notions of state violence, while maintaining a clear trajectory of its own. For instance, the practice of war can draw a distinction between combatants and non-combatants, but this is never the case with genocide. This does not mean however that war might not become genocidal and that war and genocide do not share certain features. Helen Fine (1990) offers the following definition:

> Genocide is sustained purposeful action by a perpetrator to physically destroy a collectivity directly or indirectly, through interdiction of the biological and social reproduction of group members, sustained regardless of the surrender or lack of threat offered by the victim. (Fine, 1990: 24)

In addition, Fine further qualifies this statement by adding that genocide is usually practised by the state, and seeks forcibly to destroy social collectivities that are based upon birth rather than choice.

Perhaps the most theoretically accomplished investigation of genocide has been proposed by Zygmunt Bauman's (1989) study of the Holocaust. Bauman argues that the Holocaust radically questions the assumption that modernity acts as a civilising force that would eventually remove violence from the fabric of everyday life. In fact what has happened is that violence has become ambiguously both more and less visible. While the media, increasingly it seems, focuses on violent events, the growth and specialisation of the military has institutionally separated the organisation of violence from public spaces and converted it into a rational and calculable phenomenon free of emotion. The broader problem is that the use of technical and bureaucratic reason has removed questions of violence from those of moral responsibility. This is instituted through a formal division of labour where orders and commands are issued from an internal heirarchy,where technical tasks become rationally separated and actions are measured in terms of their effectiveness. That is, in formal bureaucratic criteria the destruction of human beings can be reduced to questions of efficiency. The Holocaust in general and genocide in particular becomes part of the modern drive to achieve a 'fully designed, fully controlled world' (Bauman, 1989: 93). Genocide then tends to occur through the intermixing of an ideologically motivated political authority and rational bureaucratic institutions. If we take Bauman and Fine together this helps build up a picture of genocide as being less about 'emotional excess' than a form of purposive–rational action that attempts systematically to eliminate an 'other' group. Genocide, in this definition, becomes a peculiarly modern form of utopianism that seeks to destroy a sense of the interconnected nature of human society, and with it any shared sense of moral responsibility we might harbour for others.

Rwanda: the social and historical context

Why focus on Rwanda one might ask? There are perhaps two answers to this question, one of which is personal and the other intellectual. First, I can vividly remember the television pictures of Rwanda refugees pouring into the camps in Zaire. I was struck by how shocking and genuinely moving such images were, but also by how little, despite the huge amounts of television news and documentary I consumed, I actually 'found out' about a place very distant from where I live. Indeed, only later, conducting this research, did it strike me that the pictures revealed as much as they obscured. The other reason is perhaps less emotional and more cognitive; that is, that I wanted a case study that would more sharply focus some of the theoretical questions that have been posed on globalisation and media elsewhere in this book. The aim here was to move the discussion to a different level of abstraction opening out some of the complexities of inter-cultural exchange.

To comprehend the Rwandan massacre, I shall argue, it has to be under-stood as a genocide rather than a 'tribal conflict'. But to do this, the events leading up to the genocide have to be placed within a historical context that addresses the problem of Rwandan state formation and the construction of the identities Batutsi and Bahutu. The original Rwandan state was based upon the domination of the Batutsi (pastoral aristocracy) over the Bahutu (landed peasantry). This was not a caste-like relationship as the two groups shared a common culture, religion and language with opportunities for the Bahutu to rise in the hierarchy of the precolonial state (Mamdani, 1996). After the First World War, the Belgians colonised Rwanda and used the pre-viously created state to operate a form of indirect rule transferring colonial powers to a Batutsi aristocracy (Heush, 1995). The Belgians, who as colonists took over from the Germans, ruled on the basis of a racialised distinction between the Batutsis and Bahutus. The colonists through mechanisms of scientific classification (measuring of skulls, noses, height) sought to distin-guish the Tutsis from the Hutus and thereby racialise more fluid ethnic distinctions. The bureaucratic classification of Batutsi and Bahuti into hier-archical groups enabled the Belgians to rule through a caste of Batutsi chiefs. To mark this distinction further the Belgians issued security cards in 1926 which strictly categorised people by racial group.

The Batutsis' economic and political dominance in the 1940s and 1950s began to be undermined by developments in the education system and opportunities for economic advancement other than through cattle owner-ship. Many of the Bahutu graduates, who were excluded from numerous other professions, found a career in the church which they used as a plat-form to articulate their grievances. It was in the context of loosening Batutsi economic and social power that a process of decolonisation was commenced after the Second World War. This period, still under colonial dominance, witnessed an unstable period of power sharing between the political repres-entatives of the two main ethnic groups. For instance, after serious violent exchanges the Belgians decided to replace the existing Batutsi chiefs with those of Bahutu origin, which eventually led to the Bahutus winning the first national elections in 1960. After the Belgian withdrawal in 1962, the Bahutus used their new-found political power to drive Batutsis off their land creating a flood of refugees into Barundi, Zaire, Uganda and Tanzania. The displaced Batutsis responded by mounting a retaliatory invasion which led to 10 000 people being killed by the Bahutu dominated state in 1963. The raids by the Batutsis and the reprisals by the Bahutus took place in the context of almost zero international interest and press coverage. The Bahutus legitimated this strategy by claiming that the Batutsis wished to reinstate the old colonial regime and deprive Bahutus of their newfound social posi-tion. The 1970s and the 1980s witnessed the setting up of one-party rule in Rwanda through the Republican Party for Democracy and Development, and the emergence of the Rwandan Patriotic Front (RPF) based in nearby Uganda campaigning for the return home of the refugees. This increasingly unstable stand-off between the Rwandan state and the RPF lead to an invasion of Rwanda in October 1990 by 700 000 RPF soldiers. The unsuccessful invasion led to yet more massacres of Batutsis living within Rwanda and further political measures being taken against internal political opposition. During this period the government was largely dependent upon foreign aid from France and Belgium (supplying 60 per cent of the budget in the early 1990s) who also supplied the state with military support and largely ignored the communal violence (Human Rights Watch, 1995). The historical development of Rwanda's state therefore exhibits a relative absence of internal pacification, and the increasing intersubjective polarisation of the identities of Batutsis and Bahutus into racialised groups. These factors along with the continued support of the international community and former regional colonial powers provide the historical context for any appreciation of the complexity of the Rwandan genocide.

The build-up to the genocide itself can probably be traced from a report published in March 1993 on human rights abuses by the Rwandan state written by the International Rights Commission. The report reflected on the history of basic human rights abuse, and catalogued the numerous massacres (killing 2000 people) that had been inflicted mostly on the Batutsi population over the past three years. The report culminated in increasing international pressure for the institution of a multi-ethnic democracy within Rwanda. The then president Habyarimana signed an agreement with the RPF allowing for a transitional government to be set up. Yet all the evidence points to the fact that the government had no real intention of giving up power, and in fact mounted an ideological campaign to maintain their authority at all costs. For instance, the incredibly detailed report of the genocide drawn up by the organisation African Rights (1995) provides evidence of the sophisticated preparations for the genocide that were set in place well before the outbreak of violence. These procedures involved the militarisation and development of further racist attitudes of civil society. The two most important institutions governing this process being the creation of a special militia or home guard, and the direct control of the local media. The killing was directly orchestrated by the government using police-men, the militia, armed forces and ordinary civilians. The genocide was sparked off by the shooting down of the president's plane, which was immediately (despite lack of clear evidence) blamed on the RPF. From this point onwards the new prime minister Theodore Sindikubwabo began a systematic genocide against the political opposition and Batutsi ethnics. As the journalist Fergal Keane (1995: 29) has remarked, the genocide is marked by the fact that 'in one hundred days up to one million people were hacked, shot, strangled, clubbed and burned to death. Remember, carve this into your consciousness: one million'. Indeed, such is the horror of the genocide, one of the most difficult aspects to convey is that most of the killing was a largely passionless affair. The African Rights report tells a chilling story of how low technology (machetes being the principal weapon used) was combined with terror (ordinary Bahutus were forced to kill and denounce friends, relatives and sometimes their own children) and bureaucratic procedures (the principal means of targeting Batutsis was through the use of the Identification cards first introduced by the Belgians). The fascistic politics of the government sought to eradicate the presence of the Batutsis from civil society by mass killing, threats and extreme forms of intimidation. These practices were only stopped by the invading RPF finally defeating the government in the middle of July 1994.

Small media and genocide

The social significance of small as opposed to large media has recently been drawn out by Annabelle Srebery-Mohammadi and Ali Mohammadi (1994). They argue, in the context of the Iranian revolution, that it was the political importance of small media such as audiotapes and leaflets that provided the focus for social change. Despite the mainstream media being dominated by the state and Western imports, 'smaller' media were utilised to carry subversive and alternative messages. The Iranian experience, they argue, points to the limits of mechanical notions of cultural imperialism which supposedly overwhelms the cultures of 'Third World' nations with Western values. The centre and periphery model of international power is problematised by the fact that in Iran rapid economic development was coupled with authoritarian politics. Indeed the introduction of the 'Third World' into the equation radically disrupts Eurocentric notions of development in terms of the public sphere moving through progressive oral, literate and electric phases. For instance, in many 'Third World' societies the support for the development of electronic media is more intensely felt than the need to develop mass literacy. Since the 1980s, the disordered flux of communicative mediums that are available in many 'Third World' nations has meant that exile communities are able to send messages to people 'back home', that many of the world's peoples can tune into 'foreign' broadcasts and that an interactive underground can be sustained through small alternative media.

Rwanda follows this example in so far as the main problem with 'local' media was not the dominance of Western perspectives. However, the Rwandan experience does point towards a media which was easily dominated by the government thereby closing down the social space for alternative and contradictory viewpoints. In Rwanda 'ethnic cleansing' was both a material and symbolic process. Part of the terror of the genocide inflicted upon the Rwandan civil society was the extreme sense of social isolation experienced by the government's political opponents and the Batutsis. Due to the government's domination over the media and the systematic elimination of the political opposition the victims of the genocide had little hope of constructing a 'realistic' picture of the outside world. This sense of social isolation and media control is reflected in many of the testimonies gathered by African Rights. These are the words of a nun called Marianne living in a convent in Kigali:

> As the days went by, we felt increasingly cut off from the world and starved for information. The radio was beaming extremist propaganda that was frightening to listen to. It was impossible to have an accurate picture of what was taking place. It was therefore very difficult to know what to do, how to escape this panic, fear and what had become a very difficult life. (African Rights, 1995: 239)

This account signifies one of the most terrifying and inhuman aspects of the genocide (other than the most obvious dimensions more directly related to the killing), that is the fear that no-one is listening. Part of the terror inflicted by the genocide was not only to deny the victims any semblance of cultural citizenship in their host nation, but the sense that 'ordinary people' could be disposed of by the state without its presense being felt in the world media. This again makes the point, as I did earlier, that questions of recognition are simultaneously local, national and global.

The most important medium of communication in Rwanda, especially after the closing down of the press aligned with the opposition, was the radio. For the first 100 days of the genocide the Rwandan state managed to restrict population movement, place severe limits on the mobility of the representatives of the international media, and directly control the information distributed to its own population. The two most important sources of extremist propaganda were the state-run Radio Rwanda and the private station RTLM. Both stations were either directly controlled through formal mechanisms such as the state, or by members of the government privately owning the means of transmission. The other layer of control was that government extremists were able to pressure the journalists through the use of threats, intimidation and fear. The means of propaganda used were not particularly subtle and did not, from the evidence I have seen, require complex decoding procedures. The radio messages directly instructed the Bahutu population to kill the Batutsis, otherwise the claim was that the invading RPF would do likewise to the Bahutu. The government successfully launched a two-pronged strategy of both eliminating the political opposition and dissent in general. For instance, Sixbert Musangamfura, former editor of the Isibo (a newspaper which supported the transition to democracy), argued that before the shooting down of the president's plane, the papers' reports, while hampered by the state, were able to criticise the government. But once the state adopted the extreme 'ethnic politics' that led up to the genocide then any criticism of the government, whether it came from a Bahutu or a Batutsi, was seen as a legitimate target for attack. The control of the radio broadcasts by those promoting the genocide meant that it became converted into an agent of propaganda used to direct the genocidal violence.

Small media in this respect were less a focus for resistance, but a mechanism, due to its lack of systemic complexity, that easily became won over by the state-driven genocide. The Rwandan case would point to the fact that small media are not necessarily sites of resistance. Just as 'smallness' in some instances allows messages to pass unnoticed through grids of control and surveillance, in other contexts, their comparative lack of sophistication could mean that they are more easily subject to the agents of power and authority. The extent to which media become subject to 'outside' control is also related to the medium in question. For example, it is easier for the state to control relatively centralised systems like radio stations than it is to shut down the traffic in 'illegal' audio cassettes. However, as the Rwandan case demonstrates, the subversive potential of such mediums can be controlled by other means such as restricting population movement and other human rights violations.

Televising the genocide: Rwanda and the international media

The overwhelming focus of the television coverage in Rwanda was not on the genocide itself, but on the mass exodus of refugees to nearby Zaire. Rwanda did not translate into an international news event worthy of global television's focus until the RPF had defeated the government army in July 1994, thereby halting the genocide. This led to one million people, mostly Bahutus, fleeing to Zaire where 50 000 of them died of disease, hunger and lack of water. The first the outside world knew of the genocide was when thousands of dead bodies floated over the Tanzanian border into Lake Victoria. Until that point the government had effectively managed to confuse the international media by representing the genocide as a form of tribal violence or civil war which they could not control, and by making sure that the media were denied access to the areas where genocide had taken place. Seemingly both the African and Western media largely accepted the view that the government had very little control over events and that the killing was a mostly 'tribal' affair. The reports of a tribal or civil war spiralling out of control led initially to a reduction of United Nations troops and eventually to their withdrawal. That the 'outside world' accepted the government's line meant that it was able to pursue the practices of genocide largely unimpeded by the international community and the glare of publicity. That agencies such as the United Nations, and the French, German and Belguim governments should misread the situation as a civil war is hard to understand given they all had representatives and troops in the area leading up to the genocide. The French government in particular were actively involved in the supply of arms, military training, the provision of troops to assist the army and the extension of credit facilities, all of which aided the government in the build-up to the genocide. According to Gerard Prunier (1995), it was largely due to France's guilt over its complicity with the genocidal government and for 'internal' political reasons that they launched 'Operation Turquoise', which set up a 'humanitarian' zone within Rwanda. Despite the claims made by the French government the intervention failed to stop the genocide, and did little to address the real needs of a devastated nation.

How then, we might ask, given the complicity of the Western media and international agencies with the extremist Rwandan government, did the media represent the genocide and the subsequent refugee crisis? What were the ideological codes that were drawn upon to make sense of the Rwandan crisis? Were the media involved in the reproduction of Western notions of superiority and dominance? And finally what impact did the media have in terms of the international response to the Rwandan crisis?

In order to investigate these questions, I have analysed seven days of British television coverage of the Rwandan issues. The sample includes British terrestrial television news (BBC1, BBC2, ITV and Channel 4) from 15 July 94 to 21 July 94. This period was chosen as it shows how the Rwanda story eventually made its way to the top of the news agenda (it was a lead story for most of the period) and how the refugee crisis attracted far more attention than the problem of dealing with the aftermath of the genocide. Notably over the period it is not until the third day of the crisis that the most commercially driven network ITV (who traditionally have a higher proportion of nationally focused news stories) began to cover the influx of refugees into Zaire. Further, what was also evident, was that because each of the news stations had reporters based on the Zairean border producing dramatic pictures of over a million people literally pouring into the country, this story began to displace any reference to the genocide. The genocide, as I have already indicated, was not covered in any depth because of the government restrictions, the focus on the forthcoming South African election and the lack of visual opportunities offered by the story. This reaffirms some of Galtung and Ruge's (1973) comments about television news in that it tends to ignore the historical context, concentrate on dramatic events and largely only feature issues that have relevance to the host nation's interests. That there were no British interests directly involved in Rwanda meant that the refugee crisis would not have been covered at all if it had not involved the dramatic media spectacle of mass human suffering.

These remarks provide the backdrop to understanding the two main discourses that were evident in the news. These narratives are available to any systematic study of the news, but were rarely presented in their purest form and often became entangled within one another. Discourses are not however determining features in themselves, but are linked into the commitment particular news channels have in covering global events, and the resources that they had available. These discourses might be represented as: (1) a universalistic discourse pertaining to represent the refugee crisis as a problem for humanity and (2) a contextual discourse that attempts to view the flow of refugees in terms of Rwanda's position in national, regional and international politics. My argument is that while these discourses had different registers and frames of reference they both shared a number of distinctive features as well as common blind spots.

1 The 'universalistic' discourse was the mode of understanding mostly present on the two popular news channels BBC1 and ITV. This discourse almost completely ignored the context of the genocide and either referred to the incoming refugees as escaping from a tribal conflict or more often a civil war. This is a familiar trope in media representations of Africa in that the historical relations between Bahutu and Batutsi become naturalised in exclusive ethnic categories. If the genocide was mentioned what was not made clear was that many of the refugees had actually participated within it, and were leaving Rwanda not so much to receive 'generous' Western help as they were to escape the invading RPF army, and possibly regroup for a counter attack. The refugees themselves were either coded as helpless and passive victims requiring generous Western assistance, or as an irrational aggressive tribal people who actually cared very little for one another. This confusion about the nature of the refugees is evident in the remarks of BBC journalist George Kigali:

> Three months of strife and genocide has put paid to any sense of community. Those who might have dug graves looked around for anything useful in this land of exile. 30/40/50 dead I haven't the heart to count and it doesn't really matter- the fact is that these were innocent civilians and this was meant to be a place of refuge. (BBC News, 18.7.94, 21.00–21.30)

The innocent and yet guilty refugees are not placed inside any political/ social historical context so what we are being presented with are the essential attributes of a suffering people. The breakdown of basic civility among the refugees is often contrasted with the simple humanity of the French soldiers, the aid workers or even the journalists, all of whom are of Western origin. This, it would seem, is the basic mark of Western civility and cultural distinction. The black Africans are either violent or helpless, needy or dangerous, desperate or vicious in stark contrast to the 'giving' nature of the Europeans. This strategy of cultural distinction maintains separable categories even when it looks as though they are being undermined. Again George Kigali of the BBC comments:

> We took those we could manage to the French military hospital. At times like these it is impossible not to cross the line between the observers and the observed. (BBC1, 18.7.94, 21.00–21.30)

While appearing to cross the line drawn by 'scientific' journalism between the reporter and the event it is the newsman's 'basic humanity' that leads him both to intervene, and mark the basic distinction between himself and the refugees. Kigali's remarks code the reporter and the French military as active and humane opposed to the perceived passivity of those who are suffering. The media here represented an absolutist view of European and African cultures. The rigid binary line between them represents the West as standing for compassion, activity, reason and social order with Africa signifying violence, passivity, irrationality and disorder. This basic binarism is constantly reproduced throughout the media coverage of Rwanda. Given the repetitiveness of these stereotypes and forms of psychic splitting that help inform racial forms of thinking it is no surprise that when reports came through on the sixth day of the first cases of cholera it was the heroism of the aid workers that was celebrated. For instance, ITV's 10 o'clock news shows footage of a 'remarkable man', Kevin Noon, loading dead bodies onto a truck. The film shows 'the brave Irishman' sorting the dead from the living and the diseased from the healthy. In other words, despite the attempt by the media to represent the refugee crisis through neutral terms such as 'human tragedy' or a 'crisis for humanity', what is actually being presented is the ways in which Western superiority is rooted in media discourse and commonsense thought (Dyer, 1988).

The maintenance of binary categories of representation is important in the sustenance of social distance between the audience and the Rwandans. This sense of 'distance' is also informed by the fact that it is a television event in the first place. Fergal Keane makes this point when he writes:

> We had watched the television pictures and listened to the radio, but there was a huge distance between being a screen spectator and actually going there. The nearer we came to Rwanda, the more pressing the need to remember points of normality: home, pets, books, loved ones. (Keane, 1995: 34)

Keane's vivid account of the genocide tells of his repeated nightmares, the smell of death, the feel of terror and the sense of chaos ushered in by the genocide. He argues that it is probably impossible to convey the overwhelming social suffering of Rwanda through the usual journalistic conventions. The television screen therefore could be thought of as both a means of information, and as a barrier to 'understanding'. Morley and Robins argue that:

> The screen can allow us to witness the world's events while, at the same time, protecting us – keeping us separate and insulated – from the reality of the events we are seeing. It can expose audiences to the violence and catastrophe of war while they still remain safe in their living rooms. (Morley and Robins, 1995: 141)

The screen, then, can act as a device that protects the audience from the horror of the events being represented. The sheer horror and chaos of the genocide are managed in two respects. The first is through (as I have argued at some length) the maintenance of stable social and psychic boundaries between a civilised 'us' and a helpless and barbaric 'them'. The second is through what television 'can show' and what we might term the limits of representation. This might mean footage too disturbing for domestic contexts or more profoundly the conversion of 'suffering' into electronic images inevitably creates relations of distance. To take this argument further I would argue that the practices of the media themselves through ethnocentrism and other social practices can either heighten or lessen this degree of social distance. For example, there is evidence that many of the pictures received from Rwanda remained on the cutting room floor as they were considered too distressing to transmit. Also many of the broadcasts of the refugee crisis contained the warning that 'some of our viewers may find these pictures distressing'. Perhaps the most important source of social distancing is the conversion of the refugee crisis into a spectacle of shocking images that turns the consumption of television into a commodified practice much like any other. Turning human suffering into a voyeuristic event, where images of torn limbs, bulging stomachs and social distress are bought and sold in global media marketplaces, ultimately displaces questions related to morality and ethics. The aestheticisation of murder, warfare and extreme forms of social distress through the media means that these images have to compete for our attention amongst an array of other equally shocking mediated images. The unceasing search for new dramatic pictures, deliberately exaggerated language and a manufactured sense of shock serves to fuel contemporary compassion fatigue. These devices, amongst others, help create even further chasms between the focus of media messages and their recipients. The only creative attempt, I discovered in my analysis, that sought to bring mediated communities closer to the tragedy was the suggestion that the effort to maintain the displaced population would be the equivalent of satisfying the need requirements of a population roughly the same size as Leeds. Yet even here the comparison works through the 'quantification' of resource needs, rather than seeking to explain culturally how the Rwandans are similar to ourselves.

The representation of Western dominance is undoubtedly carried through many of the unconscious elements of racist discourse that I analysed earlier. The projection of disorder, irrationality and basic incivility onto the Rwandans has the psychic function of maintaining an untarnished 'pure' Western identity. This abolishes any lingering feelings of guilt and responsibility for the West's colonial past and for the continued poverty of the region generally. Viewed in Klienian terms then, 'we' unconsciously split away our irrational fears and prejudices onto the bodies of black Africans to preserve good feelings about ourselves. Further, Lacanian perspectives have made us aware that the crude and rather obvious nature of televised stereotypes reveal the desperate need to preserve Western omnipotence. That the news reporters adopted so readily well-worn stereotypes and metaphors that were 'ready to hand' says a great deal about the endurance of certain practices, ideological beliefs and unconscious attachments in media reporting. We might press this analysis further and argue that the categorisation of the refugees is actually an expression of our own 'inner demons'. This can be taken in a psychoanalytic and in a social sense. That is, the projection of irrational violence and passivity onto the refugees in at least some sense makes our own daily reality more endurable. It enables us to sustain the fiction of our own civilisation when we Europeans have plenty of evidence to the contrary in that the eruption of totalitarian practices permeates the diverse histories of our own societies. The squashing of our own connections to state and genocidal violence is made all the easier once we have an alien body upon which to project our darkest fears.

Both psychoanalytic traditions (Lacanian and Klienian), in their admittedly different ways, signify the 'internal' defences that offset more ambivalent forms of thinking and feeling. Less rigid forms of imagining collective identities could lead to a deeper appreciation of the ties between the Other and ourselves. Such a creative response would inevitably require more integrative and more depressive forms of linking than were evident in Rwandan news reports. These more creative responses would herald the possibility of new intersubjective relations that escape the governance of predictable patterns of representation. Such forms of creative rethinking would invoke a dialogue between universalism and difference rather than the imposition of 'our' norms or the bland insistence of the 'surface' difference between the globe's cultures.

The maintenance of a 'pure, untainted and omnipotent' identity has social as well as psychic costs. For instance, there was much media concern, given the need to maintain the notion of Western generosity in the face of 'Third World' need that 'we' were seen to do something. In fact, before the offer of American help, the British were viewed as deficient on this score. The media were counterposing images of despair and suffering backed by 'guestimates' from the aid agencies about how much help was required. For instance, Channel 4 reported that the British had provided three planes, but this was inadequate, with the United Nations claiming the refugees would need 20 flights a day and Oxfam 40 flights a day to meet people's basic needs. While it is true that these claims were mitigated by the fact that the airport was shown to be in poor repair (could it handle the required number of flights?) and the insistence that there could be no humanitarian solution to the refugee crisis, pressure mounted daily for 'something' to be done. Unless 'something' was done this would, given the media exposure given to the refugees, severely throw into question the binary identities set in play by the media. In other words, and somewhat paradoxically, one of the factors which forced Western nations directly to address the Rwandan crisis was the need to maintain the myths of cultural superiority. To have ignored the obvious need of the Rwandan refugees would not only have been deeply inhumane, but would have punctured the polarised identities that had previously been represented by the Western news agencies.

2   The other discourse, subservient to the one outlined above, was a more concerted attempt, particularly evident on BBC2 and Channel 4, to provide a more contextual understanding of the events. On the first day of my sample the *Newsnight* team (BBC2) uncovered evidence of the genocide in Rwanda and sought to link this to the arrival of the refugees in a more concrete manner than was offered above. This more informed critical discourse linked the genocide to a government desperately attempting to hold onto power, and sought to offer air space to the RPF European representative James Rwego. This perspective also explored the possibilities of a political solution realising the limitations of humanitarian aid. The most important issue explored here was the credibility of the RPF government. The questions raised were: How legitimate are the refugees' fears that the RPF will inflict genocidal retribution upon the returning Batutsi? Would the RPF welcome a United Nations force into Rwanda to act as observers? Could the RPF instigate immediate elections to secure its legitimacy? The main focus of the questions was how could Rwanda be made safe for returning Batutsis, and how could the 'international community' best seek to attend to the immediate suffering on the Zairian border. Despite this more contextual account offered largely by Channel 4 news and BBC2's *Newsnight* programme similar absences are shared with the first account. First, there was little questioning of the role the 'international community' had played in the run up to the genocide through support of the Rwandan government. Secondly, the role of the French, in setting up the humanitarian zone, was seen as mostly unproblematic, and to be supported. Next, while pressing for the return of the Rwandan refugees, there was little concern that this could actually spread the cholera epidemic to a wider population. Finally, given the question above in respect of election, there was almost no appreciation of the actual social conditions that existed inside Rwanda as well as the camps themselves. Obviously it would have been difficult for the international media, given that many of the correspondents would have been completely unfamiliar with the region, to have fully explored these aspects. However, inside Rwanda, the RPF faced a situation where 10 per cent of the population had been murdered, 30 per cent were in exile, an absence of a civilian police force, the presence of French military and general social and political collapse (Prunier, 1995). These were the conditions within which the RPF were meant to organise elections? Inside the camps themselves there was also much evidence that the former leaders of the defeated government had maintained their power base. They actually prevented people leaving the camps and returning to Rwanda, thereby evading their control (Keane, 1995; Prunier, 1995). This again radically undermines the assumption that there would have been a peaceful return to Rwanda if they could have their security guaranteed by the United Nations. These considerations seriously question the picture offered by the more critically informed sections of the Western television media.

The Rwandan story continued to appear in the Western media through-out July and August until the cholera emergency was brought under control. When the death rates began to decline, the media, with the arrival of Western aid, mostly lost interest in Rwanda. Gone was the spectacle of mass death and a sense of immediate crisis. We, it seems, had 'done' something. This is not to underrate the importance of the media in mobilising public opinion and international agencies of governance in alleviating the 'immediate' suffering of the refugees. Despite many of the problems I have indicated with the 'content' of the media's coverage, the question remains would the aid agencies have received the extra backing they required without the pictures of ordinary suffering that were being beamed into the homes of Western citizens? Although we can not be sure, I think that the answer, given that the Western powers have few strategic issues in the area, is probably negative. The response to the Rwandan crisis was primarily media driven.

Luke and Tuathail (1997) make the point that since the collapse of the Cold War (which imposed a semblance of order on questions of governance) there has emerged a recognisable discourse and set of practices of failed states. Failed states are characterised by the chaos of poverty, refugee crisis, ethnic conflict and the general absense of order. As dominant powers probably have little by the way of strategic issues at stake in regions such as Rwanda they are only forced on to a more international agenda by media attention. Unless the media are keyed into the spectacle stories such as Rwanda then they are likely to be tolerated by international agencies of control. While their plight may be picked up by human rights groups it is reasonable to assume that such 'issues' are likely to remain absent from more international forms of recognition. However, what I have termed the blind spots of the media coverage also reinforces the problem that the Rwandan's real needs remain unaddressed. These are for bread and justice. A major contributing fact to the crisis in Rwanda was the fall of the price of world coffee and tin in the 1980s, and the reduction in foreign aid. This promoted a climate whereby political groups sought to struggle over scarce resources. Further, as we have seen, the newly constituted Rwandan state encountered a situation of near social collapse and deeply ingrained social wounds. The fear remains that without international support in these areas Rwanda contains the cultural conditions for future genocides.

Castells (1998) argues that nations like Rwanda are in danger of becoming part of a fourth world increasingly excluded from the circuits of the information economy. The polarisation of the global economy, the fact that Africa remains the world's most indebted region and the increasing misery of the earth's poorest regions stack the odds against nations like Rwanda. If we add to this an ethnicised state which relies on close personal ties and the austere conditions imposed by world finance organisations then we have a set of structural conditions that may not bring about extreme conflict but certainly makes it more likely. Hence Africa's and Rwanda's plight is currently caught between marginalisation by the information economy and the disintegration of the nation-state.

Violence, democracy and the media

There is an intimate connection between communication and violence. Violence, it is often said, is in itself a form of communication in that it is a powerful message. However, it might be more productive to think of these terms as interdependent rather than overlapping. Here we might argue, along with Hannah Arendt (1958) and others, that where communication breaks down violence is most likely to take its place. The advance of democracy, recognition and meaningfulness is dependent upon a relatively secure environment where face-to-face and mediated talk provides space for a multitude of identities, positions and related arguments. Violence seeks to remove diverse multicultural groupings from a shared social space and thereby render them both invisible and silent. The importance of the visibility of minority and subordinate groups in local and global media serves to illustrate their presence in media cultures. This arena is increasingly likely to have a bearing on their access to other rights of representation. That is to say, ethnic, sexual or other cultural groupings, as part of their overall strategy to win rights and security, must aim to gain the attention of both local and global media. This will enable them to make visible forms of violence used against them as means of social control, and clearly articulate their presence to a wider population. This argument potentially applies as much to gay and lesbian groups in Britain, as Bahutus and Batutsis in Rwanda. The struggle for cultural citizensip therefore involves the need to make a rich pattern of intersubjective relations visible in a diversity of media cultures.

Dialogue and recognition are indeed what is required in the context of Rwanda's uncertain movement toward reconciliation. Yet it is clear that reconciliation is not really possible without those who promoted the violence being brought to justice, and an accompanying act of collective remembering that is the antecedent of forgiveness in the Rwandan context. These painful processes are likely to be thwarted not only by denials, but by the absence of a genuinely pluralistic civil society and media culture. The enormous loss of self-respect experienced by the perpetrators of violence and the deep anger of its victims would require a medium and a system of representation that sought both justice and the transcendence of the dualisms that continue to exist in Rwandan society. In the words of psychoanalyst Christopher Bollas (1992) the purification of the self that is characteristic of the fascist state of mind can only be mediated once we begin to take responsibility for what we have done. The fascist solution is to empty the self of all forms of ambivalence and opposition as we seek to distance ourselves from the harm we have inflicted upon others. In this construction the self ceases to be complex as it searches for certainty untainted by opposition and difficulty. The chilling fact remains that such cultural attributes were not only part of the genocide, but were also, if my account is followed, evident within Western representations of Rwanda. After all, to live within truth and democracy means we must also live within ambivalence, uncertainty and complexity. If we fail to do just this we may have to deal with problems of even greater magnitude than those ushered in by the fast moving nature of contemporary post-modern culture. Indeed, this is seemingly precisely what has occurred: the Hutu refugees have been shielded from justice by the camps, and have both become entangled in a civil war in Zaire, while using their position to send infiltrators into Rwanda (Omaar, 1997). More recent reports have also connected the Rwandan army with human rights abuses inside Rwanda itself (McGreal, 1997). The international tribunal which is attempting to bring the perpetrators of the genocide to justice are doing so in the absense of social and psychic conditions that allow for the opening of the always uncertain path towards reconcilation. Rogue bands of Hutu militia are roaming the country seeking out genocide survivors and springing the accused from prison. The Rwandan army in retaliation are reported to be killing unarmed Hutus in an attempt to drive out the regrouped militias. Notably the current lack of international concern and media reporting on these issues stands in stark contrast to the coverage of events surrounding the South African Truth Commission. While the precise dimensions of this conflict are still unfolding, the gritty human realities they represent point towards a form of human complexity poorly appreciated by the bland talk that can be associated with the arrival of a global village or cultural intermixing. The need to develop genuinely civil institutions within Rwanda, a greater degree of material and moral support internationally and more responsible forms of reporting among the Western media remains pressing.

CHAPTER 7

The future of public media cultures: questions of critique and ambivalence

A series of ambivalences and oppositions make themselves apparent if we consider the nature of globalised media cultures. These are related to a number of questions that have been raised by the development of modernity and have been touched upon in this book already. The first, and perhaps most obvious, is the capacity of electronic media to transport images, text and voice through time and space opening us to the interrogation or indifference of 'others' who live in contexts far removed from our own. The modern media in certain respects remind us of the ways in which we live on a shared planet. However, we only have to consider for a moment the contexts and social settings within which we gather information and this picture is complicated further. For most of us most of the time we engage with the media in privatised contexts where we are rendered largely passive. The media of mass communications is permanently caught between dialogue and fragmentation and engagement and boredom. The global media's capacity to make us aware of common concerns then is mitigated by the comparatively isolated contexts within which we make our interpretations. Alternatively we might view this contradiction as falling between the circulation of the knowledge necessary for us to decide upon common norms, rights and obligations and the rise of the home as an entertainment centre. Add to this the further complication that media audiences continue to be fragmented along the lines of taste, class, gender, race, age and nationality and the picture that emerges is far removed from McLuhan's idea of the global village. The modern media therefore continue to be constituted through the dual processes of unification and fragmentation. I shall call this the dialogic problem.

Secondly, the rapid development of media technologies has increased the volume of information available, imploded established distinctions between public and private, and speeded up the delivery of information more generally. The rapidly emerging information highways, the multiplication of television channels, the increasing power of communications conglomerates and the development of media technology are all driven by the instrumental logics of science and profit. The question as to whether more channels will enhance our ability to communicate with ourselves about issues worthy of public attention is rarely asked. The ambivalence here is again that while we can point to instrumental logics within communication that are contributing to processes of commodification, feelings of meaninglessness and a wider culture of superficiality we can also connect these processes to the problem of previously repressed areas of social experience. These would include questions of gender and sexual identity, ecological questions and, as we saw in the earlier chapter on Rwanda, relations between different world regions. To take one example, the current media obsession with the private lives of politicians and celebrities can be read as signifying the decline of deference, a way of trivialising public questions or as a consequence of feminist demands that intimate relations become politicised. In other words, chat shows which have become the staple diet of daytime television can be equally understood as personalising public questions or as opening up a range of concerns from child abuse to domestic violence. The contradiction here lies between the colonising logic of economics, science and technology, and more communicative concerns. I shall call this the problem of instrumental reason.

As Charles Taylor (1991) has made clear, the problem of public recognition versus the subjective turns inwards, and the problem of instrumental reason as opposed to more hermeneutic concerns can be reconfigured as questions to do with the individual and community, and strategic goal-orientated thinking as opposed to more open-ended forms of conversation. My argument then is not to press the originality of these dilemmas but to open out their inevitably ambivalent natures, and to look at the ways that they have become transformed in heavily mediated cultures like our own.

To these questions I want to add a third related issue which is the problem of identity. It seems to me that the development of media cultures not only poses questions concerning dialogic involvement and instrumental reason but also opens issues connected with identity. We have already seen how some theorists have argued that global communications can be linked to the pluralisation, fragmentation and hybridisation of modern cultures. This can be understood optimistically in opening out a form of cultural cosmopolitanism where humanity in general experiences new forms of cultural openness and engagement with previously excluded others. However, such processes can also be understood to stumble on some of the more enduring features of modernity from the powerful centres of global capitalism to the relative endurance of the national ideal. Again it seems to me that in seeking to understand the new communications environment or the development of modernity more generally we need to resist the idea that it is necessary to bet on one side against the other. Here I am questioning the impulse that makes us want definitely to decide questions rather than hold them in tension. If the question is put like this then the transformation of the media – as I have maintained throughout – holds both possibilities as well as dangers. For example, the development of a multichannel universe may well lead to audience fragmentation, the undermining of public service ethics and a relative decline in shared television experiences. Yet it might also herald new possibilities for local television companies, autonomy with the use of hand-held cameras and videos, more choice for the viewer and make it increasingly difficult for the state to censor debate. We might then equally look forward to a world which increases the power of large-scale multinationals and where new possibilities for interrupting the discourses of the powerful are utilised by citizens and new social movements alike.

Here, however, I want to press the argument that these questions can not be decided theoretically but will inevitably be the outcome of social and political processes. In order to explore these issues further I want to invest-igate a number of reactions within the literature to the ambivalences that might be associated with contemporary media cultures. Put simply, they are the arguments that the global recognition of rights to communication (as part of a human rights initiative) would empower ordinary people against states and large-scale media conglomerates, and the claim that the techno-logical development of internet cultures will lead to an energised and more participatory civil society. Both of these positions raise questions in connec-tion with dialogics, instrumental reason and identity. They differ in that the first is primarily a political initiative whereas the second is largely the result of technological change. Yet both imagine a future that has more success-fully resolved our three problems than the time we currently inhabit. I want to offer a judgement of the feasibility of these and similar perspectives by considering more pessimistic counter claims. This is done not to dismiss the imagination of the two viewpoints out of hand, but to conceive of the fate of media cultures through over-optimistic scenarios inevitably invites cri-ticism of a more pessimistic nature. To polarise the substantive debates at issue in this way not only dispenses with the ambiguities I have sought to spell out in this book, but leads to more substantive political failings and displaces many of the critical questions that come to light when we connect the themes of media, morality and globalisation.

Human rights, social movements and global media

One of the most significant moral and political achievements of humanity remains the 1948 Universal Declaration of Human Rights. The principles laid down in this document recognise that everyone irrespective of national boundaries is entitled to the rights and freedoms held out in the Charter. The Charter has provided the basis for international law setting out com-mon standards that might reasonably be expected by all peoples (Falk, 1995a). The Charter, in Article 19, contains a defence of the freedom of information and rights of expression, that includes the right to impart and receive information irrespective of frontiers. Article 19 has provided the inspiration behind attempts by Third World nations in the 1970s to challenge western media dominance, and a series of commissions and reports that issued declarations on the rights of peoples and the responsibilities of the global media. One such report, by the MacBride Commission, sought to safeguard the rights of journalists to 'exercise their profession'. That such rights are no closer to fruition than they were at the time the report was drawn up has been made evident in conflicts from the Gulf War to the genocide in the former Yugoslavia. More recently Cees Hamelink (1994, 1995) has argued that the globalisation of mass communication has led to a disempowering of ordinary people when it comes to exerting power and control over their communicative environments. Globalisation processes have increased the power of large-scale media conglomerates and flooded the world with cheap standardised media products. These processes can only be reversed through a human rights initiative that enables participation within cultural and political life by providing peoples with access to information so that they might make autonomous decisions. Thus whereas global media empires are disempowering in that they infringe upon local cultural space and privatise access to information, human rights approaches treat knowledge as a collectively owned common good to be shared, debated and contributed to by equal citizens. The reduction in cultural space enables the West to control the flow of information and disempower 'other' peoples from developing their own sense of identity.

Starting from local networks the world's peoples are encouraged to search for alternative sources of information exchange that emerge underneath the disciplinary power of the state and the commercial imperatives which govern global media empires. The development of a genuine people's media through community radio and newspapers and the burgeoning of a people's community network over the internet could form the beginning of local and global sources of information that provide alternative sources of communication. Politically we can afford to be optimistic about such movements due to the 'revolt of civil society'. By this Hamelink means that alternative networks of communication will arise along with social movements like ecology and feminism. The emergence of a 'double citizenship', or what Albrow (1996) has termed 'performative citizenship', means that such movements point to a new form of politics that seeks to link the struggles internal to nations to more global levels of interconnection. As a first step in building upon these civic initiatives, Hamelink proposes the world-wide adoption of what he calls a 'People's Communication Charter'. The main aim of the charter is to raise the awareness of individuals and social movements as to the shared importance of securing both human and cultural rights. The charter then builds upon Article 19 of the 1948 Declaration by granting people rights freely to form an opinion, gain information, enter into public discussion, distribute knowledge, protect their cultural identity and participate in a shared public culture. The aim is to make this both a movement of non-governmental forces (groups such as Amnesty, CND, Greenpeace, etc.) and to have the charter adopted by the United Nations.

The most obvious and immediate objections to such arguments are that the declaration of human rights are not legally enforceable, and without the reform of the United Nations itself, such charters have historically had little impact. The 'People's Communication Charter' on this cynical view ends up adding to the meaningless pieces of paper that are produced by the United Nations bureaucracy. These proposals could be further criticised in that they are unlikely to have any lasting impact on the dominant rationale and structures of the global media. Such arguments however are as insightful as they are mistaken about the politics of human rights and their connection to questions of cultural citizenship and the media of mass communication.

The first point to make is that the widespread acceptance of a 'People's Communication Charter' is not solely dependent upon its ability to produce legal effects. Like other human rights that are widely accepted among non-governmental organisations its 'cultural' existence gives groups something to appeal to and build a social struggle around. It is undeniable that in its perceived moral legitimacy such a process would be greatly enhanced if the charter were accepted by the United Nations. This would then give new social movements a platform on which to perform a form of immanent critique whereby signatories could be embarrassed by their refusal to uphold the principles they had formally agreed. Human rights documents are important in that they help create a set of general political and cultural expectations which when violated potentially attract the attention of the media and political movements alike.

There are of course no guarantees, but if movements for social change are able to point to international treaties or other collectively agreed documents it will aid them in making interventions into the global televisual arena. The argument being proposed here is that the economic (wealth and resources), political (influence over state policy) and cultural (modelling stocks of discourses and concepts) power of the new media order is such that an international recognition of people's rights in information exchange could indeed have an empowering effect upon the interrelation between local, national and more global public spheres.

The other argument is that without the reform of the United Nations and the eventual evolution of a world state such resolutions are unlikely to have much impact. Indeed it is significant that while media, economics and security systems have become globalised the institutional organisation of democracy remains very much on the level of the nation-state. In this view, the United Nations, if drastically reformed, could be the forerunner of a global parliament. This could be an integrated structure dependent upon local, national and regional bodies finally leading to the global level. If such a demand seems somewhat utopian in the present climate, we could begin this process by reforming the UN. Such reforms might include the empowerment of poorer nations in the Security Council, the alteration of the veto system, the creation of a new Human Rights court that did not proceed on an ad hoc basis, etc.

The argument here would be that each age has had to rework democracy to fit specific cultural contexts. Direct democracy worked in Athens as it was based on small homogeneous communities, national representative democracy was appropriate in that it came along with the rise of the national capitalism and nation-states, whereas a global age requires a global state and democracy. Further, we might continue, direct democracy implies a mostly oral public sphere of face-to-face relations, national democracy evolved along with print securing national 'imagined' communities, and what McLuhan would term the 'electric' age, makes possible political participation less dependent upon physical space and more truly global than ever before.

Arguably such views remain somewhat utopian and overly abstract from some of the more concrete pressures and practices of the present. David Held (1995), for example, argues that so-called Westphalian models of governance (based upon national sovereignty) have been displaced by a UN charter model which recognises that peoples have rights irrespective of their national citizenship. These universal human rights which should be shared by everyone on the planet offer a direct challenge to the notion that nations set the internal standards by which they are judged. Of course there is no international law requiring states directly to apply these rights; states can opt out of these treaties (a number of nations in fact refused to sign the 1948 document including South Africa and the countries of the former Eastern bloc) and human rights treaties contain considerable leeway for specifically national solutions (Archibugi, 1995). However, despite these restraints, we currently occupy an ill-defined zone between a world where nation-states were all powerful and more global forms of governance.

The last world conference on human rights took place in Vienna 1993 (with 171 states and 800 non-governmental organisations) which was the largest ever assembly on such issues. The single pressing question of the conference was, can a common commitment to human rights transform relations between the North and the South? This question allowed an uneasy consensus to emerge that sustainable development actually requires democratic participation, and that unless basic social rights are secured this is very difficult to achieve. Yet the paradox noted again was that such declarations are not legally binding and are negotiated by nation-states, not individuals. The other aspect to emerge was the growing opposition to the idea of universal rights in some Asian nations (China, Indonesia, Iran and Malaysia) who dismissed such notions as Western constructs. The argument here, strongly akin to the pessimist thesis outlined above, was that the West promoted such rights to further its own interests (Boyle, 1995; Rosas, 1995). The problem with such an argument is that it actively colludes with the interests of repressive states which are anxious to avoid being condemned by the world media.

Held suggests that instead of looking upon the United Nations as the outdated relic of the post-war era we think of it anew as offering possibilities with regard to global democracy. Indeed what he proposes is the eventual implementation of a global cosmopolitan order which is built upon local, national, regional and global levels of representation and government. The cosmopolitan order could seek to instigate a more equitable distribution of goods globally, put limits on nations' capacity to wage warfare, coordinate ecological initiatives and enforce internationally agreed standards for the functioning of the media. This would give charters such as the one proposed by Hamelink more active purchase on the structuration of political institutions and practice.

On the other hand, Richard Falk (1995b) argues that a global parliament would probably serve the interests of global capital, and what is actually required is a deeper more normative commitment to democratic principles, and the radicalisation of society through the acceptance of already agreed upon UN principles. In this respect, Falk treats democracy not just as a set of institutions, but as a binding ethical commitment. To be committed to democracy and cultural citizenship in general is to be committed to a set of norms which include reciprocity, listening, respect, responsibility and the recognition of difference. Of course these values do not exist outside of institutional structures, but neither are they likely to be ushered in by simply setting up new tiers of government. The rebirth of a more substantive democratic media then can not be assumed to be the simple 'effect' of human rights treaties or programmes of institution building. Such initiatives as communitarian and socialist humanist thinkers have long since held are the product of agency and people's projects within civil society. The faith that we might have in the 'People's Communication Charter' then is undermined not so much by the trust it places in institutions as in people's initiatives generally. Civil society is currently made up of organisations which aim to reinstate patriarchy, ethnic nationalists, religious fundamentalists and all kinds of other causes with which Hamelink would find himself out of sympathy. This begs the question as to whether a charter that emphasises the 'right' to be heard can really solve the communication crisis within civil society today.

This situation is exaggerated by the fact that Hamelink's manifesto fails to address what I shall call the 'cultural' question and notions of communicative obligation. The 'cultural' question remains how we go about imaginatively loosening the grip that the nation continues to have upon popularly constructed horizons. The fate of 'other' peoples is still extremely difficult to convert into a rallying point for change. People dying far away are unlikely to become a focus for change in the way running down 'our' welfare system or poisoning 'our' people could be. For most of the people most of the time notions of community remain local and national. Paradoxically it remains a 'real' political question as to how social movements might re-imagine relations of solidarity in an admittedly increasingly interconnected world. There are evidently new possibilities emerging with regard to new communications, diasporic population movements and the growth of tourism, but it remains an open question as to what kind of global civil society will come to represent such dimensions. We can perhaps take heart from the fact that just as the sexes have only just begun to problematise how they communicate with one another, the same could be said of different world regions. The demand that we understand rather than dominate one another occupies a comparatively short period in the history of humanity. Viewed optimistically we could all be on the cusp of a more globally informed cosmopolitan citizenship. However, as I have maintained throughout, there are just as many good reasons for thinking that the so-called global age could be equally marked by more insular forms of imagining. Secondly, the media charter's discussion of rights irrespective of obligations would, given the diverse rather than harmonious nature of civil society, not necessarily improve the quality of debate. The inclusion of more voices in an already noisy global village may have the positive benefit of getting more people heard, but actually achieve little by the way of reflexive understanding.

A more practical way of deepening democratic principles could be achieved by the United Nations right now. Ulrich Beck (1997) has offered the suggestion that the United Nations could organise global information links that seek to undermine state driven attempts to promote cultural stereotypes of neighbours and groups which are defined as 'other'. United Nations journalists therefore could be used to throw doubt upon military style preparations or consistent campaigns of hate. Such practices would undoubtedly assist the actions of human rights groups working internally for more democratic solutions to social problems. Notably actions of this kind depend upon the deepening of principles that are already held up by the United Nations, rather than the creation of new institutions. However, my argument would be that it is far too early to make a choice between the desirability let alone the feasibility of building new global structures and the development of more globally orientated social movements. What is evident, however, is that without fresh thinking on such issues 'progressive' social and cultural movements will find that the questions and the connections that they want to make will not 'necessarily' find their ways onto public agendas.

Further, the development of world regional government, with the European Union acting as a case in point, may provide a more effective means of protecting media freedom at the trans-national level than the United Nations. This can be asserted in respect of the governance of media freedoms given the development of European policies in respect of citizenship (Meehan, 1993). Europe has recently sought to balance the need to maintain collective identities and the requirement to develop super information highways to enhance financial competitiveness (Schlesinger and Doyle, 1995). While these directives arguably pull in different directions the capacity of the European Union to act over and above the national policy arena means that it is a more effective instrument of governance than the United Nations.

165

At best, the institutions of civil society can make a mostly national public sphere more globally aware (Cheah, 1997). The future development of trans-national institutions like the European Union, and to a lesser extent the United Nations, may come to play a more significant role in the governance of the media in the future. Recent experience suggests, however, that a more systematic break with the hegemony of national perspectives is required before a more fully global intersubjective dimension is likely to unfold.

My argument is then that we are some way off seeing the fully fledged development of a global public sphere underpinned by widely recognised rights to communication, More likely are other developments whereby the agendas of commercial global media are interrupted by human rights groupings in a struggle for recognition, world region organisations asserting their right to intervene in the regulation of public communications and the nation continuing to dominate the collective imagination.

Technocultures, media and community

Current debates on the development of new media technologies have a strong overlap with questions that are currently being asked about the nature of community. The media of mass communication is rapidly diversifying just at the point when old communal relations are increasingly open to question. Are new media technologies responsible for undermining a sense of community by robbing people of participatory public spaces or are they the sites where more diversified relations of solidarity can be made? Crudely, we can divide arguments in respect of the effects and transformations brought about by new media into opposing optimistic and pessimistic schools of thought. The pessimists propose that the development of new media technologies can be coupled with the continuation of modernity and the destruction of communal forms of identification and the progressive privatisation and commodification of public life. On the other hand, more post-modern frames see the emergence of internet, video, mobile phones and portable stereos as opening out new possibilities for voices that have been traditionally excluded from public cultures. New more affective attachments can be formed through underground networks, fan magazines, MUD sites and telephone chat lines. Unlike traditional communities in which 'individuals' are born into 'co-present' local relations, so-called post-modern communities are more likely to be the result of 'individual' choice and the product of mediation. Whereas one set of critics views the global triumph of capital as destroying the communal identification that allows people to resist capitalism, the other views community as a more fluid site and a potential place of radical politics. To overstate the point, where one set of critics is mournful at the passing of old ties the other is celebratory in the hope that new ones might be made.

The pessimist's camp houses a wide spectrum of political viewpoints from old-style radicals to cultural conservatives. For instance, Julian Stallabras (1996) argues that the super information highway and cyberspace will not offer a utopian domain of free communication, but the perfect marketplace which can operate through space and time at the flick of a switch. Those who are currently excited about the future possibilities of the 'Net' are failing to ask who will control the information, work out to whom its going to be made available and in whose interests it is likely to be run. The answers to these questions are all traceable back to the needs of global capital. For instance, so-called virtual communities are places built upon irony and play unlike real communities which are places of obligation and responsibility. If within cyberspace we are able to disguise our identities, this effectively denies the possibility of a genuinely democratic communicative exchange, where the individuality of the 'other' has to be engaged with. Instead it creates a 'kingdom of information, whose palatial halls we may wander without fear, free from chaos, dirt and obscurity' (Stallabras, 1996: 67). Cyberspace becomes a zone of irresponsible consumption where the poor will never appear as subjects in their own right and only very occasionally as 'objects' for discussion. Indeed the desire to create 'virtual' communities over the Web both points to the disappearance of 'real' communal relations being trampled under the atomising effect of commodity capital, and to the fact that humans desperately need a sense of belonging and will create it with whatever tools they currently have to hand. The human need and desire for community is what is being currently manipulated by the advocates of cyber solutions. The democratic and communal potential of much of the new media turns out to be an old con trick performed by capital's need for ever-expanding new markets and enthusiastic consumers.

However, as I have indicated, technological pessimism is not restricted to the Marxist left. From a markedly different political perspective, John Gray (1995a, 1995b) has similarly argued that the belief that technology is going to renew our communities, solve ethical problems and radically democratise our shared political world is the worst kind of utopian thinking. Communities are not something we change on a whim but are relatively enduring spaces of belonging and identification. The real political problem, and this is a view similar to the one presented above, is that traditional communities are being destroyed by the excesses of free market liberalism. The solution to this does not lie in the reinvention of class politics, but with the renewal of social democracy that aims to preserve and rethink community in a global age. Cyberspace, on this reading, is little more than a privatised comfort zone we retreat into to avoid increasingly dangerous public places. The image being presented here is not one of technologies modelling society, but of the reverse. New media technologies are linked to instrumental reason, processes of commodification and the individualistic retreat from the public more generally. Rather than becoming actively involved in our communities we have retreated into the cosy privacy of the home.

Significantly, the development of new communications technologies have been read differently by writers who occupy less-traditional frames of reference. Maffesoli (1996) questions the pessimistic projections of those who are concerned with the fragmentation and privatisation of the modern subject. He does this by articulating a notion of the subject that is continually searching for emotional connection with intersubjectively related others. Maffesoli rejects the idea of the isolated individual split away from others through the operation of mass culture, and points to what he calls the 'tribalisation' of the social. By this he means that through the creation of football teams, self-help groups, friendship networks, internet sites and religious associations individuals are increasingly likely to belong to a number of diverse and contradictory communities. What we are currently witnessing therefore is the de-individualisation of modernity and the growth of more effective communities based less on utilitarian notions of self-interest than on sociality. The new tribes are based upon shared sentiments, whether they are regular visitors of an internet site, readers of a football fanzine or even occasional viewers of a soap opera. These new emotional communities are constructed more upon fleeting identification and periodic warmth than the stability of traditional ties. Hence the argument here is not so much to bemoan the ways in which capitalism has destroyed traditional forms of association as to investigate the creative ways in which social solidarity might be imagined in the late modern age.

Similarly the advent of digital television, according to its most enthusiastic supporters, will rapidly expand the sheer amount of information available and provide greater interactive involvement for the viewer. Digital butlers will order and sort this information as the new smart television sets 'learn' about the preferences of their viewers. This promises no more boring nights at home slumped in front of the box, but an interactive universe where we might spend the evening e-mailing a loved one in Australia, downloading material from the *Washington Post* or creating our own camera angles at a Derby County home game (Negroponte, 1994; Gilder, 1992). In addition, the internet, due to its less centralised and hierarchical nature, opens new possibilities for oppositional voices to be heard. This is largely due to the fact that computer cultures, unlike the more traditional 'big media', are based upon a two-way flow of information and consequently are structured in less hierarchical ways (Kellner, 1995; Rheingold, 1994). The public sphere then becomes progressively unfrozen the more that technological advance allows for greater forms of participation by citizens. The net is exciting precisely because it disrupts existing regimes of power and knowledge, whether this is within the academy or decentring the power of the previously powerful media in the public sphere.

What is immediately noticeable about this debate is that the new media is subversive for the optimists for the same reasons that the pessimists find it troubling. For instance, whereas Stallabras (1996) bemoans the amount of junk and trash to be found on the World Wide Web, Sadie Plant (1996) finds the internet liberating precisely because it bypasses the usual gatekeepers of public culture. This opposition can also be seen in the related problems of dialogics, instrumental reason and identity. The pessimists read the internet as developing an individualistic withdrawal from the public, an acquisitive attitude towards commodities and the delights of consumptive freedom rather than deeper forms of social responsibility. For the optimists new media technology helps open new forms of critical engagement, makes public participation a real possibility (given the passing of old-style one-way flow media) and fosters new forms of belonging.

What is perhaps surprising is that critical theory with a tradition of dialectical reason and an awareness of the impoverished nature of thinking in binarisms can be so easily divided between optimists and pessimists in this way. My argument is in part that this sort of polarised thinking actually exhibits a fear of the future. The modernists cynically feel that the past will continue to grind on through the present in such a way that the future simply becomes the endless repetition of commodification, technological reason and other features which can all be associated with modernity. On the other hand, the post-modern view denies the more depressive aspects of social reality by splitting them off from the revolution about to be accomplished less through human agency than through technological modelling. To borrow the metaphors of lightness and weight from Milan Kundera (1994) the view that the future is actually the continuation of the past represents a heaviness through which history endlessly repeats itself. This closes down the prospect of human contingency. The other argument that new media cultures will liberate the future from the past appears to be light when it is actually heavy. By this I mean that the future is not so much viewed as an open possibility but as already predestined. My point is not so much that both perspectives continue to have something to offer – this much is obvious; more that each viewpoint attempts to colonise the future deadening itself from more ambivalent possibilities. As psychoanalytic writers have pointed out, to be a mature subject is to have an awareness of the ways of writing by wider narratives as well as maintaining a sense of the future that is open, new and 'other' (Bollas, 1994; Elliott, 1996). The message here is that whether or not the development of new communications technologies offer new opportunities for social control or the revitalisation of democratic life will be decided by wider political and social developments. While both sides of the argument raise substantive views it is as if they have allowed themselves to be defined by the discourse of the other, and in doing so robbed us of a future defined by political agency. Finally, both the technological optimists and those who wish to build a global cosmopolitan order could be found guilty of a false utopianism. I say this while remaining open minded and agnostic concerning many of the claims that they make. The utopianism of the technological optimists seems to be constructed on the desire to build a vision of the future untainted by painful limitations of the present. As Freud (1930) pointed out long ago the first requirement of a civilised social order is justice not the desire to maintain pleasure at all costs. The arguments for a more cosmopolitan distribution of power and authority then flounder on the fact that they are likely to be opposed by national interests that remain influential on the world stage. The problem then is with a kind of utopian thinking that wants to preserve its purity against the dirt of the present. However a world without any idealism ultimately ends up underestimating the continued political importance of fresh ideas and embodies a form of cynicism that ultimately always knows in advance what it thinks about a particular problem, without opening itself to the complexity of questions that are available. That we need ideals and utopias to live by and that they should concretely engage with the problems of our time is evident.[1] The coming of the global age requires a new politics with old virtues that can creatively link optimism and cynicism, the local and the global, past and present without reducing either pole to a handful of dust.

A more substantive account of cultural citizenship would seek to combine both the optimistic and pessimistic versions of the argument presented here. A genuinely sociologically informed account of the opportunities and dangers heralded by the development of new media technologies should seek to develop some of the more ambivalently conceived aspects listed below.

A culture of individual choice

The rapid expansion of new media made available by technological change will mean that our public culture will become increasingly based upon individual choice in ways that are poorly appreciated by the mass culture thesis. It is likely that much of this culture will be repetitive and conformist as the market will seek to build upon well-established formulae, but also dynamic as niche markets attempt to maintain their audience share. The problem faced by most people here will be new forms of frustration based upon cultural exclusion and cultural overload, that is too much choice rather than too little for the economically secure, and not enough for those excluded from the labour market. Such a complex culture will simultaneously offer opportunities to build new networks outside of the regulatory capacity of the state, while weakening a shared public culture. The culture of individual choice thereby offers the possibility of new communities of interest emerging, and a further atomisation of official public cultures.

A culture of sensation

The idea of a critical, rational, national public sphere is likely to become increasingly challenged by a more global agenda driven by panic, sensation and immediate opinion formation. The speeded up temporal framework evident here will need to make an impact on the audience quickly as programmes, news items and other features scramble for the audience's attention in an already overcrowded and noisy global village. Yet the increasing pervasion of economic reason, or the culture of capital, offers, within certain limits, opportunities for dramatic forms of intervention for groups within civil society, and for media of a more local and public orientation. An increasingly sensation hungry media provides spaces for movements and groups alike to make dramatic symbolic protests that are both imaginative and critical. Further, there is likely to be a reaction against a public sphere that becomes overly detached from local agendas and informed criticism, providing continued opportunities for public service provision.

A culture of escape

The large-scale media's ability to be able to impose an agenda on the public will obviously be diminished by the proliferation of new cultural forms. This offers new opportunities for cultural autonomy through developing skilled readings of horror flicks, gathering information from miscellaneous sources and participating in a diverse range of discussion groups. These groups are likely to develop their own in-house vocabulary and be a source of bemusement, indifference and occasionally cultural snobbery to those who fall outside the group. These new lifestyle communities can therefore be seen to be promoting feelings of solidarity while pursuing a strategy of distinct from other cultural groups. We could also view the autonomous capacity of the self to reconstruct itself through media narratives as a strategy to avoid more public responsibilities and issues. The economically driven world of new media is likely to promote a culture of consumption rather than old-style questions of justice, democracy and liberty. We might then find ourselves becoming experts in the pleasures of consumption rather than the gritty realities of global poverty.

A culture of interactivity

It is clear that a whole range of media are embracing a more interactive culture of consumption. More traditional media like television, magazines and newspapers regularly invite consumers' comments through phone lines, letters pages and other devices. In addition, new communication technologies including Walkmans, hand-held games and video-recorders all depend upon active participation by the subject. Further, as a younger generation grows up more used to media that depend upon active involvement this could have a profound effect upon the development of more critical and less deferential forms of subjectivity. Of course there remain evident dangers here in that the increased interactivity of the media does not necessarily make it more democratic. It is likely that powerful and manipulative forces will use the involvement fostered by more two-way cultures to make precisely this claim.

While these tendencies can be derived from current configurations it should be noted that read dialectically the new media environment is currently in the process of being formed. An already porous and dynamic public sphere is likely to become ever more so as a diverse range of issues is taken up by different groupings all attempting to secure mass public attention and recognition. The precise structure of the public sphere is likely to be formed through the interrelation of institutions, technology and the *agency* of different political organisations and cultural groups.

Manuel Castells, the media and critical theory

In a different context, Manuel Castells (1996, 1997, 1998) has come the closest of recent writers in opening some of the important political features of contemporary media cultures. Arguably, unlike the perspectives presented this far, Castells outlines a view of contemporary media cultures that both deconstructs the polarities of the earlier discussion while connecting them to processes of substantial social transformation. Castells, as we have already seen, argues that the emergent 'information society' is primarily born out of the changing relationship between global capitalism, the state and new social movements. However, he is equally clear that the development of new media, the diversification of media messages, the implosion of politics and the media, and the development of the politics of 'scandal' have all had far-reaching effects upon the public sphere. The effects of these dimensions are multifarious and move in more than one direction. Television in particular and the media in general have become central and defining institutions in modern society. Castells illustrates this by pointing to the fact that television currently frames the language and types of symbolic exchange that help define society. Unless a social movement, set of ideas, or commercial product appears on television it may as well not exist. From the advertising jingles we hum on the way to work to our opinions on the government's latest set of social policies the media frames our sets of common understandings, knowledges and languages. The media then do not so much determine political agendas, but provide the background and context to political and social struggles. The centrality of modern communications in contemporary culture therefore does not deliver a mass culture, but what Castells calls a culture of 'real virtuality'. The idea of a mass culture has now been surpassed by a media environment where messages are explicitly customised to the symbolic languages of the intended audience. The future will not so much be governed by a homogeneous mass-produced culture repressing human diversity, but by a diversified popular culture where competitive advantage comes through product differentiation and audience segmentation. For Castells (1996): 'we are not living in a global village, but in customised cottages globally produced and locally distributed'.

172

The newly emergent information society is characterised by a media culture that is more individuated and less homogeneous than before. Further, the culture of 'real virtuality' opens out a world where popular moralities and perceptions opened up by soap operas can have as much if not greater impact on modern sensibilities as the moral strictures of politicians. Indeed we can probably think of numerous examples where the 'popular' and the 'political' have become irreversibly intertwined. This might invoke soap opera's raising political questions, the development of so-called 'infotainment', politicians receiving media training, protests deliberately designed to attract maximum media exposure and the development of the art of media spin-doctoring. Taken together these aspects and others speak of a new media and cultural environment that presses the case that unless you are on the media then you are not in politics. Seemingly for Castells the new media politics can foster both domination and patterns of resistance. Here I shall open out two such examples from the many that appear in Castell's three-volume study: they are the politics of scandal and some of the avenues social movements have explored by utilising new media technologies.

Scandal politics develops within the general context of an increasingly televisual society that has come to the fore against a back drop where political concerns are frequently played out and reported as a cynical and strategic game. This privileges the presentation of political issues in a fast paced and punchy style which in turn prioritises the culture of the sound bite. Further, the visualisation and corresponding trivialisation of political issues through television gives an added emphasis to the 'personalities' rather than the substantive issues at stake in political debate. Television then produces a kind of binary politics where complex positions are boiled down into digestible categories. The personalisation of politics and the decline of ideological contrasts between the major political parties produces the grounds for the central forms of struggle in the age of informational politics. In an era where moral and ethical distinctions between political parties are increasingly being replaced by more instrumental forms of manoeuvring that seek to interrupt themes and positions previously occupied by opposing political parties, the whiff of scandal can create a sense of political division and untrustworthiness. The fact that major political parties are both involved in expensive forms of image-making while simultaneously being chronically underfunded makes them increasingly likely to accept money under the table. Once this form of corruption becomes central to the organisation of mainstream politics, this provides ammunition for journalists and opposing political forces to expose corruption at the highest level. Scandal politics, therefore, becomes a daily threat if not occurrence.

Although Castells brackets off the analysis here it is not hard to imagine a situation in the future where politicians seek to attract support by constructing agendas and political teams that are 'above' scandal. Yet, if Castells is correct, such attempts are likely to prove fruitless. We might even further extend this argument by pointing to the future possible development of a kind of 'scandal fatigue' among the electorate. Just as the reporting of distant wars, famines and human rights abuses has arguably fostered compassion fatigue, so scandal fatigue could equally lead to an unshockable form of cynical indifference among the vast majority of the population. Scandal fatigue then would open out a situation whereby the public sphere would become drained of meaning and politics detached from wider questions of value. At this point Castell's concerns come close to those of Williams and Habermas (whose ideas on the public sphere started this volume) in respect of the closing down of public space and discourse. These are all evident dangers in contemporary media saturated societies. However, if Castells retreads familiar themes within critical theory demonstrating how media politics has become detached from ideological positions, these agendas are in turn seemingly interrupted by a variety of social movements from below. Castells (1997) characterises a variety of social movements as developing highly skilful media techniques in developing largely reactive and defensive responses to economic globalisation. By this he means that the movements under review do not so much articulate a vision of a future emancipated society, but a more conservative attempt to preserve current social identities. For example, the Zapatistas in Mexico (who Castells describes as the first informational guerrilla movement) made skilful use of image manipulation (videos, internet, etc.) to convert a small local struggle for dignity, democracy and land into a movement that has caught the attention of international public opinion. Indeed the Zapatistas' media connections made it impossible for the Mexican government to use the state apparatus to repress their movement forcibly. This brings out one of the distinctive features of the network society, that is while the concentration of power and wealth is increasingly distinct from local contexts our collective forms of meaning are more ready to hand. The task then of any oppositional movement must be to connect local experiences to a more global agenda, and that absolutely crucial in this process is the media of mass communication given its capacity to shift information through time and space.

Castells argues that new media technology can contribute to the building of networks among new social movements that might serve to reinforce relations of dominance or alternatively call them into question. This picture is further complicated elsewhere in discussing who actually uses the net. Here Castells asserts that new media technologies reinforce existing social structures rather than transforming them. For instance, because access to the net is dependent upon economic and educational factors it is likely to reinforce the cosmopolitan orientation of social elites, rather than destroying social hierarchies in the way that some commentators had been expecting. New media technologies therefore simultaneously reinforce relations of cultural capital, hierarchy and distinction while enabling social movements to publicise campaigns and connect with distant publics.

My argument therefore is that Castells' concern for the cultural conditions of the public sphere in the informational age offers a more substantive agenda than questions simply linked to the granting of additional rights and tracing through the 'effects' of technological change. Rather than arguing that new social movements need to be empowered by a human rights agenda he argues that they have already had a transforming effect on modern societies. Further, he breaks with the view that we can coherently view the development of new media cultures in any straightforward way through the axis of domination or emancipation. Instead Castells' complex reading of modern informational cultures points towards a more nuanced position that views the evolution of media cultures and technologies in a structured field capable of being transformed by political agency.

By viewing Castells in terms of the tradition of critical theory we might argue that he takes a less 'pessimistic turn' than is evident in Habermas and the early Frankfurt school. What Castells most clearly provides is a social and historical understanding of the emergence of the 'information society'. Like Adorno and Horkheimer's account of the culture industry and Habermas's notion of the public sphere, the 'informational society' opens out a new critical paradigm. Yet if one of the main agendas of critical theory is present another is absent. Missing from Castells's account is a more overtly normative analysis that would provide us with a critical standpoint from which to evaluate social change. In answer to this charge I think Castells would make two responses. The first is that implicit in much of what he says there is an agenda that seeks to map out the possibilities for democracy and social justice. Secondly, it is not for 'experts' like him to hand down blueprints for social change; the history of socialism has surely put paid to the desirability (or even feasibility) of getting social reality to conform to the wishes of the intellectual vanguard. Such reasons arguably cut critical theory off from the kinds of moral and ethical questions this book has at its core. To put the point bluntly, if it is worth arguing that the public sphere is becoming increasingly infected by a form of cynical reason and 'show' politics it is also worth making some broad suggestions as to how we might begin to construct an alternative. Further, if the media are becoming increasingly central to the self-definition of democratic societies, then radical change will only come through citizens increasing their involvement and participation within wider media cultures. The question as to how democratic societies help foster public involvement as opposed to private withdrawal, communicative concerns as opposed to instrumental strategies and publically engaged pluralistic identities as opposed to passively construed cultures is central to the concerns of critical theory. In doing this we should indeed avoid adopting the legislative ambitions of the expert, while also sidestepping thinking that fails to open new critical possibilities. It is not that Castells believes that the world could not be otherwise, but that he misses the implications a moral and ethical agenda could have for media and culture. If Castells opens out a more complex view of the media's position in modern society than was evident in the other perspectives under review, he also fails to develop a more normative response to the problems of dialogics, instrumental reason and identity.

A short agenda for media and cultural citizenship

The importance of a moral and ethical dimension in media politics, this book has argued at some length, need not be seen as either turning away from the world into the comfortable certainties of the study or as pointless given the prevailing culture of cynicism and the abandonment of ideology by the main political forces. While it is true that relativistic thinking, a sense of meaninglessness, the dominance of money and power and technological reason remain determinant features of modernity, other questions and opportunities remain. New social movements, mainstream political parties, the pervasive culture of human rights, new domains of reflexivity are just some of the forces keeping moral and ethical questions alive. Indeed, unlike Castells I think that ideological debate among mainstream political organisations is far from dead. Just as the 'end of ideology' theorists in the 1960s had to revise their proclamations due to the revival of Marxism, the same can also be said of Fukuyama's more recent arguments that we have reached the 'end of history'. Fukuyama (1992) argued that ideological conflict had been brought to an end by the collapse of state socialism and the global triumph of liberal democracy. If these arguments were applied to the media then the increasing dominance of the market over the censorious state would have ensured equal rights to communication and equal forms of recognition. My argument is that, not only is this not the case, but more rights, technological advance and the capitalistic expansion of the market do not necessarily lead us to understand the points of view of strangers any better than we did before. How to make a society more genuinely communicative is, I think, the central moral and ethical dilemma concerning the study of mass communications today. Arguably then we might have a really good bill of rights protecting free speech, widespread access to the most sophisticated media technology available and the greatest range of media products in human history to choose from but still remain an uncommunicative society. Indeed one of the key questions we have to decide upon is the extent to which as a community we are willing to put limits on the determination of communications by economic and technical reason. Multichannel access, digitally enhanced television and a fast moving sound bite culture might serve our interests as consumers, but as political and cultural citizens it leaves much to be desired. The moral and ethical requirements for what I have termed cultural citizenship in the modern world requires concerted local, global and still overwhelmingly national strategies. Further, the revitalisation of our communicative sensibilities requires a cultural politics that is more communitarian than liberal in focus. That is, if the revitalisation of our culture is not to be secured through guaranteed rights and slicker forms of technology it will have to come through a reworking of civil society, journalistic practices and the dominant media institutions.

I use the term 'communitarian' guardedly in wishing to distance myself from much of the illiberal and generally repressive talk that goes on under its mantle. However, I would want to point to the importance that this tradition continues to place upon ideas of overlapping communities, the critical question of obligations as opposed to rights and the key importance of civil society. In this respect then I would like to mark out four broad areas for critical intervention.

1   The first point is to open out an ethic of responsibility and participation in respect of contemporary media and communication within society more generally. The media as a range of voices that interrogate one another should be seen as a zone of peaceful civility. One of the primary ways in which we act ethically is in the ways we choose to communicate with one another. This means that when we enter the public domain we are always seeking to judge the fine line between our rights to speak and our obligations to other members of the community. While such practices are likely to remain fraught with ambivalence all mature societies will have to learn to live with the messiness of contradictory opinions and perspectives that are voiced across a diversity of channels of communication. As far as possible the mainstream media need to become channels of 'inclusion' in terms of the overlapping cultural patterns that are allowed to interrogate one another. In this sense nations can not afford to be 'agnostic' about the cultural capabilities of their citizens. The promotion of a vibrant civil society is perhaps above all dependent upon the communicative capacity of its inhabitants. However, despite attempts to promote civil exchange (that can be linked to literacy campaigns and how the education system teaches citizenship) there will undoubtedly be groups that need to be excluded. What Beck (1998) calls 'ugly citizens' are likely to use alternative unofficial methods of information exchange to promote a sense of in-group identity and cohesion. The point here is for public systems of communication to keep the dialogue 'open' in the hope that rogue citizens will rejoin the conversation at a future date.

2   The case study on Rwanda argued that 'scientific' journalism needs to be held to question, not only over notions of bias but also in terms of the promotion of reflexivity. The media need to be opened up as far as possible in order to make sure 'alternative' voices are heard, while simultaneously making clear that any picture of a society (especially when it is distant from our own) is always incomplete. A critical democratic public sphere then depends upon how others spatially distant from the local contexts in which we live are represented on mainstream media. Journalistic culture therefore

needs to become orientated less around the search for objective factual statements (as important as this remains) and more around opening up critical questions for discussion. Media professionals will need to search for new repertoires to stimulate reflection rather than adhering to well-worn stereotypes. The promotion of a culture of critical engagement and doubt requires that journalists view themselves less as purveyors of hard truths and more as interpreters of knowledge.

3   Western European societies continue to maintain a shared tradition of public service broadcasting. Despite the growth of new and alternative technologies in media cultures, the culture of public service is likely to remain a key site. Television remains a more powerful medium than all of the other mediums combined. New pressures concerning audience share, increasing competition and the multiplication of new channels is all placing public service broadcasting under pressure. Yet reports of its demise are much exaggerated. The culture of public service broadcasting continues to have strong supporters in elite circles and needs to be robustly maintained. This is likely to become more important rather than less, given the cultural standards and guarantees that continue to regulate public service channels.

4   The move towards more trans-national levels of governance (prefigured in the EU) should open the question as to the regulation of the global media. There should be increasing concern as to the quality and type of information that is regularly crossing the boundaries of nation-states. The kind of regulation required will depend upon the different histories, traditions and sociological make-up of the societies in question. For instance, in Europe the threat to media and cultural diversity is posed by large media conglomerates commercialising public space and creating new exclusions on the basis of price. However, as we saw, there are different problems facing media cultures in different world regions. In the Rwandan context the crucial moral questions in the public sphere could not be posed in terms of the colonisation of communication by economic and instrumental reason. Instead, as we saw, the real problem was the underdevelopment of civil society allowing a so-called 'soft state' to censor and direct public debate. Again this is an issue that could be profitably taken up by different levels of governance including neighbouring African states and the United Nations.

These proposals are necessarily brief and are intended to point towards possible future debates rather than being explanatory in their own terms. What they, and hopefully the rest of this book, point towards is a future public debate that takes moral and ethical problems in the context of communications seriously. Such a venture would need to link structural questions (what would a democratic and just system of communications look like?) with those of personal and group agency (how should we go about talking to one another?) in such a way that recognises much of the ambivalence these issues inevitably open.

Notes

1 Introduction

1 See recent volumes edited by Ferguson and Golding (1997) and McGuigan (1997) for an overview of the current issues and debates in more specifically British cultural studies.
2 See Stevenson (1995a; 1995b) for a more in-depth discussion of these points. Also see Kenny (1995) for an excellent discussion of the politics of the early New Left.

2 Media, morality and modernity

1 I have discussed the interrelations of the three paradigms of mass communication elsewhere in Stevenson (1995a).
2 A short but provocative account of Mead's writing and intellectual context is provided by Jenkins (1996).
3 A good discussion of these debates is provided by Larrabee (1993).
4 Williams's contributions to media theory are more fully discussed in Stevenson (1995a).

3 Global media and technological change

1 Habermas differs in this respect from cruder propaganda models which are offered by other Leftist critics of the media like Herman and Chomsky (1994).
2 Both the arguments over handguns and the question over Paul Gascoigne's private conduct were widely covered in the British media during November 1996.
3 Habermas's descriptions of the scientised instrumental culture of modernity has a strong resemblance to Williams's (1985) discussions of Plan X.
4 An interesting discussion of Honneth's theory of recognition has been provided by Alexander and Pia Lara (1996).

4 Cultural citizenship

1 For a discussion of the diverse ways multiculturalism can be articulated by the nation culture see John Stratton and Ien Ang (1994) 'Multicultural Imagined Communities: Cultural Difference and National Identity in Australia and the USA', *Continuum*, 8(2), 124–158.
2 I am grateful to Jim McGuigan (1996) for discussing these points with me.
3 I have borrowed this term from Graham Murdock (1994).
4 I have investigated the connection between the public sphere, national identity and Europe at greater detail in Stevenson (1997a).

5 Global media cultures

1 See my discussion in Stevenson (1997b).
2 For some criticisms of Beck's account of the media and more generally see Cottle (1998) and Rustin (1994).

6 Post-colonialism and mediated violence

1 I am grateful to Greg Philo at the Glasgow University Media group for allowing me to visit and use their television resources. However a very special thank you has to be reserved for Liza Beattie (who also works at the centre) who not only collected much of the television material, but also sent me numerous articles on the Rwandan question.

7 The future of public media cultures

1 An interesting discussion of utopia and realism is provided by Giddens (1990) and Midgeley (1996).

Bibliography

Adam, B. (1995) *Timewatch*. Polity Press, Cambridge.

African Rights (1995) *Rwanda; Death, Despair and Defiance*. African Rights Publications, London.

Ahmad, A. (1995) 'The Politics of Literary Postcoloniality', *Race and Class*, 36(3), 1–20.

Ahmed, K. (1998) 'Digital TV Leaves Poor out of Picture', *The Guardian*, Saturday, Jan. 31, 1998, 7.

Albrow, M. (1996) *The Global Age; State and Society Beyond Modernity*. Polity Press, Cambridge.

Alcorn, K. (1989) 'AIDS in the Public Sphere: How a Broadcasting System in Crisis Dealt with an Epidemic', in E. Carter and S. Watney (eds) *Taking Liberties: AIDS and Cultural Politics*. Serpents Tail, London.

Alexander, J. C. and Pia Lara, M. (1996) 'Honneth's New Critical Theory of Recognition', *New Left Review*, 220, 126–136.

Amin, S. (1989) *Eurocentrism*. Zed Books, London.

Anderson, B. (1983) *Imagined Communities*. Verso, London.

Ang, I. (1985) *Watching Dallas; Soap Opera and the Melodramatic Imagination*. Methuen, London.

Appadurai, A. (1990) 'Disjunction and Difference in the Global Cultural Economy', in M. Featherstone (ed.) *Global Culture: Nationalism, Globalisation and Modernity*. Sage, London.

Archibugi, D. (1995) 'From United Nations to Cosmopolitan Democracy', in D. Archibugi and D. Held (eds) *Cosmopolitan Democracy; An Agenda for a New World Order*. Polity Press, Cambridge.

Arendt, H. (1958) *The Human Condition*. Chicago University Press, Chicago.

Baudrillard, J. (1993) *Symbolic Exchange and Death*. Sage, London.

Baudrillard, J. (1994) *The Illusion of the End*, translated by Chris Turner. Polity Press, Cambridge.

Bauman, Z. (1989) *Modernity and the Holocaust*. Polity Press, Cambridge.

Bauman, Z. (1992) *Intimations of Postmodernity*. Routledge, London.

Bauman, Z. (1993) *Postmodern Ethics*. Blackwell, Oxford.

Bauman, Z. (1994) *Life in Fragments: Essays in Postmodern Morality*. Blackwell, London.

Beck, U. (1992) *Risk Society: Towards a New Modernity*. Sage, London.

Beck, U. (1996) 'World Risk Society as Cosmopolitan Society? Ecological Questions in the Framework of Manufactured Uncertainties', *Theory, Culture and Society*, 13(4), 1–32.

Beck, U. (1997) *The Reinvention of Politics; Rethinking Modernity in the Global Social Order*. Polity Press, Cambridge.

Beck, U. (1998) *Democracy Without Enemies*. Polity Press, Cambridge.

Benhabib, S. (1992) *Situating the Self: Gender, Community and Postmodernism in Contemporary Ethics*. Polity Press, Cambridge.

Benjamin, J. (1992) *Bonds of Love*. Virago, London.

Benjamin, W. (1973) 'The Work of Art in the Age of Mechanical Reproduction', *Illuminations*. Fontana, London.

Bennett, T. (1992) 'Putting Policy into Cultural Studies', in C. Grossberg, C. Nelson and P. Treicher (eds) *Cultural Studies*. Routledge, London.

Berlin, I. (1991) *The Crooked Timbre of Humanity*. Fontana, London.

Bhabha, H. (1988) 'The Commitment to Theory', *New Formations*, No. 5, Summer.

Bhabha, H. (1994) *The Location of Culture*. Routledge, London.

Billig, M. (1995) *Banal Nationalism*. Sage, London.

Bollas, C. (1992) *Forces of Destiny; Psychoanalysis and the Human Idiom*. Jason Aronson, London.

Bollas, C. (1994) *Being a Character; Psychoanalysis and Self Experience*. Routledge, London.

Bourdieu, P. (1984) *Distinction*. Routledge, London.

Boyd-Barrett, O. (1977) *Mass Communications in Cross-Cultural Contexts: The Case of the Third World*. Open University Press, Milton Keynes.

Boyle, K. (1995) 'Stock-taking on Human Rights: The World Conference on Human Rights, Vienna 1993', *Political Studies*, 43, 79–95.

Brooks, H. J. (1995) 'Suit, Tie and a Touch of Juju' – The Ideological Construction of Africa: Critical Discourse Analysis of News on Africa in the British Press', *Discourse and Society*, 6(4), 461–494.

Castells, M. (1993) 'The Informational Economy and the New International Division of Labor', in M. Camog, M. Castells, S. Cohen and H. Condoso (eds) *The New Global Economy in the Information Age*. Macmillan, London.

Castells, M. (1989) *The Information City; Information Technology, Economic Restructuring, and the Urban-Regional Process*. Basil Blackwell, Oxford.

Castells, M. (1996) *The Rise of the Network Society; The Information Age: Economy, Society and Culture, Volume I*. Blackwell, Oxford.

Castells, M. (1997) *The Power of Indentity; The Information Age: Economy, Society and Culture, Volume II*. Blackwell, Oxford.

Castells, M. (1998) *End of Millennium; The Information Age: Economy, Society and Culture, Volume III*. Blackwell, Oxford.

Castells, M. and Hall, P. (1994) *Technopoles of the World: The Making of Twenty-first Century Industrial Complexes*. Routledge, London.

Castoriadis, C. (1997) 'Reflections on Racism', *World in Fragments; Writings on Politics, Society, Psychoanalysis and the Imagination*. Stanford University Press, California.

Cheah, P. (1997) 'Posit(ion)ing Human Rights in the Current Globe Conjuncture', *Public Culture*, 9, 233–266.

Chen, K. H. (1996) 'Cultural Studies and the Politics of Internationalization: An Interview with Stuart Hall', in D. Morley and Kuan-Hsing Chen (eds) *Stuart Hall: Critical Dialogues in Cultural Studies*. Routledge, London.

Cleasby, A. (1995) *What in the World is Going on?; British and Global Affairs.* Third World Broadcasting Project, London.

Cockburn, A. (1995) 'Fatal Attraction', *Guardian*, 12 May (Review Section), 1–4.

Cottle, S. (1998) Ulrich Bech, Irish Society and the Media: A Catastrophic View? *European Journal of Communications*, 13(1), 5–32.

Crossley, N. (1996) *Intersubjectivity: The Fabric of Social Becoming.* London, Sage.

Culf, A. (1997) 'Switch on to Two-way Television', *The Guardian*, 8 May 1997, 3.

Dirlik, A. (1994) 'The Postcolonial Aura: Third World Criticism in the Age of Global Capital', *Critical Inquiry*, 20(2).

Downing, J. (1997) *Internationalising Media Theory.* Sage, London.

Dyer, G. (1988) 'White', *Screen*, 29(4), 44–64.

Eagleton, T. (1990) *The Ideology of the Aesthetic.* Basil Blackwell, Oxford.

Economist (1995a) 'Prime-time Passions', *The Economist*, August 5, 63–64.

Economist (1995b) 'Yo quiero mi MTV', *The Economist*, February 25, 99–100.

Elliott, A. (1992) *Social Theory and Psychoanalysis in Transition; Self and Society from Freud to Kristeva.* Blackwell, Oxford.

Elliott, A. (1996) *Subject to Ourselves; Social Theory, Psychoanalysis and Postmodernity.* Polity Press, Cambridge.

Enzensberger, H. M. (1994) *Civil War.* Granta Books, London.

Etzioni, A. (1993) *The Spirit of Community: Rights, Responsibilities, and the Communitarian Agenda.* Crown Publishers, New York.

Etzioni, A. (1996) 'A Moderate Communitarian Proposal', *Political Theory*, 24(2), 155–171.

Falk, R. (1995a) 'The World Order between Inter-State Law and the Law of Humanity: The Role of Civil Society Institutions', in Daniele Archibugi and David Held (eds) *Cosmpolitan Democracy.* Polity Press, Cambridge.

Falk, R. (1995b) *On Human Governance; Toward a New Global Politics.* Polity Press, Cambridge.

Fejes, F. (1981) 'Media Imperialism: An Assessment', *Media, Culture and Society*, 3(3), 281–289.

Ferguson, M. and Golding, P. (eds) (1997) *Cultural Studies in Question.* Sage, London.

Fine, H. (1990) *Genocide: A Sociological Perspective.* Sage, London.

Flax, J. (1990) *Thinking Fragments: Psychoanalysis, Feminism, and PostModernism in the Contemporary West.* University of California Press, Berkeley.

Fraser, N. (1995) 'From Redistribution to Recognition? Dilemmas of Justice in a "Post-socialist" Age', *New Left Review*, 212, July\August, 68–93.

Freud, S. (1930) *Civilisation and its Discontents.* Hogarth Press, London.

Freud, S. (1966) *Complete Introductory Lectures.* Norton, New York.

Fukuyama, F. (1992) *The End of History and the Last Man.* Hamish Hamilton, London.

Galbraith, K. (1992) *The Culture of Contentment.* Penguin, London.

Galtung, G. and Ruge, M. (1973) 'Structuring and Selecting News', in S. Cohen and J. Young, *The Manufacture of News.* Constable, London.

Gates, H. L. (1994) *Coloured People.* Penguin, London.

Gellner, E. (1983) *Nations and Nationalism.* Blackwell, Oxford.

Giddens, A. (1990) *The Consequences of Modernity.* Polity, Cambridge.

Giddens, A. (1991) *Modernity and Self-Identity: Self and Society in the Late Modern Age.* Polity Press, Cambridge.

Giddens, A. (1994) *Beyond Left and Right; The Future of Radical Politics.* Polity Press, Cambridge.

Gilder, G. (1992) *Life After Television; The Coming Transformation of Media and American Life*. W. W. Norton and Company, New York.

Gilligan, C. (1982) *In a Different Voice*. Harvard University Press, Harvard.

Gilroy, P. (1987) *There Aint No Black In The Union Jack*. Hutchinson, London.

Goonatilake, S. (1995) 'The Self Wandering Through Cultural Localization and Globalization', in J. N. Pieterse and B. Parekh (eds) *The Decolonization of Imagination*. Zed Books, London.

Gray, J. (1995a) 'The Sad Side of Cyberspace', *The Guardian*, 10. Apr.

Gray, J. (1995b) 'Virtual Democracy', *The Guardian*, 15 September.

Griffiths, R. (1993) 'The Politics of Cultural Policy in Urban Regeneration Strategies', *Policy and Politics*, 21(1), Jan.

Gurevitch, Z. D. (1990) 'The Dialogic Connection and the Ethics of Dialogue', *British Journal of Sociology*, 41(2), 181–196.

Habermas, J. (1971) 'Technology and Science as "Ideology"', *Towards a Rational Society; Student Protest, Science and Politics*. Heinemann Educational, London.

Habermas, J. (1979) *Communication and the Evolution of Society*. Heinmann, London.

Habermas, J. (1981) *The Theory of Communicative Action; The Critique of Functionalist Reason*. Polity Press, Cambridge.

Habermas, J. (1989a) *The Structural Transformation of the Public Sphere*. Polity Press, Cambridge.

Habermas, J. (1989b) *The New Conservatism; Cultural Criticism and the Historians Debate*. Polity Press, Cambridge.

Habermas, J. (1990a) 'Morality and Ethical Life: Does Hegel's Critique of Kant Apply to Discourse Ethics?', *Moral Consciousness and Communicative Action*, trans. C. Lenhart and S. Weber Nicholson. Polity Press, Cambridge.

Habermas, J. (1990b) 'What Does Socialism Mean Today? The Rectifying Revolution and the Need for New Thinking on the Left', *New Left Review*, 183, Sept./Oct., 3–22.

Habermas, J. (1990c) 'Moral Consciousness and Communicative Action', in *Moral Consciousness and Communicative Action*, trans. C. Lenhart and S. Weber Nicholson. Polity Press, Cambridge.

Habermas, J. (1992) 'Individuation Through Socialization: On George Herbert Mead's Theory of Subjectivity', in *Postmetaphysical Thinking; Philosphical Essays*, trans. W. M. Hohengarten. Polity Press, Cambridge.

Habermas, J. (1993a) 'On the Pragmatic, the Ethical, and the Moral Employment of Practical Reason', in *Justification and Application: Remarks on Discourse Ethics*, trans. C. P. Cronin. Polity Press, Cambridge.

Habermas, J. (1993b) 'Remarks on Discourse Ethics', in *Justification and Application: Remarks on Discourse Ethics*, trans. C. P. Cronin. Polity Press, Cambridge.

Habermas (1994) 'Citizenship and National Identity', in B. V. Steenbergen (ed.). *The Condition of Citizenship*. Sage, London.

Habermas, J. (1995) 'Reconcilation through the Public Use of Reason: Remarks on John Rawls's Political Liberalism', *Journal of Philosophy*, 92(3), 109–131.

Habermas, J. (1996) *Between Facts and Norms; Contributions to a Discourse Theory of Law and Democracy*, trans. W. Rehg. Polity Press, Cambridge.

Hall, C. (1996) 'Histories, Empires and the Post-Colonial Moment', in Iain Chambers and Lidia Curti (eds) *The Post-Colonial Question: Common Skies, Divided Horizons*. Routledge, London.

Hall, S. (1987) 'Minimal Selves', in *Identity: The Real Me*. ICA Document 6.

Hall, S. (1996) 'New Ethnicities', in D. Morley and Kuan-Hsing Chen (eds) *Stuart Hall: Critical Dialogues in Cultural Studies*. Routledge, London.

Hallin, D. C. (1994) *We Keep America on Top of the World; Television, Journalism and the Public Sphere*. Routledge, London.

Hamelink, C. (1994) *The Politics of World Communication; A Human Rights Perspective*. Sage, London.

Hamelink, C. (1995) *World Communication; Disempowerment and Self-Empowerment*. Zed Books, London.

Hannerz, U. (1992) *Cultural Complexity; Studies in the Social Organisation of Meaning*. Columbia University Press, Columbia.

Hartmann, P., Patil, B. R. and Dighe, A. (1989) *The Mass Media and Village Life; An Indian Study*. Sage, London.

Harvey, S. and Robins, K. (1994) 'Voices and Places: The BBC and Regional Policy', *The Political Quarterly*, 65(1), 39–52.

Hebdige, D. (1990) 'Fax to the Future', *Marxism Today*, January 18–24.

Held, D. (1995) *Democracy and the Global Order; From Modern State to Cosmopolitan Governance*. Polity Press, Cambridge.

Herman, E. S. and Chomsky, N. (1994) *Manufacturing Consent; The Political Economy of the Mass Media*. Vintage, London.

Heush, L. D. (1995) 'Rwanda: Responsibilities for a Genocide', *Anthropology Today*, 1(4), August.

Hill, J. (1993) 'Government Policy and the British Film Industry', *European Journal of Communication*, 18(2), June, 203–224.

HMSO (1994) *The Future of the BBC; Serving the Nation Competing World-wide*. HMSO, London.

Holsten and Appadurai (1996) Cities and Citizenship, *Public Culture*, 18(2), 187–204.

Honneth, A. (1995) *The Struggle for Recognition; The Moral Grammar of Social Conflicts*. Polity Press, Cambridge.

Hooks, B. (1992) *Black Looks: Race and Represenation*. Routledge, London.

Human Rights Watch (1995) *Slaughter Among Neighbours; The Political Origins of Communal Violence*. Yale University Press, New Haven and London.

Innis, H. (1951) *The Bias of Communication*. Oxford University Press, Oxford.

Jameson, F. (1991) *Postmodernism or, the Cultural Logic of Late Capitalism*. Verso, London.

Jenkins, R. (1996) *Social Identity*. Routledge, London.

Jonas, H. (1985) *G. H. Mead: A Contemporary Re-examination of His Thought*, trans. R. Meyer. Polity Press, Cambridge.

Julien, I. and Mercer, K. (1996) 'DeMargin and DeCentre', in D. Morley and Kuan-Hsing Chen (eds) *Stuart Hall: Critical Dialogues in Cultural Studies*. Routledge, London.

Karikari, K. (1993) 'Africa: The Press and Democracy', *Race and Class*, 34(3), 55–66.

Kasler, D. (1988) *Max Weber; An Introduction to his Life and Work*. Polity Press, Cambridge.

Keane, F. (1995) *Season of Blood; A Rwandan Journey*. Penguin, London.

Keane, J. (1989) *Democracy and Civil Society*. Verso, London.

Keane, J. (1996) *Reflections on Violence*. Verso, London.

Keegan, V. (1996) 'Highway Robbery by the Super-rich', *The Guardian*, 2, July 22, 2–3.

Keegan, V. (1997) 'What a Web we Weave', *The Guardian*, 2, May 13, 2–3.

Kellner, D. (1992) *The Persian Gulf TV War*. Westview Press, Boulder, Co.

Kellner, D. (1995) 'Intellectuals and New Technologies', *Media, Culture and Society*, 17(3), 427–448.

Kenny, M. (1995) *The First New Left; British Intellectuals After Stalin*. Lawrence and Wishart, London.

King, A. D. (1995) 'The Times and Spaces of Modernity (Or Who Needs Postmodernism?' in M. Featherstone, S. Lash and R. Robertson (eds) *Global Modernities*. Sage, London.

Kovel, J. (1995) 'On Racism and Psychoanalysis', in A. Elliott and S. Frosh (eds) *Psychoanalysis in Contexts; Paths Between Theory and Modern Culture*. Routledge, London.

Kundera, M. (1994) *The Unbearable Lightness of Being*. Faber and Faber, London.

Lacan, J. (1977) *Ecrits: A Selection*. Tavistock, London.

Larrabee, M. J. (1993) (eds) *An Ethic of Care; Feminist and Interdisciplinary Perspectives*. Routledge, London.

Lash, S. and Urry, J. (1994) *Economies of Signs and Space*. Sage, London.

Luke, T. W. and Tuathail, G. O. (1997) 'On Videocameralistics: The Geopolitics of Failed States, the CNN International and (Un) governmentality', *Review of International Political Economy*, 4(4) Winter, 709–733.

Luke, T. W. (1995) 'New World Order or Neo-World Orders: Power, Politics and Ideology in Informationalizing Glocalities', in M. Featherstone, S. Lash and R. Robertson (eds) *Global Modernities*. Sage, London.

Mader, R. (1993) 'Globo Village; Television in Brazil', in T. Dowmunt (eds) *Channels of Resistance: Global Media and Local Empowerment*. BFI Publishing, London.

Maffesoli, M. (1996) *The Time of the Tribes; The Decline of Individualism in Mass Society*. Sage, London.

Maingard, J. (1996) 'Transforming Television Broadcasting in a Democratic South Africa', *Screen*, 38(3).

Mamdani, M. (1996) 'From Conquest to Consent as the Basis of State Formation: Reflections on Rwanda', *New Left Review*, 216, 3–36.

Mann, M. (1993) 'Nation-states in Europe and Other Continents: Diversifying, Developing, not Dying', *Daedalus*, Summer 93.

Marshall, T. H. (1992) *Citizenship and Social Class*. Pluto Press, London.

Martin-Barbero, J. (1993) *Communication, Culture and Hegemony: From the Media to Mediations*. Sage, London.

Mattlelart, A., Delcout, X. and Mattelat, M. (1984) *International Image Markets*. Comedia, London.

Mattlelart, A. and Mattlelart, M. (1992) *Rethinking Media Theory: Signposts and New Directions*, trans. J. A. Cohen and M. Urquidi. University of Minnesota Press, Minnesota.

McGreal, C. (1997) 'Hutus Raid Genocide Jail', *The Guardian*, December 5, 19.

McGuigan, J. (1996) *Culture and the Public Sphere*. Routledge, London.

McGuigan, J. (1997) (eds) *Cultural Methodologies*. Sage, London.

McLuhan, M. (1994) *Understanding Media; the Extensions of Man*. Routledge, London.

McLuhan, M. and Fiore, Q. (1967) *The Medium is the Message*. Penguin, London.

McLuhan, M. (1969) *Counterblast*. Harcourt, New York.

Mead, G. H. (1934) *Mind, Self and Society: From the Standpoint of a Social Behaviorist*. University of Chicago Press, Chicago.

Meehan, M. (1993) *Citizenship and the European Community*. Sage, London.

Mercer, K. (1994) *Welcome to the Jungle; New Positions in Black Cultural Studies*. Routledge, London.

Midgley, M. (1996) *Utopias, Dolphins and Computers; Problems of Philosophical Plumbing*. Routledge, London.

Millar, S. and O'Neill, B. (1996) 'From Cradle to Grave on Memory Chip', *The Guardian*, 18 July, 1.

Mitchell, J. (eds) (1986) *The Selected Melanie Klien*. Penguin, London.

Mohammadi, A. S. and Mohammadi, M. (1994) *Small Media, Big Revolution; Communication, Culture and the Iranian Revolution*. Minnesota Press, Minneapolis.

Morley, D. (1996) 'EurAm, Modernity, Reason and Alterity or, Postmodernism, the Highest Stage of Cultural Imperialism?', in D. Morley and Kuan-Hsing Chen (eds) *Stuart Hall: Critical Dialogues in Cultural Studies*. Routledge, London.

Morley, D. and Robins, K. (1995) *Spaces of Identity: Global Media, Electronic Landscapes and Cultural Boundaries*. Routledge, London.

Mulgan, G. and Worpole, K. (1986) *Saturday Night or Sunday Morning: From Arts to Industry – New Forms of Cultural Policy*. Comedia, London.

Mulgan, G. (1997) *Connexity; How to Live in a Connected World*. Chatto and Windus, London.

Mullholland, J. (1998) 'ITV Failing Quality Standards Says Report', *Guardian Newspaper*, Janurary.

Murdock, G. (1994) 'Money Talks: Broadcasting, Finance and Public Culture', in S. Hood (ed.) *Behind the Screens: The Structure of British Television in the Nineties*. Lawrence and Wishart, London.

Murdock, G. (1989) 'Televisual Tourism: National Image-making and International Markets', in C. W. Thomsen (ed.) *Cultural Transfer or Electronic Imperialism?* Reihe Siegen Heidelberg.

Nairn, T. (1997) *Faces of Nationalism; Janus Revisited*. Verso, London.

Negroponte, N. (1994) *Being Digital, Coronet Books*. Hodder and Stoughton, London.

Offe, C. (1984) *Contradictions of the Welfare State*. London, Hutchinson.

Ogden, T. (1989) *The Primitive Edge of Experience*. Jason Aronson Inc, New Jersey.

Omaar, R. (1997) 'A Bitter Harvest', *The Guardian*, April 30, 21.

Parekh, B. (1991) 'British Citizenship and Cultural Difference', in Geoff Andrews (ed.) *Citizenship*. Lawrence and Wishart, London.

Parekh, M. (1993) 'The Cultural Particularity of Liberal Democracy', in D. Held (ed.) *Prospects for Democracy*. Polity Press, Cambridge.

Petley, J. and Romano, G. (1993) 'After the Deluge', in Dowmunt, T. (eds) *Global Television and Local Empowerment*. BFI Publishing, London.

Phillips, A. (1991) *Engendering Democracy*. Polity Press, Cambridge.

Phillips, A. (1993) *Democracy and Difference*. Polity Press, Cambridge.

Pieterse, J. N. (1992) *White On Black; Images of Africa and Blacks in Western Popular Culture*. Yale University, Yale.

Pieterse, J. N. and Parekh, B. (1995) 'Shifting Imaginaries: Decolonisation, Internal Decolonization, Postcoloniality', in J. N. Pieterse and B. Parekh (eds) *The Decolonization of the Imagination*. Zed Books. University Press, New Haven and London.

Plant, S. (1996) 'Connectionism and the Post Humanities', in Warren Charnaik, Marilyn Deegan and Andrew Gibson (eds) *Beyond the Book; Theory, Culture, and the Politics of Cyberspace*. Office for Humanities Communication Publications, Number 7.

Plummer, K. (1995) *Telling Sexual Stories; Power, Change and Social Worlds*. Routledge, London.

187

Porter, R. (1996) 'The Keeper of the Global Gate', *The Guardian*, October 29, 2–4.

Poster, M. (1990) *The Mode of Information*. Chicago Press, Chicago.

Poster, M. (1995) *The Second Media Age*. Polity Press, Cambridge.

Prunier, G. (1995) *The Rwanda Crisis 1959–1994; History of a Genocide*. Hurst and Company, London.

Rawls, J. (1972) *A Theory of Justice*. Harvard University Press, Cambridge, Mass.

Rawls, J. (1996) *Political Liberalism*. Harvard University Press, Cambridge, Mass.

Real World Coalition (1996) *The Politics of the Real World*. Earthscan, London.

Reeves, G. (1993) *Communications and the 'Third World'*. Routledge, London.

Rheingold, H. (1994) *The Virtual Community – Surfing the Internet*. Martin Secker and Warburg, London.

Richardson, D. (1996) 'Heterosexuality and Social Theory', in Richardson, D. (eds) *Theorising Heterosexuality*. Open University, Buckingham.

Ricoeur, P. (1978) 'The Language of Faith', in C. E. Reagan and D. Stewart (eds) *The Philosophy of Paul Ricoeur; An Anthology of his Work*. Beacon Press, Boston.

Ricoeur, P. (1991a) 'Narrative Identity', in D. Wood (eds) *On Paul Ricoeur; Narrative and Interpretation*. Routledge, London.

Ricoeur, P. (1991b) 'Life: A Story in Search of a Narrative', in M. J. Valdes (eds) *A Ricoeur Reader; Reflection and Imagination*. Harvester and Wheatsheaf, Hemel Hempstead.

Robertson, R. (1992) *Globalization; Social Theory and Global Culture*. Sage, London.

Robins, K. (1993) 'The Politics of Silence: The Meaning of Community and the Uses of Media in the New Europe', *New Formations*, 21, Winter, 80–101.

Roche, M. (1992) *Rethinking Citizenship: Welfare, Ideology and Change in Modern Society*. Polity Press, Cambridge.

Rorty, R. (1998) *Achieving Our Country; Leftist Thought in Twentieth-Century America*. Harvard University Press, Cambridge.

Rosas, A. (1995) 'State Sovereignty and Human Rights; Towards a Global Constitutional Project', *Political Studies*, 43, 61–78.

Ross, K. (1996) *Black and White Media; Black Images in Film and Popular Television*. Polity Press, Cambridge.

Rustin, M. (1991) *The Good Society and the Inner World; Psychoanalysis, Politics and Culture*. Verso, London.

Rustin, M. (1994) 'Incomplete Modernity: Ulrich Beck's Risk Society', *Radical Philosophy*, 67.

Said, E. (1978) *Orientalism*. Routledge and Kegan Paul, London.

Said, E. (1993) *Culture and Imperialism*. Chatto and Windus, London.

Schiller (1992) *Mass Communications and American Empire*, 2nd edn, Updated, Westview Press, Boulder, Col.

Schiller, H. (1996) *Information Inequality; The Deepening Social Crisis of America*. Routledge, London.

Schlesinger, P. (1993) 'Wishful Thinking: Cultural Politics, Media and Collective Identities in Europe', *Journal of Communication*, 43(2).

Schlesinger, P. and Doyle, G. (1995) 'Contradictions of Economy and Culture: The European Union and the Information Society', *Cultural Policy*, 2(1), 25–42.

Seaton, J. (1998) *Politics and the Media*. Blackwell, Oxford.

Shaw, M. (1995) *Civil Society and Media in Global Crisis; Representing Distant Violence*. Pinter, London.

Shawcross, W. (1995) 'Reaching for the sky', *New Statesman and Society*, 24 March.

Simmel, G. (1950) *The Sociology of George Simmel*, trans. Kurt H. Wolf (Ed.). Free Press, New York.

Simpson, L. C. (1995) *Technology, Time and the Conversations of Modernity*. Routledge, New York and London.

Sinclair, Jacka and Cunningham (1996) New Patterns in Global Television; Peripheral Vision. Oxford University Press, Oxford.

Smith, A. (1980) *The Geopolitics of Information; How Western Culture Dominates the World*. Faber, London.

Smith, A. D. (1995) *Nations and Nationalism in A Global Era*. Polity Press, Cambridge.

Smythe, D. (1977) 'Communications – Blind Spots of Western Marxism', *Canadian Journal of Political and Social Theory*, 1(3), 1–27.

Somers, M. R. (1994) 'The Narrative Consitution of Identity: A Relational and Network Approach', *Theory and Society*, 23, 605–649.

Sorensen, J. (1991) 'Mass Media and Discourse on Famine in the Horn of Africa', *Discourse and Society*, 2(2), 223–242.

Stallabras, J. (1996) *Gargantura; Manufactured Mass Culture*. Verso, London.

Steiner, G. (1974) *Extraterritorial*. Penguin, Harmondsworth.

Stevenson, N. (1995a) *Understanding Media Cultures; Social Theory and Mass Communication*. Sage, London.

Stevenson, N. (1995b) *Culture, Ideology and Socialism; Raymond Williams and E. P. Thompson*. Avebury, Aldershot.

Stevenson, N. (1997a) 'The European Public Sphere; National Culture, Identity and Cultural Citizenship', *European Studies Journal*, 14(1), 47–61.

Stevenson, N. (1997b) 'Critical Theory and Television', *Rethinking Marxism*, 18(4), 75–88.

Stratton, J. and Ang, I. (1994) 'Multicultural Imagined Communities: Cultural Difference and National Identity in Australia and the USA', *Continuum*, 8(2), 124–158.

Straubhuar, J. D. (1997) 'Distinguishing the Global, Regional and National Levels of World Television', in A. Sreberny-Mohammadi, D. Winsek, J. McKenna and O. Boyd-Barrett (eds) *Media in a Global Context*. Edward Arnold, London.

Taylor, C. (1989) *Sources of Self; The Making of Modern Identity*. Cambridge University Press, Cambridge.

Taylor, C. (1991) *The Ethics of Authenticity*. Harvard University Press, Cambridge.

Taylor, C. (1992) *Multiculturalism and 'the Politics of Recognition'*. Princeton University Press, Princeton.

Taylor, C. (1995) 'Liberal Politics and the Public Sphere', in A. Etzioni (eds) *New Communitarian Thinking*. Virginia University Press, Virginia.

Tester, K. (1997) *Moral Culture*. Sage, London.

Therborn, G. (1995) 'Routes to/Through modernity', in M. Featherstone, S. Lash and R. Robertson (eds) *Global Modernities*. Sage, London.

Thompson, J. B. (1994) 'Social Theory and the Media', in Crowley, D. and Mitchell, D. (eds) *Communication Theory Today*. Polity Press, Cambridge.

Thompson, J. B. (1995) *The Media and Modernity: A Social Theory of the Media*. Cambridge, Polity Press.

Tomlinson, J. (1991) *Cultural Imperialism*. Pinter Publishers, London.

Toynbee, P. (1998) 'Murdock Takes a Hit', Wednesday, 11 Feb., 17.

Traynor, I. (1995) ' A Question of Who Calls the Shots', *The Guardian*, 28 January, 27.

Turner, B. S. (1993) 'Contemporary Problems in the Theory of Citizenship', in B. S. Turner (Ed.) *Citizenship and Social Theory*. Sage, London.

Turner, B. S. (1994a) 'Postmodern Culture/Modern Citizens', in B. V. Steenbergen (Ed.) *The Condition of Citizenship*. Sage, London.

Turner, B. S. (1994b) *Orientalism, Postmodernism and Globalism*. Routledge, London.

Turner, T. (1994) 'The Mission Thing', *Index on Censorship*, Sept./Oct.

Urry, J. (1995) *Consuming Places*. Routledge, London.

Van Dijk (1992) *Racism and the Press*. Routledge, London.

Verdery, K. (1993) 'Wither Nation and Nationalism', *Daedalus*, Summer, 122(3), 37–46.

Walerstein, I. (1974) *The Modern World System*. Academic Press, New York.

Walzer, M. (1994) *Thick and Thin; Moral Argument at Home and Abroad*. University of Notre Dame Press, London and Notre Dame.

Wasko, J. (1994) *Hollywood in the Information Age*. Polity Press, London.

West, C. (1993) 'The New Cultural Politics of Difference', in S. During (Ed.) *The Cultural Studies Reader*. Routledge, London.

West, C. (1994) *Race Matters*. Vintage Books, New York.

Wexler, P. (1990) 'Citizenship in the Semiotic Society', in B. S. Turner, *Theories of Modernity and Postmodernity*. Sage, London.

Weymouth, T. and Lamizet, B. (1996) *Markets and Myths; Forces for Change in European Media*. Longman, Harlow.

Williams, R. (1962a) *Communications*. Penguin, Harmondsworth.

Williams, R. (1962b) *The Existing Alternatives in Communications: Socialism in the Sixties*. Fabian Pamphlet, June.

Williams, R. (1965) *The Long Revolution*. Penguin, Harmondsworth.

Williams, R. (1974) *Television: Technology and Cultural Form*. Fontana/Collins, London.

Williams, R. (1976) *Keywords: A Vocabulary of Culture and Society*. Fontana, London.

Williams, R. (1979) *Marxism and Literature*. Oxford University Press, Oxford.

Williams, R. (1980) 'Means of Communication as Means of Production', in *Problems in Materialism and Culture*. Verso, London.

Williams, R. (1983) 'Culture', in D. McLellan, *Marx: the first 100 years*. London, Fontana.

Williams, R. (1985) *Towards 2000*. Penguin, London.

Williams, R. (1989a) 'Distance', in *What I Came to Say*. Radius, London.

Williams, R. (1989b) 'Culture is Ordinary', in *Resources of Hope*. Verso, London.

Williams, R. (1989c) 'Art:Freedom as Duty', in *Resources of Hope; Culture, Democracy, Socialism*. Verso, London.

Wolfe, A. (1989) *Whose Keeper? Social Sciences and Moral Obligation*. University of California Press, California.

Index